THE MENTAL HEALTH WORKBOOK (4 IN 1)

A PRACTICAL GUIDE TO COGNITIVE BEHAVIORAL THERAPY (CBT), DBT & ACT FOR OVERCOMING SOCIAL ANXIETY, PANIC ATTACKS, DEPRESSION, PHOBIAS & ADDICTIONS

WESTLEY ARMSTRONG

DEVON HOUSE
PRESS

CONTENTS

COGNITIVE BEHAVIORAL THERAPY (CBT) & DIALECTICAL BEHAVIORAL THERAPY (DBT) (2 IN 1)

BEAT ANXIETY & PANIC
ATTACKS (2 IN 1)

COGNITIVE BEHAVIORAL THERAPY (CBT) & DIALECTICAL BEHAVIORAL THERAPY (DBT) (2 IN 1)

HOW CBT, DBT & ACT TECHNIQUES CAN HELP YOU TO OVERCOMING ANXIETY, DEPRESSION, OCD & INTRUSIVE THOUGHTS

I

IDENTIFYING WHAT IS WRONG AND LEARNING TO FIGHT IT

1

THE THINGS THAT ARE WEIGHING YOU DOWN: A LOOK INTO MENTAL ILLNESS

There was a time when our population had to deal with things like civil war, violent crime, the black plague, violent crime, and the struggle for food and water. These were stressful times. That level of stress, commonly referred to as acute stress, was tough. Perhaps our ancestors often died from stress than any other disease but just didn't know it.

Unfortunately, stress is still a problem today, even though we are more developed and civilized. Why? Because although we're not dealing with war and other external threats, there continues to be an increase of low-level chronic stress that's silent and hidden. A person gets up in the morning, drowns themselves in coffee, and reports to an office job where they sit in their cubicle from 9am to 5pm dragging themselves from one task to another and periodically faking a smile at the watering hole. To all their colleagues, they're just aloof, absent-minded, sometimes moody, and often slow to complete projects.

Unknown to them is that this person is fighting a hidden battle that no one else knows about. Every morning is a drag. The sun never seems to shine, and there seems to be a grey cloud looming over them wherever they go.

This is a common experience for many suffering from low-level chronic stress. Yet, there are many more symptoms that could vary from individual to individual. The natural process of the body's stress response is to trigger heightened alertness and energy for a short period as the fight, freeze, or flee response is activated. When this becomes a regular everyday occurrence, devastating consequences follow. But here's what I want you to understand. Stress doesn't necessarily lead to mental illness unless left unmanaged for prolonged periods. And if you are struggling with mental illness, there's nothing wrong with you.

WEIGHED DOWN BUT NOT ALONE

Contrary to what the voices in your head might be telling you, you're not crazy or making things up. Something is wrong, and you do need to heal from this current state. However, you shouldn't feel shame, remorse, or assume that you're weak for falling mentally ill.

In fact, you're not the only one struggling with mental illness. Take a look at some of these statistics.

970 million people worldwide have a mental health or substance abuse disorder, according to Our World in Data. The same report issued in 2018 showed that anxiety is the most common mental illness in the world. Pre-pandemic (COVID-19, which impacted all of us in

2020), there were 248 million reported cases of people suffering from this mental illness. Females are more affected by mental illness (11.9%) than males (9.3%). JAMA Psychiatry also reported an alarming statistic back in 2015 when they said that an estimated 14.3% of deaths worldwide are attributed to mental disorders. As if that's not disheartening enough, here's what we know from 2020.

- More than 264 million people suffer from depression globally. (source: World Health Organization).
- Depression is the leading cause of disability in the world. (source: World Health Organization).
- 17.3 million adults in America (that is, 7.1% of the adult population) have had at least one major depressive episode.
- Adolescents between 12 to 17 years of age had the highest rate of major depressive episodes (14.4%), followed by young adults between 18 to 25 years of age (13.8%). 11.5 million adults also had a major depressive episode. (source: Substance Abuse and Mental Health Services Association).
- Anxiety is affecting approximately 40million adults in the United States each year, according to the Anxiety and Depression Association of America.

Given the dramatic global pandemic that devastated all of us, I antici-pate these numbers will continue to rise. I'm sharing these painful statistics with you for one reason. I need you to realize that you're not the only one struggling.

There are millions of us across the globe silently struggling with the difficulties of life. Some are fortunate enough to make it through the dark storms of life better than others. When crises or challenges show up, these individuals seem to have the power to transform into their own superhero and face the obstacle head-on. Ultimately, they emerge out of the difficulty more resilient and victorious. But not everyone comes in-built with this natural ability. Some of us get hit, and we lack the strength or mental power to get back up.

 I am writing this book for you if you can feel in your heart that you're ready to follow simple, proven techniques to heal yourself and conquer all mental disorders from your life. If what you want is a new chapter of your life to begin where you are stronger, healthier, happier, more confident, and at peace, this book can become your guide.

It is not written with sophisticated medical jargon that makes me sound impressive and smart but yields no results for you. I've deliberately simplified every technique, concept, and suggestion so that anyone from any background can understand and apply these teachings.

One thing I must mention before going any further is that you cannot use this book to self-diagnose or as a substitute for professional medical help. It is not intended for that, so always make sure to consult a qualified medical professional, especially if your case is extreme.

ANXIETY, DEPRESSION, OCD, INTRUSIVE THOUGHTS: WHAT ARE THEY?

Mental illness, also called mental health disorders, refers to a wide range of mental health conditions, the most common of which are anxiety, depression, OCD, and intrusive thoughts.

People will experience mental health concerns at different stages of their lives, especially when there has been prolonged stress. And should those concerns persist, i.e., continued and uncontrollable mood disorders, eating disorders, etc., this can quickly turn into a mental illness. Let's touch on the most common ones.

ANXIETY

Anxiety is usually a natural reaction of the body when under stress. It's a strong feeling of fear about what's to come. Think of it like worry on steroids. It's expected that we experience some anxiety when doing something like a job interview, giving a speech, a big final exam, or anything else that triggers your nerves and causes you to be fearful. What causes anxiety? We don't really know, but researchers are still working on an answer. It's probably a combination of genetic disposition, lifestyle, brain chemistry, and other environmental factors.

There's a great story of the famous Opera Singer Caruso that's often told. He got nervous, and anxiety kicked in just before one of his big performance. Minutes to curtain raise his throat dried up, he couldn't sing, and he experienced stage fright. Thankfully, he was aware of how to handle his anxiety and calm his nerves. That single performance put his name on the map in the world of Opera, and the rest, as they say, is history.

So, anxiety is not so much a problem as it is a defense mechanism. However, what goes wrong is that these extreme feelings don't just last a few minutes for some of us. They go on for months on end. Daily functioning at work and at home becomes a problem.

There are many types of anxiety disorders, including panic disorders, phobia, social anxiety disorders, obsessive-compulsive disorders, separation anxiety, illness anxiety disorder, and post-traumatic stress disorder.

- **An anxiety attack** - is a feeling of overwhelming apprehension, worry, distress, or fear. Different people will experience this in diverse ways. Some might feel dizzy, sweat profusely, get hot chills or hot flashes, become restless, etc. Others might get dry in the mouth, become distressed, experience shortness of breath, and so much more.
- **Panic disorder** - occurs when you experience panic attacks at unexpected times. Most people who suffer from panic attacks live in constant fear of the next episode.
- **Obsessive-compulsive disorder** - recurring irrational thoughts that lead you to perform specific, repeated behavior.
- **Phobias** - these are due to extreme fear of a specific activity, situation, or object.

- **Social anxiety** - occurs when one fears being judged by others in social situations.
- **Separation anxiety** - is fear of being away from loved ones or extreme homesickness.
- **Illness anxiety disorder** - occurs when you get too anxious about your health.
- **Post-traumatic stress disorder (PTSD)** - is anxiety following a traumatic event.

Depending on your personality, temperament, and environment, anxiety will take many forms. It can be as easy to spot as Caruso's story of getting a dry throat and being unable to activate his voice, or it can be in the form of butterflies in your stomach or a racing heart. It can also feel overpowering and out of control to the point where you have trouble breathing, and you feel a disconnect with your mind and body. Some people experience repeated nightmares, painful thoughts, or memories that they can't seem to shut out or control. But typical symptoms that we see across the board is a deep feeling of constant fear and worry. You might also have noticed rapid breathing, increased heart rate, trouble concentrating, difficulty falling asleep, restlessness, among a multitude of other discomforts.

How to diagnose anxiety

A single test will likely not diagnose anxiety. So, you will need to see a professional and go through a lengthy physical examination process, mental health evaluations, and psychological questionnaires. Some doctors might even put you through blood and urine tests to rule out underlying medical conditions.

Treatments for anxiety

Depending on how severe your anxiety disorder is, you may need medical treatment, or you might be able to self-heal with some lifestyle and mindset changes. Officially, there are two categories of treatment: medication and psychotherapy. Unless you're dealing with something extremely severe, I ask that you also consider a third alternative - natural remedies and self-healing. The central aspect of using this third method is to increase your awareness and understanding of your mind and body. It's about learning to take better care of yourself and your mind. You'll notice that although this book teaches lots of therapy-based techniques, I will continue to encourage you to eliminate unhealthy habits and develop healthy mind-body practices.

DEPRESSION

Most research points out that depression affects more women than men. Still, it could be because most men don't immediately seek professional help when they realize something is wrong. Although depression is high in teens and young adults, it can strike at any age for various reasons. Since the global pandemic of 2020, where many people had to struggle with financial uncertainty, job loss, and social distancing, causing them to see loved ones less, it's probably triggered an increase in depression for adults in their 30s and 40s. According to the Centers for Disease Control and Prevention (CDC), adults in the United States reported elevated levels of adverse mental health conditions, substance use, and suicidal ideation in the United States in June 2020. The prevalence of anxiety disorder symptoms was approximately three times those reported in the second quarter of 2019

(25.5% versus 8.1%). The prevalence of depressive disorder was about four times what was reported in the second quarter of 2019 (24.3% versus 6.5%).

But what is depression?

It is a mood disorder that causes a persistent feeling of sadness that just eats away at your heart, health, happiness, and productivity. You can't shake this deep sense of loss no matter what you do. It affects how you think, feel, behave, and leads to various emotional and physical problems. Most people suffering from depression can barely get out of bed, let alone carry out normal day-to-day activities. Contrary to what others might think, depression isn't "holiday blues," and it's not a weakness you can just snap out of. For most people, treating depression happens over a long period of time. It often requires both medicine and some form of psychotherapy.

Symptoms of depression:

- Overwhelming sense of sadness, tearfulness, emptiness, and hopelessness.
- Angry outbursts, irritability, and frustration even over trivial matters.
- Slowed thinking, speaking, and body movements.
- Inhibited thinking and creativity.
- Difficulty concentrating, memory loss, and poor decision-making skills.
- Sleep disturbances, including insomnia or sleeping too much.
- Serious fatigue and lack of energy and enthusiasm to do anything. Small tasks require a lot of extra effort.

- Unexplained physical problems such as back pain or headaches.
- No interest or pleasure in most or all normal activities such as socializing, sex, hobbies, physical exercise, etc.
- Feeble appetite and weight loss, or for some, it's the opposite with increased food cravings and weight gain.
- Anxiety, agitation, or restlessness.
- Feelings of worthlessness or guilt.
- Self-loathing, fixation on past mistakes and failures, and a lot of self-blame.
- Frequent or recurrent thoughts of death, suicidal thoughts, a suicide attempt, or suicide.

Did any or all of these symptoms trigger something in you? Have you noticed that you're having noticeable problems handling your day-to-day activities such as school, work, relationships with others, etc.? Perhaps you've been feeling like a dark grey cloud looms over your head wherever you go, and it's not going away no matter what you try. If so, it's time to get some help because you might be suffering from depression.

It's good to recall that your experience of depression may not be as obvious as what you read online because depending on your gender, age and environment, it may show up different. For instance, men usually experience symptoms related to their mood such as anger, restlessness, irritability or they may become too aggressive. It could also be a feeling of emptiness or a deep sadness. Sometimes it can be a rapid shift in behavior e.g., no longer finding pleasure in their favorite activities or losing sexual interest. Physically it can be digestive problems, fatigue, pains and headaches. For women, it's mainly a feeling of hopelessness, thoughts of suicide, thinking or talking more slowly, changes in appetite, increased menstrual cramps and sleep problems.

Types of depression

Atypical features - This type of depression includes the ability to temporarily become cheerful when outer circumstances such as a happy event occur. It also comes with increased appetite, excessive need for sleep, sensitivity to rejection, and a heavy feeling in the arms or legs.

- **Melancholic features** - This type of depression is quite severe. You hate waking up in the morning, struggle with feelings of guilt, agitation, and sluggishness. Your appetite also changes drastically.
- **Anxious distress** - This type of depression causes you to be unusually restless with constant worry about possible events or loss of control.
- **Peripartum onset** - This type of depression occurs during pregnancy or in the weeks or months after delivery, in which case we call it postpartum.
- **Mixed features** - Simultaneous depression and mania, including elevated self-esteem, talking too much, and increased energy.
- **Psychotic features** - This type of depression is accompanied by delusions or hallucinations, which may involve personal inadequacy or other negative themes.

- **Seasonal pattern** - This type of depression relates to changes in seasons and reduced exposure to sunlight.
- **Catatonia** - This type of depression includes motor activity that involves either uncontrollable and purposeless movement or fixed and inflexible posture.
- **Premenstrual dysphoric disorder** - This is a condition that causes depressive symptoms. It's due to hormone changes that begin a week before and improve within a few days after the onset of your period. They should become minimum or completely gone after the completion of your period.
- **Disruptive mood dysregulation disorder** - This condition commonly occurs in children. It often leads to depressive disorder or anxiety disorder during their teen years or adulthood and includes chronic or severe irritability and anger with frequent extreme temper outbursts.
- **Bipolar I and II disorders** - These are mood disorders that are usually hard to distinguish from depression itself. They both include mood swings that range from highs (mania) to lows (depression).

If you're reading this as a parent of a young child or teen trying to identify whether or not they might be suffering from a depression disorder, look out for the symptoms already mentioned and realize that depending on your child's age, there could be other subtle warning signs.

For example, younger children tend to become clingy, refusing to go to school or leave the house. They might get extremely irritable. You might also notice they complain of constant aches and pains, they seem to have a worried look all the time, and their weight might drop drastically. In teenage children, their body language speaks volumes. You might notice your child is extremely negative, always self-loathing, carrying around a sad, defeated look all the time. Their grades often drop due to poor performance and low attendance. You might notice getting to school is a chore. Even if they go to school, they find ways to ditch class, hang out with the wrong kids, start using recreational drugs or alcohol, and their sleeping and eating habits will become anything but healthy. They might also avoid social interaction or even try to get out of family time with you.

Should you see a doctor when you recognize these symptoms?

If you feel depressed, it's a good idea to make an appointment to see a family doctor or a mental health professional as soon as possible. But if you don't like seeking medical treatment, then reach out to a trusted loved one, a friend, your faith leader, or something respectable that you trust. Going through this book and implementing the ideas discussed will also help you heal and get back to your truly happy and energetic state. But I will insist that you seek emergency help by calling your local emergency number if you feel you're at a point where you may hurt yourself or attempt suicide.

The cause of depression isn't entirely known, as is the case for almost all mental disorders. It's always going to be various factors, including brain chemistry, changes in your body's balance of hormones, genetics, and other biological differences. Research is still ongoing to determine exactly what causes this mental disorder. Regardless, I wouldn't fret too much about the cause. Instead, I would be more focused on the journey of healing from depression before it completely debilitates your life.

Do you know your triggers?

Research has shown certain factors increase the risk of getting into major depression. These include a traumatic or stressful event such as the death of a loved one, financial problems, sexual abuse, etc. It could also be triggered by abuse of alcohol or recreational drugs. Suppose you suffer a chronic illness like heart disease or stroke. In that case, depression might get triggered, especially if you are predisposed to get it due to a family medical history of depression. If you have a history of other mental disorders such as eating disorders, anxiety, or PTSD, you could also trigger depression. All this to say, it's crucial to understand self-care and to monitor yourself when faced with triggers so you can mitigate their influence.

Depression can also influence some chronic health conditions making it worse. It is considered a serious medical condition and even especially when one is already fighting a chronic illness such as cancer, cardiovascular disease, asthma, diabetes, or arthritis. If you notice something is off with your emotional state and cognitive functions for an extended period of time, don't just assume it's the blues. Ask for a professional diagnosis to avoid further medical complications as you work on your chronic illness.

Treatment options for depression

If you have severe depression, you may need a hospital stay or an outpatient treatment program until symptoms improve. However, for most people, healing depression requires a combination of medication, some form of therapy, and a lot of self-care. When it comes to medicine, don't wing this. Speak to your doctor and learn about the different options so you can figure out which antidepressant will be right for your case. You might also need psychotherapy, and this book will help you understand some of the best therapies for treating depression. Besides that, you will need to make some changes to your current lifestyle, and we'll be talking more about this in upcoming chapters. Recently, doctors have started recommending other procedures known as brain stimulation therapies such as electroconvulsive therapy (ECT) or Transcranial magnetic stimulation (TMS), both of which are expensive.

OCD

Obsessive-compulsive disorder (OCD) has become a ubiquitous term. It's considered a long-lasting condition that can develop in childhood and worsen or dampen with time, depending on various factors. What is OCD? Well, to answer that, let me first paint a common scenario.

Have you ever left your home to go to a friend's party only to find yourself wondering whether you turned off the cooker and locked the door? For the average person, this thought might come, and in a little while, he or she will conclude that all is well at home and move on to enjoy the party. For someone with OCD, it would become an obsessive thought that keeps replaying over and over. Behavior and mood would be impacted as a result, and it would probably ruin the whole party experience. This is what OCD is. It's an obsession and compulsive behavior.

Depending on how mild or severe your OCD is, you're likely to portray certain symptoms. Ongoing research is starting to point to genetic disposition, environment, and particular brain structure and functioning as the factors that lead to developing this mental disorder. Some individuals with OCD also develop a tic disorder. These are sudden, brief, repetitive moments that include eye blinking, facial grimacing, shoulder shrugging, throat clearing, sniffing, or grunting sounds, among a multitude of other signs.

Treatment options

Typically, your doctor will prescribe mediation, psychotherapy, or a combination of the two if you're diagnosed with OCD. The techniques we will learn in this book may also be beneficial in your journey to healing.

Intrusive Thoughts

What are intrusive thoughts? These are thoughts that seemingly come from nowhere and set up camp in your mind. No matter how hard you try to chase them away, they don't budge. They frequently reoccur without your volition and usually create anxiety within you because they are negative, violent, disturbing, and out of integrity with your true self. Anyone can experience intrusive thoughts (in fact, we all do from time to time). Reported cases of patients range over 6 million in the United States alone, and those are just the few who have enough courage to ask for professional help. Although having these intrusive thoughts doesn't automatically mean you need medical attention, it can be an excellent way to determine whether you have a developing mental health condition. Unsolicited ideas of violence or inappropriate sexual fantasies that keep recurring aren't signs of a healthy mind. So, if you've been dealing with any thoughts that interfere with your mood, character, and daily activities, it might be a good idea to speak with a mental health professional.

When those intrusive thoughts become uncontrollable, they turn into obsessions, which may lead to compulsions. A great example of something small that can grow is the story I shared of worrying about locking your door and turning off your cooker. Suppose you realize that each time you leave the house for something important like a job interview, a friends' party, etc., you struggle to be present because of the constant worry and thoughts such as "did I lock the door?" or "I think I forgot to turn off the cooker." These thoughts aren't just passing warning signals; they literally set camp in your mind and hijack your attention, making it almost impossible for you to remain calm and focused in the present. In that case, you might want to monitor yourself more to figure out if perhaps you're suffering from intrusive thoughts.

The cause of intrusive thoughts in some individuals is an underlying mental health condition such as PTSD or OCD. It could also be due to brain injury, Parkinson's disease, or dementia. I want to invite you now to notice how disruptive your thought patterns have become. Do you frequently have obsessive thoughts? Are these thoughts seemingly glued to your mind? Are they thoughts of disturbing imagery?

Treatment for Intrusive thoughts

Don't feel ashamed if you realize you suffer from this. The best thing to do is to reduce your sensitivity to the thought and its contents. That's where the techniques you'll learn throughout this book become highly valuable. Through Cognitive Behavioral Therapy (CBT), you can relieve and ultimately heal this condition. It's more like talk therapy, where you'll learn new ways of thinking and reacting so you can become less susceptible to intrusive thoughts.

Another critical thing is to focus on self-care. You can create healthy coping strategies and manage your stress better. By recognizing that these intrusive thoughts are just thoughts and that you don't need to label them, you already begin the soothing process that will weaken their grip. You should also figure out the simple things you can do to manage your stress levels so you can bring your mind to a sense of calm.

However, if your condition is pretty bad, I suggest speaking with your doctor so they can recommend medication or a therapist to discuss these thoughts.

WHY DO I HAVE IT?

It took me a long time to finally own responsibility for my mental health. For most of my life, I knew I had an illness that haunted my life ever since I was a child, but I hadn't yet acknowledged what it was or that I had the power to heal. As a young child, I had a loving family, and all my needs were met. I went to the best schools in my hometown, and many could argue I had an ideal childhood. But here's the thing. I didn't feel that way. There was a nagging feeling like something was wrong with me that I just couldn't shake. I have flashbacks of being six years old and probably even before that, and I felt like an outsider looking in when I considered my peers. Things bothered me that didn't bother anyone else. I felt like I didn't belong, and I was different in a way that wasn't loveable. I constantly worried and tried to get as much validation from my parents as I could. But always felt like I was failing them. Depression first kicked in as I became a teen, but long before that, I would have meltdowns, anxiety attacks, and struggled with eating disorders pretty often. But somehow, I managed to grow up with these recurring cycles and fell in love. That was when things went south, and I fell into the worst depression I had ever experienced.

After recognizing that I had a mental disorder that I needed to heal, the question that kept lingering in my mind was, "why me?" I was already having a hard-enough time accepting that my six-year relationship with the woman I intended to marry had just gone up in flames.

Consumed by my rage and her betrayal, I felt the ground beneath my feet open up and swallow me alive. One moment I was the happiest man in the world with dreams to accomplish, and the next, I couldn't eat, sleep, and quite frankly, life lost all meaning. My fiancé didn't just break my heart with her betrayal. She left me feeling hopeless and lifeless. I could not carry out daily activities, and a few weeks after our breakup, I was in major depression.

What I didn't realize at the time is that asking the question "why me?" does nothing productive for your brain or personal recovery. The question is rooted in victimhood (pretty much how I felt all the time). When mental health problems arise, the first thing we want to do is acknowledge, embrace, and find simple ways of empowering and soothing ourselves. I was doing the opposite, and I think many of us are guilty of it too.

But, if you're wondering why you're struggling with mental health issues or why you keep falling into depression, it's good to know that mental illness isn't caused by any particular thing. Several factors contribute, including your family genes, family health history, personal life experiences (childhood abuse or trauma), chemical imbalances in the brain, traumatic brain injury, having a severe medical condition like cancer or AIDS, loneliness, and a deep sense of isolation, etc. Most of the time, it's a combination. In my case, it was the combination of family health history, losing my job, and catching my fiancée cheating on me. Although scientists would like to find a one-size-fits-all root cause, this isn't yet possible. Certain disorders, such as schizophrenia and bipolar disorder, fit the biological model. However, other conditions, such as depression and anxiety, do not.

The brain is extremely complex and more powerful than any super-computer known to mankind, so it's naive to assume every mental disorder can fit into one category. The journey to having proven scientific causes for every mental illness is at infancy, so we best give scientists time to help us accurately answer this question. For now, we need to focus on doing the best we can with the available knowledge.

The other thing I want you to know is that you're not alone in this fight for your life back. You're also not the only one struggling with mental disorders. More than half of Americans will be diagnosed with a mental illness at some point in their life, especially as our society continues to change. I suspect this will be true of almost any developed country you can name. As economies become more volatile, life becomes more fast-paced, and our relationship dynamics continue to evolve, we will likely see more and more people struggling to cope with all these changes and experiences.

If things seem to be going wrong in your life and your mind feels out of control, it's advised that you take steps to see a medical professional who can diagnose what's ailing you. Usually, the diagnosis is pretty simple, and the earlier you catch your condition, the better. It will involve getting to know your medical history, doing some physical examinations, and taking some lab tests depending on your symptoms. You will also take a psychological evaluation where you'll be asked to share your thoughts, feelings, and how you've been reacting lately.

WHAT TO NOTE: THE SIGNS AND SYMPTOMS

While every mental disorder carries its own set of symptoms, some commonalities act as initial red flags. These are the warning signs you need to look out for if you suspect something is terribly wrong, whether or not you've received a diagnosis from a medical professional.

- Drastic sleep or appetite changes.
- Mood changes.
- Significant drop in productivity and ability to function well at school, work, or social activities such as physical exercise.
- Difficulty thinking.
- Apathy.
- Withdrawal and loss of interest in activities previously enjoyed.
- Feeling disconnected from oneself and one's surroundings.
- Nervousness, constant fear that doesn't go away.
- Difficulty focusing and concentrating.
- Unusual behavior.
- Substance abuse.
- Feeling guilty or worthless.
- Constant heaviness and sadness.
- Extreme worry that also brings about physical effects such as shortness of breath, recurring headaches, heart palpitations, restlessness, or a racing mind.

A BATTLE THAT CAN BE WON

It's important to know that regardless of your specific mental health problem, the options available for treatment are numerous. You should consult with a qualified professional on your best options depending on how chronic your case might be. In some instances, medication is necessary and must be part of your treatment. However, therapy can be enough, especially if you feel self-empowered enough. This book focuses on healing through therapy and self-care techniques. We tackle Cognitive Behavioral Therapy (CBT), Dialectal Behavioral Therapy (DBT), and Acceptance Commitment Therapy (ACT). By the end of it, you will know what they are, how they work, and how to apply them now.

2

PRINCIPLE BEHIND COGNITIVE BEHAVIORAL THERAPY (CBT) AND MORE

C ognitive Behavioral Therapy or CBT helps people understand how their patterns of thinking influence their actions and feelings. It's a form of therapy that takes into account how behavior impacts thoughts and feelings.

Many experts in the world of psychotherapy consider this form of therapy the industry's gold standard mainly because it's proven very effective. It's also the most researched form of psychotherapy. It aligns with most international guidelines for psychological treatments making it the first-line treatment for many disorders.

WHY HAS CBT BECOME SO POPULAR?

Many consider CBT the new face of psychology because, unlike the traditional form of therapy that most of us hear about (where a patient spends years lying on the couch in a therapist's office passively trying to get to the root of his or her problem), this new form of treatment is more proactive. The patient and therapist have to work together to develop solutions to the issues at hand. What I like best about this approach is that it's focused on moving forward, creating healthier patterns, and learning to let go of unhealthy ones instead of focusing on events from the past.

Most patients who have experienced this treatment report that they loved the feeling of being empowered and working as a team with their therapist. It's very liberating to feel like you have control over your life. After all, a key aspect of mental health issues is the racing mind and sense of loss over one's power. Even for those dealing with chronic cases where medication is required, this form of therapy still works. It may also help when:

- Coping with a severe medical illness.
- You need to prevent a relapse of mental illness symptoms.
- Coping with grief or loss.
- You want reliable, simple techniques for coping with stressful situations such as job loss, global pandemic, relationship conflicts, etc.

HISTORY OF CBT:

This form of psychotherapy is founded on Albert Ellis and Aaron Beck's work back in the 1950s. Since then, other psychologists and psychiatrists have put together their own techniques and treatment programs based on these ideas. Even DBT (you'll learn about that shortly) evolved from CBT.

In 1955 Albert Ellis proposed his ABC model founded on his belief that external events don't automatically trigger negative emotional responses. What matters is the belief one has about that event. ABC is an acronym for **A**ctivating events, **B**eliefs, and **C**onsequences.

A simple way to think about this is that our emotions and behaviors, i.e., **C**onsequences, are not directly determined by life events, i.e., **A**ctivating Events, but rather by the way we cognitively process and evaluate those events, i.e., **B**elief. Furthermore, this model states that it's not a simple matter of unchangeable process in which events lead to beliefs that result in consequences. Instead, it's the type of belief that's held that matters, and we have the power to change those held beliefs. Albert Ellis's model played a significant part in the form of therapy known as Rational-Emotive Behavior Therapy (REBT), which is like a precursor to the more commonly applied CBT. In REBT, beliefs are divided into "rational" and "irrational" beliefs. Using the ABC model, the aim is to help you accept the rational beliefs and dispute the irrational ones. The disputation process is what results in the model being referred to as the ABCDE model after it was upgraded to include these two steps. Applying it today might look something like this:

A: *Activating Event* (something happens to you or around you).

B: *Belief* (the event that causes you to believe either rational or irrational).

C: *Consequence* (the belief leads to a consequence, with rational beliefs leading to healthy consequences and irrational beliefs leading to unhealthy consequences).

D: *Disputation* (if one had held an irrational belief which has caused ill consequences, they must dispute that belief and turn it into a rational belief).

E: *New Effect* (the disputation has turned the irrational belief into a rational belief, and the person now has healthier consequences of their belief as a result).

Aaron T. Beck evolved and expanded on Ellis's works in the 1960s that contributed significantly to the modern CBT that we know. Beck noticed that many of his patients had internal dialogues that were almost a form of them talking to themselves. He also observed that his patients' thoughts often impacted their feelings and called these emotionally charged thoughts "automatic thoughts." Thus, he developed CBT as a newer form of therapy that looks at patterns and beliefs that can contribute to self-destructive behaviors. CBT can treat anxiety disorders, mood disorders, personality disorders, eating disorders, sleep disorders, psychotic disorders, and substance abuse.

WHAT'S THE PRINCIPLE BEHIND CBT?

Cognitive Behavioral therapy assumes that both the individual and the environment are of fundamental importance and that treatment outside of a holistic approach would be an injustice to the client. Three basic principles are underlying this approach:

1. CBT assumes that problems are based in part on unhelpful and unhealthy ways of thinking.
2. Those problems are rooted in part in learned patterns of unhealthy and unhelpful behavior.
3. An individual suffering from any psychological problem can learn better ways of handling them.

In so doing, the individual can relieve the symptoms and become more empowered and effective.

For these core reasons, Cognitive Behavioral therapy is about collaboration and participation. It emphasizes the present and requires an excellent client-therapist relationship. CBT is an ever-evolving formulation of the patient and their problems in cognitive terms, which aims to teach the client to be his or her own therapist. CBT sessions are time limited. Each session is carefully structured to aid in the successful execution of this form of therapy. It is goal-oriented and uses a variety of techniques to change thinking, mood, and behavior. From personal experience, I can see that CBT values and empowers an individual to take control of his or her problems and manage life in a healthy adaptive way. This is accomplished through psychoeducation.

3 WAYS IT CAN HELP YOU OVERCOME YOUR MENTAL ILLNESS

Three simple steps you can take to start implementing this form of therapy are:

The first step is to identify the negative thought.

Your therapist or someone you trust, and respect can help you uncover some of those unhelpful and unhealthy thoughts contributing to your current mental disorder. For example, using my story of how I started using CBT. It took me a while to see progress, but after a little effort, I realized that I had been carrying around thought patterns and feelings of unworthiness. I always felt like my fiancé was too good for me. Like I didn't deserve happiness or to be loved. And I quickly made the connection that I had always been carrying around these thoughts since childhood.

The same process will apply to you. While working together with your appointed therapist or guide, you can start talking about your feelings toward the current problem and name some of the dominant thoughts associated with those feelings.

The second step is to challenge that negative thought.

Once you've identified some unhealthy thoughts, the next step is to question the evidence for your ideas, analyze the beliefs behind those thoughts, and really challenge their validity. At this point, it helps to have someone objectively help you through this process. Then you'll discuss why you feel as you do and the corresponding behavior these thoughts have created. Finally, you'll need to test your negative thinking by separating your thoughts and feelings from reality. Often, we realize that our thoughts and feelings aren't based on facts when we go through this step.

The third step is to replace that negative thought with a realistic one.

If you change your negative thought to the extreme opposite, the new one won't stick in your mind for very long. Even personal development students have figured this out. When someone with a strong belief in poverty tries to shove the affirmation "I'm a billionaire" down their throat, it never yields any fruitful results. Saying "I am super-rich" when the belief of being poor is dominant might offer temporary relief at that moment, but it won't help you permanently shift your thought patterns, feelings, actions, or attitude toward wealth. When working with CBT to eliminate anxiety, depression, or whatever else, your therapy should help you formulate a new thought that is realistic enough for your mind and brain to accept as real for you. It's about creating new bridge thoughts that can ultimately get you to the desired final thought. The further away you feel from where you want to be in your thinking, the more you should create little bridges instead of trying to make a huge jump from where you are now to that new thought reality. So, for example, if you suffer from social anxiety, instead of saying, "I'm the coolest person in the world, and everybody loves being around me," a more constructive thought that will easily get anchored in your mind would be "just because it's awkward for me to be around people doesn't mean others see me that way." Build the new thought reality from that foundation, and it is likely to yield better long-term results.

This is the skill that Cognitive Behavioral Therapy gives us. It puts us in the driver's seat of our own lives and equips us with tools for navigating what would otherwise be overwhelming events. Since we know negative thoughts lead to negative feelings and actions, we reframe our thoughts into positive, constructive thoughts, leading to corresponding feelings and behaviors. Every mental health issue will be approached differently by your chosen therapist but let me share the foundational techniques that will always be included.

- You will identify specific problems in your current state and daily life.
- You'll become aware of the unproductive thought patterns and how they are impacting your life.
- The therapist will show you how to start reshaping your thinking in a way that changes how you feel about yourself and the problem or issues at hand.
- You'll learn new behaviors and begin putting them into daily practice.

Then you'll be advised to implement one of these techniques.

#1. COGNITIVE RESTRUCTURING OR REFRAMING

Do you have a tendency of assuming worst-case scenarios? Are you often expecting people to mistreat you, events to turn out wrong, or for you to mess up things that are important to you? Thinking this way affects almost everything you do. Fussing over minor details or getting too worked up and taking any small conflict personally will create a lot of disharmony in your life, and unfortunately, expecting the worst tends to become a self-fulfilling prophecy.

That's why it's crucial to identify your negative patterns and how you often react to situations. Once you become aware, you can reframe those thoughts, so they are more positive and productive.

For example, I was sitting at Starbucks with a friend soon after starting my journey to recovery. I had just spent countless hours studying cognitive-behavioral therapy. Because I had joined the college to major in psychology (before calling it quits), it wasn't too long before I started recognizing some of the dominant thought patterns that were ruining my life, like that one time sitting with John who was trying to comfort me after my breakup. The waitress brought his order and completely forgot about mine. It sounds ridiculous, but it's almost like I had been invisible the whole time, and everything she heard while we placed our orders evaporated into thin air. As you can imagine, when his coffee and eggs on toast came, I was infuriated. I told him, "See John, it's like women are out to get me. And every time I get a female waiter, something always goes wrong with my order." I was just about to flip the lid (he was used to it), but this time, a little voice stopped me from having a momentary outburst. And I just reflected for a moment on what I was saying and where that thought came from. Surely this girl wasn't out to get me. She had never seen me before. Why do I assume the worst all the time?

When I started having these "moments of awakening," things began shifting within me. That particular day, my friend was utterly shocked that I didn't have a temper tantrum with that waitress. Instead, I called her back and didn't even ask why she ignored my order. I simply asked her to pay close attention and retake my order.

#2. EXPOSURE THERAPY

This technique is used to confront fears and phobias. Your therapist should slowly expose you to the things that evoke fear or anxiety and offer guidance on coping with them in-the-moment. For example, if you suffer from social anxiety and the thought of being at a party full of people triggers a lot of fear, then you might want to incrementally expose yourself to how it would feel to experience that event. Break it up into chunks and experience different aspects such as arrival and greeting new strangers. Choose a technique that helps you get through that phase first, and when you can feel calm enough while replaying that scene, move into the next phase, e.g., striking a conversation with a few people who capture your interest. Keep working on it until you feel less vulnerable and more confident to cope with such an experience.

#3. RELAXATION AND STRESS REDUCTION TECHNIQUES

In cognitive behavioral therapy, you'll learn some progressive relaxation techniques such as:

- Muscle relaxation
- Deep breathing exercises
- Imagery

All these exercises lower stress and increase your sense of calm and control. They also help you deal with triggers in real-time, which gives you enough buffer time to prevent relapses.

#4. ACTIVITY SCHEDULING AND BEHAVIOR ACTIVATION

In this technique, you finally learn to deal with procrastination and other habits that are rooted in fear and anxiety. We help you do this by encouraging you to block time on your calendar for these anxiety causing activities. Once it's on your calendar, you are more likely to see it through, and it helps you develop the right habits needed to make you a high performer. Combining this with other techniques such as deep breathing can help you accomplish things that previously seemed impossible.

#5. JOURNALING AND THOUGHT RECORDING

I find writing an effective form of therapy, and now there's plenty of research to back this technique. You can start by listing the negative thoughts that hijack your brain and mood as they occur and then write out their opposite (or bridge thoughts) depending on how severe your case might be. A particular technique I regularly practice to-date is called clarity through contrast. Basically, I grab a piece of A4 paper and draw a horizontal line. On my left, I title it what I don't want, and on my right, I title it what I would love. I put my current thoughts or whatever ails me on the left side. All those ridiculous voices and feelings come out and on to that paper. Once I feel I have put out everything, I take three deep breathes and switch to the right side of the paper, filling in the thoughts and feelings I would love to feel and think. Most of the time, I don't even believe I can ever get to that other side, but just making this list of what I would love opens me up to a better feeling state and calms me down, which allows me to handle matters better.

Another exercise that works well, especially at the early stages of your healing, is noting down in a journal all the new thoughts and behavior you're putting into practice as you go through your therapy. Putting things down in writing helps you see your progress, which keeps you encouraged and focused on healthy thoughts and behavior.

#6. ROLE PLAY

Role-playing is an excellent technique if you struggle with expressing yourself and communicating with others. You can use this technique to practice social skills (e.g., if you want to ask a woman out but struggle with anxiety), improve your problem-solving abilities, gaining familiarity and confidence in certain situations, and so much more.

#7. GUIDED DISCOVERY

This is best done with your therapist or someone qualified who can listen to your problem and learn your viewpoint. Then he or she will ask questions designed to challenge your current beliefs. They will assist you in broadening your thinking by offering different perspectives. You might be asked to give evidence that supports your assumptions as well as evidence that does not. As you go through this process and open up your mind to see things from other perspectives, you become empowered to see and choose a new, more beneficial path.

#8. PROGRESSIVE MUSCLE RELAXATION

This technique is similar to the body scan (if you practice mindfulness, this should sound familiar). You do it by instructing your muscles to relax (one muscle group at a time) until your whole body gets into a state of relaxation. You can use audio guidance if doing it by yourself (you can even find videos on YouTube) or simply in a quiet relaxing ambiance with some candles or whatever stimulates relaxation for you. It can be beneficial when soothing a busy and unfocused mind or when you feel too nervous or anxious about something.

#9. BEHAVIORAL EXPERIMENTS

This technique allows you to become your own prophet in this sense. If you're fearful or anxious about something, ask yourself what you think is going to happen. What is it that is so bad that causes this reaction in you? Detail it out as much as possible. Then carry out your activity and take note of the actual outcome you experience. For example, if you're anxious about standing in front of an audience because you think you'll die or someone will throw rotten eggs at you because you suck, detail out that prediction, then go make your speech regardless if only to test whether your prediction was valid or not. Take note of how many of your predictions will come true. Over time you might discover that the predicted catastrophes that typically hold you back from things you want to do hardly ever happen. That alone is transformational therapy because it gives you the confidence and mental freedom needed to approach things with a healthy attitude and mindset. Ultimately, your anxiety to do things that are out of your comfort zone will dissipate. As Mark Twain once said, "I've had a lot of worries in my life, most of which never happened."

A PRACTICAL LOOK AT COGNITIVE BEHAVIORAL THERAPY

From a practical viewpoint, CBT is meant to be something short-term. It doesn't deny that your past is real but simply emphasizes the current present and what you can do to make things better for yourself. This talking therapy follows a simple model of thoughts (cognition) - feelings - actions (behavior), and by starting to make adjustments at that thought level, the end result is bound to change.

Take into consideration some of the techniques shared above. Techniques like deep breathing, journaling, and progressive muscle relation are simple yet profound practices that can help you alleviate some of the symptoms that afflict you and, in some cases, completely eradicate them from your life. The goal of cognitive behavior therapy is to teach you that you can control how you interpret and deal with situations and your environment even when the world around you is less than pleasant.

DOES IT WORK?

CBT has helped many people with certain types of emotional distress that don't require psychotropic medication. People suffering from depression, anxiety, anger issues, eating disorders, nightmares, phobias, addictions, panic attacks, and so much more. It's empirically supported and has been shown to effectively help patients overcome and heal a wide variety of life-crippling behaviors. The best part about this is that you can also combine it with medication if your case is chronic. You can get a therapist for more advanced CBT strategies or DIY if you feel capable. The techniques shared in this book are simple enough to start implementing now, making it one of the most affordable forms of therapy.

3

DIALECTAL BEHAVIORAL THERAPY (DBT): WHAT YOU NEED TO KNOW

P sychotherapy is one of the best forms of treatment methods for numerous mental health illnesses. So far, you've learned about the umbrella term CBT which is often referred to as talking therapy. For many of the common mental health problems, CBT works exceptionally well in helping the patient overcome their problems. However, not all patients can see the positive effects of this form of therapy (especially those suffering from borderline personality disorders and post-traumatic stress disorders). A doctor by the name of Marsha Linehan began to notice this back in the 80s. By the end of the 1980s, Linehan and colleagues decided to evolve CBT to create a more effective treatment for problematic, suicidal women. Linehan combed through the literature on efficacious psychological therapies for other disorders and assembled a package of evidence-based, cognitive behavioral interventions that directly targeted suicidal behavior. That was the birth of DBT.

Branching Out from CBT to DBT

DBT (dialectical behavior therapy) was initially focused on changing cognitions and behaviors of patients who felt criticized, misunderstood, and invalidated. Linehan weaved into the treatment interventions designed to convey the patient's acceptance and help them accept themselves entirely. That includes emotions, thoughts, the world, and others. This therapy was intended to treat borderline personality disorder, but it has since been adapted to treat other mental health conditions as well, including but not limited to eating disorders, substance use disorders, and post-traumatic stress disorders. As an extension of CBT, dialectical behavior therapy incorporates the philosophical process known as dialectics. The standard DBT treatment package consists of weekly individual therapy sessions, a weekly group skills training session, and a therapist consultation team meeting.

WHAT IS THE PRINCIPLE BEHIND DBT?

To understand DBT and its founding principles, you need to learn a thing or two about dialectics. So, what is dialectics anyway? It's a concept that states everything is composed of opposites and that change occurs when there is "dialogue" between opposing forces. The idea originates from ancient Greek philosophy, and according to Wikipedia, it is a discourse between two or more people holding different points of view about a subject but wishing to establish the truth through reasoned methods of argumentation. How does this become a helpful form of therapy for you?

Using this process, you are encouraged to resolve the apparent contradiction between self-acceptance and change to bring about positive changes in your life. There are three basic assumptions applied to this form of therapy. The first is that all things are interconnected. The second is that change is constant and inevitable, and the third is that opposites can be integrated to form a closer approximation of the truth. Another important aspect of DBT developed by Linehan is known as validation. Linehan and her team found that when validation was used along with the push for change, patients were more cooperative and less likely to quit or become distressed as they went through the changes. In practice, the therapist validates that a patient's actions "make sense" within the context of their personal experience without necessarily agreeing that the actions taken are the best possible approach to solving their desired problem.

HOW IS IT DIFFERENT FROM COGNITIVE BEHAVIORAL THERAPY?

From the name, we can tell that CBT and DBT share some similarities. DBT evolved from cognitive behavior therapy, but its approach is distinct enough to merit being considered a unique model. Both CBT and DBT are supported by extensive evidence-based research. So, we can feel confident about their effectiveness. They can each be used to treat a wide variety of mental health problems, but in some instances, one is more suitable than the other.

That's why it's good to understand some of the differences between these two therapy models.

The main difference is the kind of change they create for the patient, according to scientific research. CBT can help a patient recognize and change problematic patterns of thinking and behaving. On the other hand, DBT is best when a patient needs help regulating intense emotions and improving interpersonal relationships. Through validation, acceptance, and behavior change, DBT can help a patient create those required shifts. In DBT, there's no heavy reliance on changing thoughts. There's an implicit process that happens so that as the client is mindful, more accepting of themselves, and as they learn to validate themselves and ask for validation, they start to change any resistance they may have. Ultimately, they become kinder to themselves, get more grounded in reality, and accept reality without catastrophizing everything in their world. But they don't go through the process of actively challenging their thoughts like in CBT.

One thing to note here is that research doesn't say there's a one-size-fits-all. Although the doctor who evolved DBT was focused on suicidal patients, this model has worked for other mental health disorders. So, we must remain open-minded enough and avoid making the mistake of assuming that one is better than the other. Mental health disorders affect cognition and behavior differently, so neither CBT nor DBT is the best option in all cases. You need to figure out which is the best option for your particular case.

Research shares so far that depression, anxiety, OCD, phobias, and PTSD are typically better approached through cognitive behavior therapy. For borderline personality disorders, chronic suicidal ideation, and self-harm behaviors, dialectical behavior therapy is usually more effective.

THE STRATEGIES OF DBT THAT HELPS TRANSFORMS NEGATIVE BEHAVIORS INTO POSITIVE ONES

Using DBT, you get to learn and develop four core skills to cope with emotional distress in healthy, positive, and productive ways. These skills are sometimes referred to as modules and are considered by Linehan as the "active ingredients" of successfully utilizing DBT. They are mindfulness, emotion regulation, distress tolerance, and interpersonal effectiveness. Let's examine each skill.

Mindfulness

What is mindfulness? Mindfulness means maintaining a moment-by-moment awareness of our thoughts, feelings, bodily sensations, and the surrounding environment through a gentle nurturing lens (definition from greatergood.berkley.edu).

The roots of mindfulness can be traced back to Buddhism, more specifically, Buddhist meditation. Today, most people only know of the more secular practice of mindfulness, which entered mainstream America in the late 1970s. Many studies have been documented since the 70s to show the physical and mental health benefits of adopting mindfulness practices.

We also need to consider the aspect of mindfulness that is about acceptance. What do I mean? In mindfulness, we are encouraged to pay attention to our thoughts and emotions without judging them, without believing even for an instant that it's wrong or right for you to feel how you're feeling in any given moment. For example, as you're going through this chapter, notice how you feel in this moment as you read my words. If you're feeling soothed and encouraged by what you're learning, that's great, and you can embrace those thoughts and emotions. If you're struggling to agree with or even see value in what you've learned so far, perhaps you're starting to get frustrated and impatient with me; it's also okay. As you begin to notice what's happening within you and how you respond to the activities and interactions you have throughout the day, you begin to practice mindfulness. That helps you tune into what you're sensing in the present moment. It also keeps you grounded in the NOW instead of being pulled back into the past or dashing into an imaginary future.

In the context of using this practice in DBT, acceptance plays a significant role. The more you notice and accept your thoughts and feelings through that nurturing less, the easier it becomes to progress with your healing. So DBT breaks down mindfulness into the "what "skills and the "how" skills.

The "what" skills are about noticing what you're focused on. That includes the present moment, your awareness in the present, your thoughts, emotions, and sensations, and separating emotions and sensations from thoughts.

The "how" skills teach you how to be more mindful. You do this by learning to balance rational thoughts with emotions, using radical acceptance to learn to tolerate aspects of yourself as long as they aren't harmful to you or others. It's also about taking effective action and overcoming things that make this practice of mindfulness challenging to execute. Things like restlessness, fatigue, sleepiness, and doubt all inhibit your ability to practice mindfulness, so they need to be managed effectively. And lastly, you need to use these mindfulness skills that you learn regularly. It cannot be a one-time thing or only when it's convenient for you.

Emotion regulation

While mindfulness practices are extremely powerful, we know that sometimes it's just not enough, especially when you feel like your emotions have a life of their own and you've been kidnaped by them. For those of us who've battled with mental health issues long enough, we know how crippling emotions can be. There are moments in my life when I felt like there was no escape from the hellish experience of my feelings. If you've had those moments too, I feel for you. And I want you to know that as difficult as it might be, it's possible to manage them. That's what this skill of emotion regulation teaches you.

Emotion regulation teaches you how to deal with immediate emotional reactions before they lead to a chain of distressing secondary reactions. You will learn how to recognize emotions, reduce your sense of vulnerability and insecurity. You'll overcome barriers to emotions that have positive effects and increase those emotions with positive effects. That will help you become more aware and mindful of your feelings without judging them and expose you to your emotional self. The more exposed you are to your emotions, the easier it will be to avoid giving into emotional urges because you'll be able to recognize them and that in turn will solve problems in helpful ways. In case you're wondering what, a primary emotion might be, let me share an example.

Suppose you're about to get extremely angry for whatever reason. Still, because you've practiced emotion regulation, you get a buffer time that enables you to recognize that you're about to explode with anger. In that case, you can practice these core skills that you're learning in this chapter (depending on what feels most effective in that situation) and calm yourself down. That will enable you to avoid entering into a downward emotional spiral, which might lead to guilt, unworthiness, shame, and even depression depending on how bad things would get if you didn't regulate yourself while in that particular situation.

Distress tolerance

While regulating your emotions is wonderful and prevents you from falling into bouts of depression and other terrible states, some environments are just rigged with triggers that seem out to get you. In a moment of crisis, even with all your mindfulness and commitment to regulating your emotions, how can you best avoid that pit of despair if nothing else seems to be working? The short answer is by activating distress tolerance.

You learn distress tolerance skills so you can get through moments of crisis and rough storms without the need for potentially destructive coping techniques. That's why I love this module. Before developing distress tolerance skills, I would be fine until something unexpected throws me off my game. Then I would try to use coping mechanisms like self-isolating, avoidance, and alcohol to deal with situations that I just couldn't control. Suffice to say, the results weren't what I wanted. Many have had a similar experience, so I encourage you to learn these skills instead of seeking temporary coping mechanisms that might cause more harm. By learning distress tolerance skills, you learn to distract yourself until you become calm enough to deal with the destructive emotion or situation. You learn to self-soothe by relaxing and using your senses so you can reconnect to that feeling of peace. These skills are priceless because they always help you find ways to improve the moment even if you're in great pain or difficulty. If you must use some coping technique, you won't blindly pick the easiest one. Instead, you'll be mindful and thoughtful about the pros and cons of your choices. Using this technique, I recognized that drinking as my coping mechanism was only making my life worse. I could catch myself in that moment when the idea of getting a drink popped into my head and would reach for a better feeling solution instead, like calling my support group or going for a jog to get the steam out. That's when things really started shifting permanently. I got to a point where I stopped being fearful and anxious about relapsing into depression.

Interpersonal effectiveness

Relationships are always going to be integral to our growth and happiness as human beings. No matter how heartbroken you feel or how betrayed you felt, learning how to better connect and relate to others is still important, and it should be part of your recovery process. Interpersonal effectiveness skills help you view relationships from a new lens. It gives you clarity and perspective. These skills combine listening skills, social skills, and assertiveness training so you can learn how to change situations and still remain in integrity with your values. These skills include learning how to work through conflict and challenges in relationships and learning how to ask for what you want. It's also about building great respect and love for yourself.

WHAT TO EXPECT IN DBT

DBT uses specific techniques to achieve the treatment goals that will help you get better. It usually includes a combination of individual sessions and group support.

Individual therapy typically comes first.

In these weekly sessions, the emphasis is on recognizing and self-monitoring your thoughts, emotions, and behavior by using a form of diary card that will be processed by your therapist. This card helps you and your therapist keep track of the treatment goals. The goal here is to bring about greater awareness of your triggers, thoughts, emotions, behaviors, and actions so that you can elicit change strategies. It is usually a 50-minute session. During individual therapy, you will also work on emotion regulation, traumatic experiences, and any other issues that arise.

You can expect your therapist to be active in teaching and reinforcing adaptive behaviors between and during sessions. The emphasis should be on teaching you skills that will empower you to manage your emotional trauma. It's about working together with your therapist so you can learn to improve many of the necessary social and emotional skills needed to help you feel more in control. You might also receive some homework assignments during these individual sessions.

Weekly group therapy sessions are the second component of DBT.

These sessions are typically two and a half hours long. These structured gatherings led by your therapist will help you learn, incorporate and practice one of the four different modules discussed earlier. After all, unless you can practice these core skills, it won't stick or produce lasting effects in your life. In the group, you also get the chance to discuss homework assignments, practical applications of the new skills you're learning, etc.

During your DBT treatment, you will have access to your therapist by phone or virtually if you need help dealing with any crises that show up.

As you commit and go through this process, you will start to experience the benefits of learning skills that improve your tolerance to distress and emotional regulation. If you were dealing with any self-harming behaviors or suicidal thoughts, these would be addressed first. And as you combine the individual psychotherapy sessions with the supportive group experience, you'll start practicing more of the interpersonal skills you'll learn from your therapist, decreasing maladaptive behaviors and thoughts affecting your quality of life and relationships. In short, you'll finally start getting your life and peace of mind back in order. As your self-confidence, self-respect, and self-belief increases, you'll learn how to set reasonable goals to improve your lifestyle.

DBT, ARE YOU THE ONE FOR ME?

How will you determine whether DBT is right for you, and can you be sure it will work?

Well, some signs and symptoms would make DBT seem like the best therapy form. Do you suffer from any of the following?

- Self-destructive behaviors such as alcohol or drug abuse, binge eating and purging, sexual promiscuity, and other impulsive behaviors like gambling, gaming, or spending sprees.
- Repeated suicide threats or attempts.
- Chronic problems with depression, anxiety, and anger.
- Self-harm behavior such as cutting, burning, and picking yourself.
- Hypersensitivity to criticism, rejection and disapproval, fear of abandonment, and a pattern of unstable interpersonal relationships.
- Intense and volatile emotional reactivity and difficulty returning to a stable mood.
- Poor and unstable self-image with a strong sense of emptiness.
- Feelings of paranoia and victimization.
- Detached thinking that ranges from difficulty maintaining attention to episodes of complete disassociation.

If you are struggling with one or more of these issues, DBT can be the right one for you. There are many success stories where using Dialectical Behavior Therapy has been the ultimate treatment that helped avert suicide. In fact, one of the best stories I can share with you is that of Dr. Linehan, the woman behind this form of treatment. In 1961, at the age of 16, she was admitted to a psychiatric hospital. She was there for over two years, and almost all the therapists that came to treat her proved ineffective. She says some of them were so bad, she often felt like they were driving her deeper into what can only be described as hell. She considers it a miracle that she was able to heal and make a successful life for herself, getting a Ph.D. in social and experimental psychology. Out of that, she was able to evolve existing therapy treatments into the kind of treatments she once needed. "I developed dialectical behavior therapy (DBT) for people who suffer unimaginable emotional pain and resort to desperate behavior amid suffering. The people I most wanted to help were those at very high risk for suicide, and DBT turned out to be extremely successful in helping suicidal people stay alive." Dr. Marsha M. Linehan.

HOW DAVID HEALED HIMSELF FROM PAIN MEDS ADDICTION

David is a friend I met years ago in my support group, and we've continued our friendship long past our old lives when everything seemed unbearable. Our connection might be because we both struggled to recognize that something was terribly wrong and that we needed help until it was almost too late. Although he didn't get heartbroken by a woman, he still underwent his own version of a living hell. According to David, he couldn't remember a time in his life when he actually felt like life was worth living. What's worse is that he was referred from one specialist to another, all of whom seemed to only bury him deeper in his depressive state. He was also prescribed various psychotropic medications, which had severe side effects.

To make matters worse, his depression was getting more chronic. So, to make things a little more bearable, David started soothing himself with some strong pain meds his mother was taking. It wasn't too long before that became his new coping mechanism, and over time, he became a serious addict. That's when his mother decided to try a different form of therapy. By the time his mom was able to get him into DBT, he was suffering from Major Depression and Substance Abuse Disorder. He was also starting to develop certain self-destructive behavior that his mother worried would lead to suicidal threats. The treatment that David reluctantly joined is what connected us, and the rest, as they say, is forgotten history.

After going through DBT, David was able to develop new skills, heal, and transform his life. There was a time in his life when he couldn't get out of bed for days on end because of the despair and emotional suffering he was undergoing. Today, David is a successful entrepreneur running his own business, and he volunteers at his local community to pay it forward. He's also started a YouTube channel to encourage men suffering from mental health issues to seek out support and treatment because he feels it was more of a struggle for him due to his reluctance to speak up. He tried to ignore the warning signs and didn't want to appear "weak," but now he recognizes the importance of getting help when one feels mentally unwell.

4

A CLEAR OVERVIEW OF ACCEPTANCE & COMMITMENT BASED THERAPY (ACT)

Researchers continue to work tirelessly to develop and discover the most effective ways to help people overcome mental challenges. Long-term recovery and relapse prevention still remain a huge obstacle that many strive to resolve because there's nothing worse than putting someone through a program successfully only to have them relapse shortly after. There's also the issue that not all standard therapy programs effectively help people overcome psychological pain. That's where ACT comes in.

GETTING INTO THE ACT

Acceptance and commitment therapy (ACT) is a new form of treatment developed more recently (in the 90s) with the hope of increasing long-term success in the treatment of mental health conditions. It's based on relational frame theory (a school of research focusing on human language and cognition). This therapy is more action-oriented and also has its roots in traditional behavior therapy and cognitive behavioral therapy. ACT teaches you how to stop denying, avoiding, suppressing, and struggling with your inner emotions and instead start accepting that you are not flawed or broken. These negative, often shunned feelings are appropriate responses to specific situations, but that should never inhibit you from moving forward in your life. In other words, ACT enables you to accept your issues and hardships and to commit to making necessary changes in behavior regardless of what's going on around you. Treatment using ACT has been successful when applied to chronic pain, eating disorders, depression, psychosis, anxiety, and substance abuse.

WHAT'S THE BASIS OF IT?

At a fundamental level, ACT is concerned with helping you realize the fullness and vitality of your life. It's about bringing new meaning to your life and helping you discover your values so that you can lead a value-based lifestyle that ultimately brings a greater sense of worth. It also emphasizes the importance of embracing that a full life includes a broad spectrum of emotions and human experiences, including pain. Acceptance of things as they come without evaluating or attempting to change them is one of the core skills you learn, making it easier to shift and manage painful or difficult situations.

THE 3 KEY FUNDAMENTALS TO ACT

#1. Acceptance

Accepting one's emotional experience can be described as the process of learning to experience the range of human emotions with a kind, open, and accepting perspective. Whether it's a situation you cannot control, a personality trait that's hard to change, or an emotion that overwhelms you, ACT invites you to accept reality and work with life as it is instead of trying to fight or control things beyond your control.

#2. Choosing the Desired Direction

You get to choose the best direction that you can take based on your values during this process. To do this, you'll be guided through a values clarification process that will help you define what's most important to you. Your mental health professional will share exercises to help you identify your core values then you can align them with your actions to respond to pain and difficulty from that frame of mind. It's also a great way to clarify how you wish to live life and what's meaningful to you.

#3. Taking Action

The last key is taking action and committing to the changes you've made in behavior and moving in the direction of your identified values. These three keys are interconnected and cannot be treated as separate when going through the therapy. What underlies all of them is that each one must be approached through the lens of mindfulness. So, let's touch on the role of mindfulness in the ACT.

During ACT, mindfulness will allow you to connect with the observing self (the part of you that is aware but separate from your thinking self). ACT uses mindfulness so that you can detach from thoughts and experiences that make it hard for you to see clearly or even remain present. Challenges related to painful feelings and past situations that no longer serve you are first reduced and eventually accepted through mindfulness practices. So, for example, if like me you struggle with thoughts of unworthiness and you've had a painful experience like what I had where someone I loved betrayed me in the worst possible way, which had me believing that I really am unworthy and unlovable, then instead of replaying that thought "I'm unworthy and unlovable," you might be asked to instead say "I'm having the thought that I'm unworthy and unlovable." This effectively separates you (the individual) from the cognition, thereby stripping it of its negative charge.

The Single Key Difference That Separates ACT From Other Therapies

Thus far, you've learned about three types of psychotherapy treatments that all work in helping people overcome mental health problems. CBT (cognitive behavior therapy) is the foundation of both DBT and ACT. However, they are all distinct in their own ways, which is why they are considered separate. When it comes to understanding the core difference between ACT, DBT, and CBT, the key difference is that ACT emphasizes facing painful emotions and experiences head-on and taking positive action forward. It focuses on embracing, accepting, and transforming the feelings through a committed effort to shift one's behavior and perceptions about the problem. It's also more focused on accepting oneself and seeing the good instead of believing that we are flawed in some way for developing mental issues. Through acceptance and positive action based on one's values, tackling life's difficulties can become manageable, and life can once again become fulfilling and enjoyable.

PRACTICAL STEPS IN APPLYING ACT

Whether you have a therapist guiding you through the acceptance and commitment therapy or not, you can still apply some of the exercises to your current situation. Many of the mindfulness exercises are practical and easy for anyone to implement. For example, if you want to practice Acceptance, a simple exercise to do is "Opening up."

If unpleasant feelings are showing up for you right now, see if you can take a few deep breaths and just allow them to be there with you. Instead of suppressing or sweeping them under your mental carpet, embrace these feelings. Explore what there is to experience and notice your body's sensations and the thoughts, images, and emotions running through your mind. Can you stay present with these difficult feelings and keep in touch with them without judging yourself? Do these feelings remain the same or do they start changing as you allow them non-judgmental space to just be with you? Stay with them a while longer and notice whether there's any fluctuation. Are they getting heavier, lighter, or still the same? Notice how you're talking to yourself as these feelings are experienced. What interpretations are you making about your experience, and is it really based on reality?

Now, see if you can counter some of the negative self-talk with more realistic ones and then re-evaluate that experience from your newly found perspective.

Other practical strategies that can be useful in your daily life include:

- Acknowledge the difficulty in your life without escaping from it or avoiding it.
- Give yourself permission to not be good at everything.
- Allow feelings or thoughts to happen without the impulse to act on them.
- Realize that you can be in control of how you react, think, and feel in any given situation.

NO NEED TO ACT, ACT WORKS!

ACT was developed in the late 1980s by Steven C. Hayes, and most academics like to consider it the "third wave" of behavioral psychotherapy approaches. Think of it as an updated version of CBT, yet with more mindfulness and present-moment processing. There's a lot of scientific evidence that mindfulness practices and cognitive behavior therapy positively affect treating mental health problems such as anxiety, depression, substance abuse, and trauma. With ACT, metaphors, paradoxes, and experiential exercises are frequently used. Many interventions are playful, creative, and innovative ranging from short ten-minute interventions to some that extend over many sessions. An ACT-informed therapist usually takes an active role in guiding the client by exploring their values and building skills associated with mindfulness. For example, I have a friend (let's call her Ann to protect her privacy) who recently completed an ACT program. She shared that during her sessions, she felt guided into developing more compassion and mindfulness. She changed her relationship to her thoughts and started to feel the shift after just a few sessions.

Ann initially sought help because she felt so dissatisfied with her life, but at the same time, she was beating herself up and feeling guilty for having these thoughts and emotions. According to the status quo standards, Ann has a great life, and her husband is highly successful. Her days are occupied by their three young children, and although she has the lifestyle most housewives only dream about, she still felt dissatisfied. Not wanting to share this with her family for fear of being thought of as selfish and ungrateful (especially her traditional southern mom), she decided to seek professional guidance. Through ACT, she was guided to explore her values through a values exercise, which enabled her to examine whether or not she was living within her value system and in what ways she might desire to change things. Through this exercise, she has finally accepted her dissatisfaction and figured out ways to shift her current routine so she can live more aligned with her own values.

Besides personal stories that I have encountered of the success and viability of ACT as a form of treatment, there's enough scientific evidence backing up the validity of this form of psychotherapeutic approach. One such evidence is the result shared in the European Journal of Psychiatry Volume 32, Issue 4. Sixty-seven inpatients of a German psychiatric department were assigned to either ACT or

CBT+ condition assessed with respect to symptom measure and ACT-specific outcomes. The results showed that both groups improved on measures of symptom severity as well as ACT-specific components. There were no significant between-group differences. (Source. Effectiveness of Acceptance and Commitment Therapy compared to CBT+: Preliminary results).

II

USING THE PRACTICAL METHODS IN CBT, DBT, AND ACT IN YOUR DAILY LIFE

5

YOUR IRRATIONAL THOUGHT PATTERNS AND RISING ABOVE THEM

Have you ever been in a situation where someone is talking to you, and you get an image in your head of punching them till they bleed? Or perhaps you're just minding your own business while having your morning coffee at Starbucks, and all of a sudden, you start thinking about what everyone around you would look like naked. As Rihanna would say, these are "wild thoughts," and it is quite normal to have an irrational thought pop up every once in a while. In fact, I think every human experiences some fleeting irrational thoughts in some way, shape, or form at some point in their life. It usually comes and disappears quickly.

The problem is when the thoughts are persistent, and they hijack your attention and emotions. If you keep catching yourself drowning in an inner dialogue or mental movie scene that feels out of control and is rooted in harmful or destructive ideas, then you've landed in the realm of distorted thinking.

Irrational thoughts can be self-directed or directed toward others. Regardless of whom they are focused on, these thoughts are usually sad, disturbing, negative, and at times destructive in nature. Letting them hang out in your mind is often the reason stress, anxiety, and depression accelerate, so it's best to become aware and to devise healthy ways of dealing with them as they show up.

IRRATIONAL THOUGHTS AND WHY WE HAVE THEM

The first thing to realize is that we have thousands of thoughts each day. Out of these, the majority are recycled thoughts. The implications of knowing this is that many irrational thoughts aren't originally yours. They are simply recycled, and you just happened to pick them up and call them your own.

There are many different types of irrational thoughts (expertly known as cognitive distortions in CBT), but at a fundamental level, they all seem to be unrealistic and definitely harmful to your mental well-being. These thoughts might include unjustified worry of financial hardships, fear that no one likes you, that you're unlovable and will always be alone, they might be thoughts of harming yourself or others. It could be a persistent thought of others falling ill or dying. As they come up, they seem to hijack your senses and attention, which sends you spinning off on a downward spiral with no hope.

From what research shows, we tend to have these irrational thoughts when under emotional distress. Strong, intense fear or anger is usually the culprit behind cognitive distortions. Pessimists and people who hate change typically struggle with irrational thinking.

HAVE YOU HEARD OF COGNITIVE REFRAMING (CR)?

Cognitive reframing, sometimes called cognitive restructuring, is a therapeutic process that helps the client discover, challenge, and modify, or replace their cognitive distortions. This is a staple tool in cognitive behavior therapy used frequently by therapists because many of our problems stem not so much from the crisis or unexpected situation but from the faulty way of thinking that we have about ourselves and the world around us. Through cognitive reframing, you will finally learn to reduce stress in your life as you develop healthy ways of restructuring your thought patterns and cultivate more positive and functional habits. Of course, this is easier said than done. Anyone who has suffered mental health issues and irrational thinking can attest to the fact that changing one's thoughts can feel almost impossible. But can you recall a time when doing something felt overwhelmingly hard? Perhaps it was learning to drive or getting through pre-calculus or any other skill you've picked up throughout your life. At first, it does feel strenuous, but just like any other skill, the more you practice, the easier it becomes. Challenging your own negative thoughts and beliefs and even catching yourself when your emotions are getting hijacked by distorted thoughts becomes manageable. We want to use this tool to develop the curiosity of what's real whenever thoughts and images hijack our mental space. When looking for a solution to overcome mental health issues, a good rule of thumb is to know that automatically trusting all your thoughts might not be the best idea. So, with a tool like cognitive reframing, you have the ability to test those thoughts for accuracy so you can better respond to the situation.

GETTING TO KNOW THE IRRATIONAL PATTERNS

The ways in which irrational thoughts play tricks on us are so numerous it's almost laughable. These tricks are called cognitive distortions in psychology, and you must start recognizing some of the patterns and beliefs that are playing out in your life. These beliefs and thought patterns may seem real, but they won't stand the test of light when analyzed accurately. They make your recovery hard and relapse after treatment a real possibility because as long as they are dominating your mental space, they are silently causing damage to your well-being. Unfortunately, many of these are ingrained during our formative years and feel like part of who we are. But that's false information, and it's crucial to start catching yourself when these culprits are threatening your well-being. Here are a few you should become aware of:

Catastrophizing

Are you one of those people who is always expecting the worst to happen? For example, you're sitting at a restaurant waiting for your date to arrive. You've been looking forward to this evening for such a long time. And then you realize your date is running late. Twenty minutes into it and still waiting. There's no answer when you call. It just rings and rings, so you automatically assume the worst and leave the restaurant. Of course, that reinforces the thoughts in your head that you're not loveable; she was playing you all along and never even liked you,, etc. You start thinking about how worthless you are and how much women suck!

Irrational thoughts of the girl out with another man and laughing about you and what an idiot you are for thinking that she would ever go on a date with you fill up your mind. No matter what soothing words or solutions you try to apply, there's no remedy. This is an example of catastrophizing. It's about seeing only the worst possible outcome in everything.

Magical thinking

This distorted thought pattern is most common in children and adults with obsessive-compulsive disorder. Magical thinkers believe that they can avoid harm to themselves or others by doing some sort of ritual. Sometimes these rituals pose a threat to the person, but they don't see it that way. You might also find some bipolar cases with magical thinking tendencies.

Paranoia

In its extreme forms, paranoia sips into the realm of delusion. Many bipolar people experience less severe forms of paranoia because of personalizing events, catastrophizing, or making leaps in logic. If you've had thoughts that make you feel like everyone at the cocktail party you went to was watching and judging you, then you've probably experienced this. The truth is, most of the time, people are too consumed in their own issues to judge us in the way we tend to think.

Minimization

I see this one as the opposite of catastrophizing because it's about devaluing ourselves or the things that happen to us. It can apply to oneself or in relating to others. For example, if a person fails to meet your high expectations in one way, like telling a lie on a single occasion, you will now write that person off forever, refusing to see any good characteristics that may exist. Another way this expresses itself is through refusal to see the good or bad qualities in yourself and others.

Personalization

As the name implies, this is about taking everything personally and assigning blame to yourself without any logical reason. It can be as simple as blaming yourself when that date didn't show up for dinner or as severe as believing that you are the cause of every bad thing that happens around you. You might even call yourself a bad luck charm.

Control fallacy

A control fallacy manifests as one of two beliefs. Either you believe you have no control over your life and are nothing more than a helpless victim with a pre-determined fate or that you are completely in control of yourself and your surroundings and thus responsible for the feelings of those around you. Both beliefs are equally inaccurate.

All or nothing thinking

In this type of perception, you only see things through the binary black and white lens. Life has no shades of gray, and you are either an abject failure or a complete success. There's absolutely no in-between for you, which can often lead to despair and major misperceptions about your life and goal achievement.

These are but a few of the various irrational thought patterns that might be dragging you down and inhibiting your full recovery despite all your efforts to get better. While these distortions are common and potentially extremely damaging, you don't have to live with them any longer. There are various techniques you can use to identify, challenge and erase or at least minimize them. The first step is, of course, increasing your awareness of your thoughts.

THE NEXT STEPS TOWARDS A POSITIVE OUTLOOK

To overcome cognitive distortions, the first thing you need is a healthy way of identifying and understanding your irrational thinking. A useful tool you can use is an automatic thought record.

Create a six-column worksheet for yourself either in your private journal or Google document. The six columns should be date/time, situation, automatic thoughts (ATs), emotions, your response, a more adaptive response. If you need something more flexible, you could also use your smartphone's notebook so you can record throughout the day.

First, you need to record the date and time of the thought you're recording. You can do an hourly check-in or something more frequent.

In the second column, write down the situation you just experienced. Ask yourself:

1. What led to this event?
2. What caused the unpleasant feelings I am experiencing?
3. Who was involved?

In column number three, you will write down the negative automatic thoughts that came up, including any images that accompanied the thought. You will consider the thoughts and images that went through your mind, write them down, and determine how much you believed these thoughts. Examples can include *I'm such an idiot, no one loves me, I can't cope with this, I'll never get better, I'll never find another relationship, the world is always working against me, I'll never find a job, I suck at everything I do, etc.*

The purpose of this exercise is to find the "hot" thought or the one with the most significant electrical charge that messes with your entire system. That thought is the one that needs to be worked on first.

After identifying the thought, take notice of the emotions and sensations that accompanied said thoughts. This should go into the fourth column. What emotions did you experience at the time, and how intense were they on a scale of 1 (barely felt it) to 10 (completely overwhelming). Examples can include anxious, guilty, ashamed, depressed, afraid, helpless, angry, happy, etc. You might wonder why I've included "happy" in this example list, but it's because I want to show you that thought recording is about getting in touch with and observing all your emotions at that designated time. So, you need to monitor both the negative and positive thought patterns.

In column five, I invite you to come up with an adaptive response to those thoughts. This requires courage and some effort on your part as you identify the distortions that are cropping up and challenging them.

Answer the following questions here.

1. Which cognitive distortions were you employing?
2. What is the evidence that the "hot" thought(s) is true, and what evidence is there that it's not true?
3. You've thought about the worst that could happen, but what's the best that could happen? What's the most realistic scenario?
4. How likely are the best-case and most realistic scenarios?

Since your current thinking is biased to that negative thought, this step should be easy. I want you to do your best to stick with verifiable evidence such as data, percentages, facts, and real proof. Avoid opinions and interpretations. A simple example to help illustrate this could be:

Suppose it was you who was waiting at a restaurant for over 15 minutes for your date to show up, and she didn't pick up the phone when you rang to find out where she was. When working out this process after that event, credible evidence that would be considered acceptable are:

- I was sitting at the restaurant for over twenty minutes, and she didn't show.
- I rang her cellphone once, and there was no answer or response.
- I was disappointed she went cold and didn't even call to explain that she wanted to cancel.

However, the following statements are not proof of evidence:

- She hates me and wanted to humiliate me in public.
- She had no intention of going out with me since the beginning.
- She's ruined my chances of finding love.
- I will never find a woman who genuinely loves me.

In the last column, I want you to consider the outcome of this event. Think about how much you believe the automatic thought, now that you've come up with an adaptive response, and just rate your belief out of ten. If you feel the grip of that initial thought lessening, then the process is working. Write out what emotions you're feeling now and at what intensity you're experiencing them.

ADDITIONAL TECHNIQUES THAT YOU CAN PRACTICE

To avoid being hijacked by irrational thoughts, I encourage you to practice at least one of these methods.

#1. Personalization

This cognitive distortion is about seeing yourself as the cause of all negativity around you, including others' misfortunes or everyday mishaps. It can take many forms. For example, you made dinner reservations for yourself and friends, but your name isn't on the list when you show up. Or, in my case, I'm sitting with a friend at a coffee shop, and the waitress gets his order right but not mine. Another scenario could be going on a beach vacation with your family only to have it rain the entire time. Yet on the last day, as you head to the airport, it's sunny clear blue skies. If you recognize that you usually take things personally when something happens, or someone says or doesn't say what you want, here's how to challenge those irrational thoughts as they come up.

How to handle it:

Notice how you're quick to take responsibility for something that's out of your control. Ask yourself, "could I factually control or contribute to this problem and how?" Then consider all the other factors that may have contributed to the problem. For example, in the case of the dinner reservations with friends, perhaps you could have double-checked they got the right date and time and that they didn't misunderstand your information. Could there be a glitch in the software system, or did the person who took the reservation forget to confirm it? When it comes to rain during a vacation, did you really cause rain just because you wanted good weather so badly? What facts can prove that you are the rainmaker and that it's your fault? Get curious, not judgmental, and have an open dialogue with yourself about these thoughts.

#2. All-or-nothing thinking

The do or die mentality will not serve you in most cases and only causes distress as you move through life because, in reality, life isn't binary. People aren't binary, and it will serve you well to question those thoughts whenever they come up.

How to handle this:

Notice the times when they come up and question if there's no other possibility other than that extreme thought trying to hijack your mind. For example, if you're thinking you didn't get hired at that interview because you're the worst, perhaps you can introduce the thought, "Is that really the only reason they didn't hire me? Couldn't there be another possibility? What if there's another reason?"

I like to play "what if there's another reason? What could it be?" when this type of irrational thought comes up. I find it breaks the doom and gloom pattern, enabling me to process the situation from a new perspective.

#3. Decatastrophizing

This tool is a great one to talk yourself out of the habit of catastrophizing situations or seeing the worst in people.

How to apply this:

When that worst-case scenario shows up, take a deep breath, find your journal or a piece of paper, and then write down your worry. Identify the core of the issue. What are you worried about? Do your best to identify the actual problem causing you to think this way. Now, picture for a moment how horrible it would be if what you're thinking actually came to pass. That worst-case scenario that you're so afraid of. Does it feel better thinking about this? When have you ever even experienced that same event or something similar in the past? How often has it happened? If it doesn't feel good playing out this worst-case scenario, and since you're not 100% certain that it will actually happen even if it did in the past, why not consider a different outcome. What if something good happened instead, and you got the opposite of that unpleasant outcome. What would that look like? Invest some time painting that scenario in your mind with as much color (if not more) as you did when thinking about the negative outcome. Sit with it until your emotions catch up. Consider the details of this new scenario and write them down. How does it feel to sit with this outcome?

Next, think about your chances of surviving in one piece. How likely are you to be okay if your fear comes true? How are likely is it that you'll be okay in one month or one year?

Finally, come back to the present moment and think about how you're feeling now. Are you still just as worried, or did the exercise help you think a little more realistically? Write down how you're feeling about it.

#4. Facts or Opinions exercise

I find this one to be incredibly therapeutic and use it all day, every day. One of the first lessons you learn in CBT is that facts are not opinions. These might seem obvious for people without mental health issues, but you and I know how hard it can be to remember and apply it in day-to-day interactions. I encourage you to start exercising with facts and opinions as you go through your day. To help you practice this immediately, here are some of my statements that I began playing with years ago. First, I made a long list of the common thoughts that dominated my day at the time, then I would sit for five minutes three times a day and go through each of them, labeling them either fact or opinion to help me remember what's real and what's not.

You can borrow my list or make one of your own.

- I am a failure.
- No one likes me.
- I am uglier than [name him/her].
- I suck at everything.
- I'll never find love again.
- I will never get better.
- She didn't care about hurting me.
- No one understands me in this world.
- I'm a terrible person.

- Bad things always happen to me.
- I am so unlucky.
- This will be an absolute disaster.
- Nobody could ever love someone like me.
- I ruined everything.
- I'm too fat.
- I'm selfish and uncaring.
- I can't do anything right.
- I'm too old.
- It's too late for me now.
- I ruined the evening.
- I failed the exam.
- A friend in need said "no" to me.
- I made a mistake and caused us to miss the movie.

Once you have your list of the most common thoughts, go through each, identifying which is fact and which is an opinion. Here's what mine looked like.

- I am a failure. *False*
- No one likes me. *False*
- I am uglier than [name him/her]. *False*
- I suck at everything. *False*
- I'll never find love again. *False*
- I will never get better. *False*
- She didn't care about hurting me. *False*
- No one understands me in this world. *False*
- I'm a terrible person. *False*

- Bad things always happen to me. *False*
- I am so unlucky. *False*
- This will be an absolute disaster. *False*
- Nobody could ever love someone like me. *False*
- I ruined everything. *False*
- I'm too fat. *False*
- I'm selfish and uncaring. *False*
- I can't do anything right. *False*
- I'm too old. *False*
- It's too late for me now. *False*
- I ruined the evening. *False*
- I failed my exam. *True*
- A friend in need said "no" to me. *True*
- I made a mistake and caused us to miss the movie. *True*

#5. The Socratic method

The Socratic method, sometimes referred to as Socratic questioning, involves a disciplined and thoughtful dialogue between you and your therapist or by yourself (if you can be objective enough to carry it out). It has its roots in the great Greek teacher, and philosopher Socrates and the method is applied between teacher and student, coach and coachee, and mentor and mentee. In CBT, the Socratic method is used as an umbrella term for using questioning to clarify meaning and elicit emotions and consequences. It's a great tool to help one gradually create insight and explore alternative action. Instead of using the didactic approach, which emphasizes teaching, this method focuses on personal reflection and questioning.

When applying this method either on your own or with a professional, remember the intention is to thoughtfully question yourself, not engage in confrontation or judgment. It should be a guided discovery in an open interested manner to acquire insight and enlightenment. There are certain qualities that all the questions you ask should possess. They should be concise, directed and clear, open, yet with purpose, focused but tentative, and above all else neutral and free of judgment (as much as possible).

Using this method, you can thoughtfully reflect on those distorted thought patterns to figure out how realistic they are.

How to apply this to your irrational thoughts:

Identify the thought and the beliefs that are trying to run your mind, ask open questions to bring to the surface further knowledge so you can uncover assumptions, inconsistencies, contradictions, etc. Challenge the assumptions and inconsistencies that come up. See if you can identify and replace that "hot thought" that's creating the problem or, at the very least, restate it more precisely so it can stop having a strong negative grip on you.

Create a list of the go-to questions that you could ask yourself when irrational thoughts threaten to hijack your mind and emotions. Here's a list to help get you started.

1. What is the meaning behind that "hot thought"? Why have I attached that meaning and those accompanying feelings to that thought?
2. What assumptions am I making here?

3. Is there a different point of view I could have?
4. Is there evidence to validate that what I am thinking, and feeling is real?
5. Are there alternative viewpoints to consider?
6. What are the long-term implications of feeling and thinking this hot thought?
7. What would be a better thought to have? Is there a better question I could ask myself to understand why I am having this thought?

If you're at a loss on how to come up with the best questions for your particular case, then a good rule of thumb is to use the 5 W's and an H. What happened? Who is involved? When did it happen? Where did it happen? Why did it happen? How did it happen?

6

THE LINK BETWEEN PROCRASTINATION AND MENTAL HEALTH & HOW TO OVERCOME IT

Most people are quick to judge procrastination as a sign that one is just plain lazy but is that really accurate? I personally disagree. In fact, I find myself working long and hard just to beat a deadline after procrastinating for weeks. Even back in my college years, I would put things on hold till the 11th hour when a paper was due. Then I'd pull an all-nighter and get it done. Did I enjoy that pressure and anxiety? Not really. But eventually, I got the job done. Surely procrastination isn't about being lazy because I doubt a lazy person could have the stamina of putting in such long hours and hard work. So, what is the real reason, so many of us procrastinate, and is there a correlation between this habit and mental health? Finally, can we overcome procrastination?

FACING THE CONSEQUENCES OF PROCRASTINATION

Whether you justify why you procrastinate or hate it entirely, the fact is there are always negative consequences of procrastinating on anything. Feelings of anxiety, stress, fatigue, and disappointment are typical experiences for procrastinators. There's also that dreaded feeling of looming failure and the fear that something might go wrong, and it might not be possible to fix the issue because there wouldn't be enough time anyway. I mean, imagine waiting till the last minute to complete a work project only to have the computer crash hours before you're supposed to present it to your boss, thereby losing everything. That's cause for severe stress and anxiety. According to a 2009 Ferrari, Barnes & Steel research, nearly 25% of adults living in the United States and other countries are classified as chronic procrastinators.

Procrastination is actually a condition, and it has negative impacts on our mental and physical health. In a 2007 study published in the Psychology Bulletin, psychologist Piers Steel defined procrastination as "self-regulatory failure leading to poor performance and reduced well-being." In other words, it's a form of self-sabotage. Several studies show just how debilitating procrastination can become.

One such study in 2010 titled "I'll Go to Therapy Eventually" found that procrastination and stress are interconnected. It also linked poor mental health to procrastination. There's also growing evidence that procrastination affects physical health and is a factor that can lead to hypertension and cardiovascular disease. (2015 study by Fushia M.

Sirois). Of course, that naturally leads to poor performance both at work and school. If your mental and physical health is jeopardized, how can you possibly become a high performer? Procrastinators tend to earn less, spend shorter periods of time in any given job, and hold positions with lower intrinsic value. This condition is also frequently linked to poor financial decision making in adults and low grades in students.

Despite all these negative consequences, we need to realize that it is a condition, not just about poor time management or being lazy. Procrastination for many of us can be traced back to some underlying psychological reasons. Most of the time, our reasons for procrastinating and avoiding things are rooted in fear and anxiety about failure or underperformance. Sometimes it's because we are afraid of looking stupid or being judged harshly by others. Low self-esteem and the belief that "I'm not good enough to do this" can amplify this procrastination condition. Whatever the reason might be for you, it's good to address it because being a procrastinator makes you your own worst enemy and only heightens any underlying mental issues. In cases where procrastination is a symptom of underlying mental health problems, you will need some professional help. That's where CBT is useful because, for the most part, it can help you understand and recognize your unhelpful thought patterns and behavior, which contribute to issues like depression. And, of course, most people suffering from depression tend to be professional procrastinators. Through CBT and recognizing that you need to work on the underlying problem, you can start creating structures that help you take on procrastination and finally beat it.

THE ONLY METHOD YOU NEED TO OVERCOME PROCRASTINATION

The only way to overcome procrastination is to understand that your brain is complex, and it can be your best friend or your worst enemy. There are specific chemical releases within the brain that either make it easier or more challenging for you to beat procrastination, depending on whether these chemicals are naturally released in ample quantity or not. One such crucial chemical hormone is dopamine.

What is dopamine?

Dopamine is a type of neurotransmitter that's naturally produced by your brain. Your nervous system uses it to send messages between nerve cells, which is why it's sometimes referred to as a chemical messenger. Perhaps the most important thing for you to know about dopamine is that it's your "feel good" neurotransmitter, and it plays a huge role in how you feel, think, and plan out things. It is involved in neurological and psychological functioning, which includes your mood and ability to make decisions.

Too much or too little dopamine means your ability to focus, find life exciting, and even the lens through which you interpret life will be thrown out of balance.

Aside from making you feel good, dopamine is also involved in blood flow, digestion, heart and kidney function, sleep, pleasure and reward-seeking behavior, stress response, executive functioning, memory, and focus.

How does dopamine function in the brain?

From infancy, dopamine plays a huge role in your development, and in fact, research links various mental disabilities to low levels of dopamine. Genetic conditions like congenital hypothyroidism are said to be linked to insufficient dopamine. Even Alzheimer's, depressive disorders, binge-eating, addiction, gambling, and so much more have recently been associated with dopamine deficiency.

Scientists who study neurobiological and psychiatric disorders have been interested in uncovering how dopamine works and how imbalanced levels (either too much or too little) can affect behavior and lead to disability. For the sake of our particular quest of healing from mental health issues, we are going to focus on how you can increase dopamine as a method to overcome procrastination. Here are tips for implementing immediately.

- **Get plenty of rested sleep.** Proper sleep is mandatory for your mental well-being, and it also fuels dopamine production. If you have nights of restless sleep, insomnia, or poor-quality sleep, it's essential to get help because the better you sleep, the more dopamine you will naturally produce.
- **Nutrition.** Eat foods rich in tyrosine, such as meat, fish, cheese, nuts, beans, lentils, soy, and dairy, among others. On that same note of watching your nutrition, I encourage you to avoid processed foods, high fats, sugar, and caffeine.
- **Body Movement.** Exercising daily in the way you most enjoy is an excellent hack for increasing dopamine in your brain.

- **Consider using natural nootropics**, including L-Tyrosine and L-theanine.

With the right amount of dopamine, you will feel more alert, motivated, happy, focused, and almost euphoric, which are all necessary feelings for overcoming procrastination and getting things done. The critical takeaway here is that dopamine increase can help you beat procrastination because it serves many vital neurological and cognitive functions. The effects on mood and pleasure, as well as the motivation-reward-reinforcement cycle that is created when dopamine is released in your brain, is all you need to stop procrastinating and start engaging more in your projects, whether at school or work.

TIME MANAGEMENT STRATEGIES THAT WILL HELP YOU ALONG THE WAY

Aside from increasing dopamine levels in your brain (naturally and healthily), you also need to get better at time management. This is a huge topic. There are countless books written on productivity and time management, yet it still remains a huge obstacle for most people. So, let me share a few simple time management hacks that have been working for me in recent years.

#1. Block out time for critical time-sensitive projects. In other words, schedule time to boldly face this thing that's giving you so much apprehension. By creating a chunk of time where you sit with your project, assignment, or problem, you can intelligently organize yourself and figure out how to apply the second tip.

#2. Salami Slice your tasks. This essentially means you need to chunk it down into a bitesize task so you can have mini-milestones on your way to completing the entire thing. By breaking things down into something small and manageable, the overwhelm immediately dissipates. During the depths of despair as I was going through my depression, I would break things down into small 5-minute tasks. So, all I had to do was focus on that small five-minute task. That felt manageable for me then as I got better, I added more time.

#3. Get the most unpleasant tasks out of the way as early in the day as possible. I know it might seem like it's best to start with something easy but trust me, the best time to beat procrastinating is earlier in the day. The thing that you fear most or overwhelms you the most and thus stirs up procrastinating is what you should do first thing in the morning.

#4. Don't obsess about time management. Instead, focus on managing your activities and your energy. For most of us, this will be the best-kept secret of managing time and getting things done. You need to realize that what fails us is our energy, focus, and motivation levels, not that time isn't enough (although we might think that). So instead of fussing over getting more time (which is impossible as there are only 24 hours in a day), focus on increasing your dopamine and stamina. That way, you'll stay engaged in the activity for the allocated time and actually produce something good at the end.

#5. Use the Pomodoro technique (25min sessions) to give yourself breaks in between the task, so it doesn't become overwhelming. Once you can consistently work on a task for 5 minutes at a time without losing focus, you can advance to this Pomodoro technique. It's used by leaders all over the world. Both students and professionals can develop this habit of chunking down into 25-minutes of work and 3-5 minutes of rest time. Do two or three Pomodoros at a time, then take a longer break to reward yourself for the excellent work put in. During the Pomodoro, however, there should be no distractions.

OTHER STRATEGIES THAT CAN HELP YOU BEAT PROCRASTINATION

#1. Apply the decatastrophizing technique

We learned this in a previous chapter, so you should now recognize that catastrophizing something is an irrational thought and often accompanies procrastination. For example, has there been a time where you made a huge deal out of something (an upcoming exam, a research paper, a project, etc.), and you thought, "*Oh, this is going to be painfully tough.*"? In that belief of making it seem unbearable, your brain automatically rejected the idea of taking action. Even if you were right about the fact that it would be challenging, arduous, uncomfortable, or boring, that still should trigger procrastination unless it turns into irrational thought.

So, follow the technique you learned of decatastrophizing and keep things in proper perspective. For example, you might counter that same irrational thought with "*sure, this isn't my favorite task, but I can get through it, and the sooner I do, the better I'll feel.*"

#2. Get an accountability partner.

I have found this beneficial because by asking someone to keep me accountable and cheer me on, I stay focused long enough to see it through. If you're at work, you could ask a close colleague or your boss (if you get along) to become an accountability partner. If in school, it could be a classmate, friend, or your favorite teacher. If none of those options are viable, consider joining a support group, hiring a coach, or even a therapist. Not wanting to go back or break your word to someone who matters to you is an excellent incentive to squash procrastination.

#3. Optimize your environment

The environment you work in matters a lot. A dimly lit and dull workspace for someone with mental health problems is perfect for - getting more depressed and producing nothing! An environment with lots of distractions for someone with attention deficit disorders or a person who loves being on social media is the perfect way to promote procrastination. In both these scenarios, we end up with the massive problem of low production and poor performance. Therefore, I encourage you to be extra thoughtful about your workspace. Whether you work from home or in a big office, make sure the area you do your best work is off-limits when it comes to distractions such as cellphones, magazines, and so on. Install proper lighting and create a warm, bright, and inviting ambiance. Even if you're a student, you can always ensure your desk and workspace is neat, clutter-free, and near a window or in a position that makes you feel good.

#4. Develop a reward system for your efforts

In other words, always give yourself a treat when you accomplish something that triggered feelings of procrastination. Each time you manage to beat it, reward yourself for that good behavior so you can release more dopamine and reinforce that action-oriented behavior. The reward can vary depending on how big the task was and how much procrastination you had to squash. See if you can come up with a list of things (big treats and small treats) that are healthy and make you feel good. For example, if you like flowers, buy yourself some flowers when you accomplish something. Take yourself out for a nice dinner or give yourself an ice-cream treat!

PROCRASTINATION GONE: REAPING THE BENEFITS

There are so many benefits of overcoming procrastination, and the more you do it, the more you'll enjoy them. Remember, your mental and physical health are all impacted by this habit, so the more you defeat it, the better you'll feel. It will also increase your sense of accomplishment, sense of confidence, and self-esteem. When we procrastinate, we end up disappointing ourselves because, deep down, we know it's not possible to perform at our highest and best if we are always in a mad rush to meet a deadline. You're here because you want to transform your life and create a better future for yourself. The best way to secure that better, brighter future is to eliminate unhealthy habits such as procrastination. Keep reminding yourself "why" you're choosing to make this change and keep your eyes on the new life you wish to experience. The more you stay focused on unleashing that new, healthier, better version of yourself, the easier it will be to leave procrastination behind.

7

BREAKING AND BUILDING HABITS THAT SUPPORTS A HEALTHY LIFESTYLE

Automatic habits and behaviors drive nearly half of your daily life. Did you know that? Well, consider this. You probably have a morning routine that you do almost without thinking. You wake up, brush your teeth, shower, dress, etc., without giving any conscious thought to the process. And if you look back at your routine this morning, yesterday, last week, and even last year, you'll notice it's pretty much the same. Right? We are creatures of habit because it's the most efficient way for our brain to get through the day. And while habits and routines can be useful, they can also make it feel impossible to overcome a mental health issue. The condition's persistence shows certain habits and behavior have become your default operational setting, fostering the disorder. So, the path to recovery (whether you have a therapist and an on-going program or you're self-healing) is to commit to changing some of the habits that contribute to your current situation. But we don't just want to give up bad habits without replacing them with new ones, so this one will be a two-step process that happens simultaneously. It's easy to recognize the things that harm your physical health. For example, binge-eating McDonalds and KFC will drive up your cholesterol, increase your waistline and probably even give you heart disease. But there are habits you might have that make you easily relapse back into depression, anxiety, etc.

BAD HABITS THAT YOU SHOULD CHANGE

Guilt

This is a habit, yes, and a very dangerous one. Though unseen to others, your learned behavior (perhaps since childhood) feeds your mental health problems. If left unchecked, you may find yourself in a state of perpetual guilt that prevents you from leading a healthy, happy lifestyle.

If you want to know whether this is a problem, do a thought recording exercise for twenty-one days. Notice how much you magnify issues and how often you claim responsibility for creating problems with little or nothing to do with you. Are you usually blaming yourself for things, perceiving yourself as a bad person, and struggle with self-forgiveness? Then you likely have guilt as a habit, and that thing has to be changed.

Lack of proper exercise

This isn't about getting a gym membership. It's about developing the habit of daily performing some form of exercise to get your brain and body moving. The challenge is when we feel at our worst (depressed, anxious, suicidal), that's when we need the benefits of exercise the most. Yet, it's so hard to get it done.

Regular exercise is proven to ease depression by releasing endorphins and other "feel good" hormones. It not only enhances your mood and immune system but as well your sense of confidence. There's no particular form of exercise that is mandatory, but you will need to make an effort and start doing something. Consider trying different things at home, in the gym, or dance studio until you find something you enjoy doing at least six times each week. You can experiment with Yoga, Pilates, Strength Training, High-Intensity Interval Training, Dance, etc.

The worst thing you can do when overcoming a mental health issue is to exercise irregularly or not at all.

Poor quality sleep

Many people with mental health issues spend a lot of time in bed supposedly sleeping, but it's usually very crappy sleep. On the other extreme, there are those who barely get any because of insomnia. In both these cases, insufficient sleep is a massive struggle during recovery and treatment. It should be addressed as early on in the treatment as possible because it's hard to heal without a night of good restful sleep. The Sleep Health Foundation reports that 60 to 90 percent of patients with depression also have insomnia. According to the Harvard Mental Health Letter published by Harvard Medical School, poor sleep can result in mental health problems, and treating sleep disorders can relieve mental health symptoms. So, if you weren't taking this seriously, it's about time you start.

A CHALLENGE TO SELF: 3 STRATEGIES TO BREAK THE BAD HABITS

Now that you have an idea of some of the habits that need to change in your life let's talk about how to break them. I want you to challenge yourself with these three strategies:

First, figure out your triggers

For example, if your habit is procrastination or stress eating, pay attention to the circumstances surrounding you when you do those things. Once you identify your triggers, take notice of the impulsive behaviors that follow as you act out. So, if it's procrastinating, do you reach for your phone instead and drown in social media instead of starting the project? When someone stresses you, do you immediately go for junk food or something sweet as you sob and worry?

The second thing you must do is:

Increase your awareness and become mindful of your feelings as you're doing this

It's vital to employ mindfulness at this point so that you don't attack yourself once you catch yourself in the act of a bad habit yet again. As you start doing "the thing," pay attention to how you feel when partaking in it. If you're stress eating and down to your second box of cookies even though you're not hungry, just pause for a moment and get in tune with how you're really feeling. What is your state of mind right now? Do you really feel good? How good will your mind and body feel after another hour of getting through those boxes of cookies? Is this really the kind of lifestyle and behavior that makes you happiest? Grab your journal and just write what you're feeling deep in your heart as you ask these questions and self-reflect.

As your awareness increases, your brain will accurately update the reward value of the habit you want to break, and it will begin to see that "X" behavior leads to "Y" consequences, which isn't what truly makes me happy.

The third thing you must do is:

Let go of your failure mindset

It's hard to be perky and enthusiastic when struggling with depression, anxiety, and so on, but your healing can only work when you let go of that doom and gloom mindset. Those negative thoughts are actually a habit that can be released, but they've been around so long you probably assume that's the only way to think. Ugly irrational thoughts will tell you that this won't work or that there's no hope for you, but you can and must choose to think differently. This will work this time, and you do not need to be tortured by your own thoughts of failure anymore. As you learn to disregard these thoughts and allow them to float away from when, they came, you'll find the courage and optimism needed to continue on this quest of breaking the habits that have caused you so much psychological pain and suffering.

BUILDING ON THE GOOD HABITS

Breaking bad habits isn't enough. You also need to build the right ones to replace the old, outdated ones that no longer serve you. But how does one start doing this? I recommend starting simple. Take small steps forward and implement one habit change at a time. Don't do too much too soon. Here's a scientifically proven technique that will help you build new habits.

THE HABIT STACKING AND THE ANCHORING TECHNIQUE

Habit stacking is a method created by Dr. BJ Fogg as part of his Tiny Habits Program. It's about building new habits by stacking them on top of a current one that already exists. The formula is quite simple:

After/Before [current habit] I will [new habit].

When it comes to helping your brain form new habits, the best thing to do is leverage existing habits that are working well. Ever noticed how efficient you are at remembering to take a shower and open the blinds each morning as you start the day? Or how you automatically know where to throw the keys as soon as you walk into the house? It's not something you have to consciously plan. Your brain has built a strong network of neurons to support that behavior of getting out of bed, drawing up the curtains and getting into the shower or opening the door and immediately offloading your keys and coins, placing them in the same location each time. The more you do something, the stronger and more efficient the connection becomes. So how would this apply in the creation of a new habit?

Instead of pairing your new habit with a particular time and location, pair it with a current routine.

Examples of implementing habit stacking:

After I sit down to dinner, I will say one thing I'm grateful for that happened today.

Before I pour myself my morning cup of tea, I will meditate for five minutes.

Overall, habit stacking allows you to intentionally implement new actions with will be ingrained in your brain more quickly because you are stacking them into something you're currently doing. It's like creating a game plan for which action should come next. Once you get comfortable with this approach, you can develop general habit stacks to guide you in all situations. For example, when I walk into a party, I will introduce myself to anyone I don't know yet, or when the phone rings, I will take a deep breath and smile before answering.

GOOD HABITS YOU'D LIKE TO HAVE

#1. Work on your posture

Most of us don't realize how much poor posture affects how we feel. Evidence shows poor posture can cause one to feel more depressed, anxious, and insecure. Therefore, it's time to correct your posture. Start by standing up and sitting up straight. Notice the difference it makes even if you're just practicing in front of the mirror for a few minutes each day until it becomes the new norm.

#2. Drinking plenty of water

Hydration can mess with your focus and mood because the brain requires a lot of water to function optimally. Research also shows that water boosts mood and energy levels. Most of us forget to hydrate enough, so a good habit to develop is drinking at least 10-12 glasses of water daily. Consider using the habit stacking and anchoring technique in the morning for drinking 2-3 glasses of water as part of your morning routine.

#3. Spend some time with the morning sun

The morning sun is excellent for aiding your body in the synthesis of vitamin D. In fact, something I noticed through sheer experiment was that five minutes with my face to the sun early in the morning significantly reduced my depressed state. Scientists seem to agree that not enough sunlight can cause depression, which is ironic because depressed people hardly ever want to be outdoors. But you don't need to leave your house, just stand next to an open window and stick your head out for a few minutes or sit on your terrace each morning. It will give you an energy and mood boost instantaneously, enabling you to tackle the day better.

#4. Read something inspiring

One of the best habits you can pick up is starting and ending the day with something inspiring, motivating, and uplifting. Reading the right materials also broadens your thinking and increases your mental power. Consider reading self-help books or even getting crosswords, jigsaw puzzles, and other mentally stimulating activities to keep your mind active.

#5. 4:55 Drill

This is a little technique that can massively improve your productivity and beat procrastination if you turn it into a habit. At the end of each workday, use the last five minutes of your day to get yourself organized for the following day. Take a moment to decide on no more than two things you'd like to accomplish first thing in the morning and assemble everything you need now so that you can hit the ground running the next day. All it takes is the last five minutes (hence 4:55 Drill), but this small shift in how you end your day can significantly help you eliminate that feeling of overwhelm or procrastination in the morning.

#6. Journal daily.

The recovery process is long, and there's nothing more therapeutic than getting into the habit of journaling your thoughts at the end of the day so you can express how you're feeling as you go through this recovery process. It's also a very effective way of monitoring your self-talk, which leads me to my next suggestion.

#7. Be self-aware and practice positive self-talk

As you practice mindfulness and increase self-awareness, you can begin to be mindful of your feelings and emotional responses. Monitor the inner dialogue you currently have and make it a habit to speak more kindly to yourself. As you speak more positively to yourself, you'll find it easier to also watch your tone when interacting with others, which improves your social skills.

#8. Clean up your environment

This is a simple action that can create a sense of ease and lighten your mood, making you feel more ready to face the day. A clean workspace, clean home, and clean bedroom are all great for promoting a sense of well-being and organization. I don't know about you, but when I am going through depression, the last thing I want to do is make my bed or clean my office space, yet these cluttered environments do very little to help with recovery. Research shows that your personal environment directly impacts your well-being. A clean home and work environment can influence your mood, affect your behavior and motivate you to take action. It also helps reduce that sense of constriction or stagnation and stress because a clutter-free area has better air circulation, less stuffiness, and a sense of expansiveness, which will impact how you feel internally.

#9. Practice gratitude daily

Invest five minutes a day to write out things you are grateful for. I started this as a morning habit, and it has helped me curb those negative thoughts that used to hijack me in the morning. I find some sunny spot in my house, sit with a pen and paper and jot down five things I'm grateful for. Some days are easier than others, but even when I feel like I have nothing good going for me, I still force myself to feel grateful for the things we often take for granted, like the fact that I had running water in my house or that I took a hot shower. Try it for one month, and you'll see the therapeutic benefits this has.

SURE-FIRE METHOD TO MAKE THE NEW HABITS STICK

Building a new habit isn't easy and doesn't happen overnight. You also can't expect to see immediate results even once you start implementing the action and behavior, so how do you ensure you stick with it long enough to reap positive rewards?

It begins with a shift in mindset. What you need to focus on is making this a part of your new lifestyle. It's not about whether something is giving you the end results you need. It's about whether it's feeling naturally integrated into your life and whether you're enjoying it as part of your journey. For example, if you decided to eliminate the bad habit of no exercise with a morning jog, your goal shouldn't be to lose weight in a week or even two. Implement the new habit and train yourself into waking up each morning and doing your morning run simply because you want it to become the new way of living. While running, you also catch that morning sun, and you're outdoors in nature, allowing you to habit stack multiple good habits all at once. The end result of losing weight and getting fitter should be a by-product that comes in its own due time. Your reward should be more centered on how you feel during and after investing in this healthy habit.

Another sure way to help you maintain your new habits is to keep yourself accountable through a habit tracker. A habit tracker is a simple way to measure whether you implemented your habit or not each day. Research has shown that people who track their progress on goals like losing weight, quitting smoking, etc., are more likely to improve than those who don't. So why not set yourself a goal of positive self-talk, drinking enough water, jogging in the morning, or making your bed first thing in the morning?

You can get an app on your smartphone or use a calendar and simply cross off each day you stuck to your routine. What you'll notice over time is that your habit will start creating streaks that you'll feel compelled not to break. That reinforces that feeling of winning and healing that's extremely desirable. This is one of the best signals and proof that you're making progress. It motivates you to keep going and feels very satisfying as you see yourself accomplishing something productive each day.

There are many options for habit trackers on iOS and Android, or simply get a journal with a calendar and do it manually. Regardless of the format, you use to track the new habit, keep it simple and easy to do. Also, remember to start small by integrating a single habit at a time until it becomes part of your daily life.

8

MINDFULNESS: WHAT IS IT AND HOW CAN IT HELP YOU

Y ou've likely seen a lot of mindfulness talk on the Internet. It seems to be the trend that many are promoting as a tool for healthy living, from celebrities to athletes and everyday busy individuals. Most of what people talk about when referring to mindfulness practices is meditation. Although meditation is a powerful tool, it's not the only way to practice mindfulness. So, if you tried it and didn't reap the benefits, don't give up just yet. I encourage you to keep reading so you can discover more ways to practice mindfulness.

A LOOK INTO MINDFULNESS

To understand mindfulness, we need to define it. What is mindfulness? According to American Psychological Association (APA.org, 2012), mindfulness is a moment-to-moment awareness of one's experience without judgment. In this sense, mindfulness is a state and not a trait. Merriam-Webster Dictionary also offers a unique understanding of mindfulness as it defines it as the practice of maintaining a non-judgmental state of heightened or complete awareness of one's thoughts, emotions, or experiences on a moment-to-moment basis. One of my favorite definitions is from Greater Good Science at the University of California at Berkley. "Mindfulness means maintaining a moment-by-moment awareness of our thoughts, feelings, bodily sensations, and the surrounding environment." While there are varying definitions, the fact is, mindfulness is about present moment awareness. When it comes to mental health problems, mindfulness is extremely helpful because it keeps you focused on the here and now instead of consumed by the past or the future. Often, our biggest problems arise from spending too much time in the past or in the future.

WHERE DID MINDFULNESS COME FROM?

Mindfulness isn't just a buzzword. It's a practice that has been around for a really long time. However, in the West, Jon Kabat-Zinn is linked to this concept of mindfulness because he re-imagined Buddhist contemplation practices for the secular world decades ago. Since mindfulness is centered around knowing the mind, training the mind, and freeing the mind when used as part of the healing treatment, it can be an effective way of healing and creating your dream lifestyle.

Two components work together to bring about relief. Awareness and an open and accepting attitude. Both are essential when you start practicing mindfulness. Research shows that people who practice mindfulness receive heightened metacognitive awareness. That means one can detach from one's own feelings and mental process. It also decreased patterns of negative thinking behavior, which positively affects the individual and reduces the chances of a relapse into depression after treatment is completed. Other studies conducted also showed that mindfulness can improve anxiety and depression symptoms and reduce stress levels. In short, anyone struggling with mental health issues can significantly benefit from this practice.

CAN IT REALLY HELP ME?

If you struggle with anxiety, depression, and other similar mental health issues, then mindfulness is definitely for you. Anyone can learn and practice mindfulness whether you have severe mental disorders or simply want to improve your current mental state. The best part is anyone at any age can implement mindfulness into their daily routine. Choosing to practice mindfulness will increase your awareness and help you detach from irrational thoughts and overwhelming emotions. It will help you center your mind, improve your memory and bring more clarity into your life.

It will make you more accepting of yourself and situations that are beyond your control. Instead of resisting or fighting your fears, doubts, or even anger when it shows up, you can simply learn to observe and let it go.

MINDFULNESS AS A THERAPY

It is possible to combine mindfulness and therapy. In fact, most research centers around two specific types of mindfulness training.

The first was pioneered by Jon Kabat-Zinn, known as mindfulness-based stress reduction (MBSR). The second is Mindfulness-based cognitive therapy (MBCT), a type of psychotherapy that combines cognitive therapy, meditation, and the cultivation of a present-oriented, non-judgmental attitude, aka mindfulness. It builds upon cognitive therapy principles by using techniques such as mindfulness meditation to teach people to consciously pay attention to their thoughts and feelings without placing any judgments upon them. This type of mindfulness training was created by a group of therapists (John Teasdale, Zindek Segal, and Mark Williams) who felt the need to develop a cost-effective method for treating and preventing relapse in depressive patients.

When treating chronic depression, the goal of MBCT is to help a patient learn how to avoid relapses by not engaging in those automatic thought patterns that often worsen depression. A recent study showed that MBCT reduces the risk for relapse by 50% regardless of age, sex, education, or relationship status.

HOW DOES IT WORK?

An MBCT program is usually a group intervention that lasts eight weeks. In the program, you attend a weekly course that lasts two hours and one day-long class after the fifth week. During this time, you'll be taught what's known as the three-minute breathing space technique, which focuses on three steps, each one minute in duration. Step one is observing your experience and how you are doing right now. Step two focuses on your breath, and step three is attending to the body and physical sensations.

When combining mindfulness and therapy, most of the work is self-directed. So even if you choose to combine mindfulness with Cognitive Behavioral Therapy, Dialectical Behavioral Therapy, or Acceptance and Commitment Therapy, you still need to make that effort to become more aware of your thoughts, feelings, and actions.

HARNESSING THAT INCREDIBLE POWER

Now that you've been introduced to the power, becoming aware, and keeping your focus in the present moment, it's time to start putting it into practice so you can harness that incredible power. You can train your mind to be more "in the present moment," freeing yourself from worry, trauma, and anxiety. By activating this power, you become more equipped to face and make peace with whatever challenges life throws you. It all begins with your willingness and decision to spend more time being present. As you eat, walk, interact with others, work, and so on, you can keep giving yourself little reminders to stay focused in the Now. You can also read books to help you understand the importance of present moment awareness, such as "The Power of Now" by Eckart Tolle. You can also learn from the great master himself, Thich Nhat Hanh, who has several books and YouTube videos on making mindfulness part of everything you do. As you train and still your mind, you will discover an aspect of you that has been thus far missing from your life. Mindfulness is a sure way to transform your life. Begin today.

MAKING A HABIT OUT OF MINDFULNESS

Let's help make this concept of mindfulness practices with simple step-by-step tips on applying it in the things you're already doing.

Tip #1: Do one thing at a time.

Forget what you hear people say. Multi-tasking will get you nowhere. It's not a productivity hack. If anything, it just spreads your attention and energy really thin, making it even harder to accomplish tasks. Therefore, give yourself permission to slow down and focus on one activity at a time. Take on each task with your full attention and bring awareness to what you're doing and how that feels. This is a simple way of increasing your power of concentration and mindfulness. In so doing, you are less prone to rush, forget details or make silly mistakes. You'll notice over time that you move through your activities with greater ease and confidence because you give yourself enough time and personal presence.

Tip #2: Sit in silence and observe your mind's chatter.

Anytime you watch your thoughts, you're actually being mindful. You can invest a few minutes during the day to listen to the voice in your head without self-loathing or criticism. Notice when repetitive thoughts enter your mind. Be an observer, not a judge and what you'll start to notice is that there are voices in your head and some thoughts are disconcerting... but... you are not your thoughts. Do this long enough, and you'll come to the full awareness that you are not your mind, and so you can choose to detach from the noisy playground called your mind.

Tip #3: Mindful walking.

This is one of my favorite things to do because I'm not a fan of the classic meditation in the lotus position. Instead, I find walking in the park or anywhere in nature to be more beneficial in restoring my sense of calm. Whether you're walking to work, around your neighborhood, from the car to the store, or through the hallways at work, you can choose to turn it into a meditative experience.

How? Well, try this.

The next time you're about to open the car door or rise out of your chair at the office, turn your attention to your intention of walking mindfully. Simply say to yourself, "I'm going to be fully present and mindful of each step I take." Then make your move. As you do, become aware of the sensations. Put your attention on your body. Pause, take one conscious breath. Begin to move your feet. If time permits, you can deliberately take slow steps to feel the moment more and more. Notice how the ground feels under your feet. Notice how your clothes feel against your body as you walk. If you're doing this outside, notice the air, birds, trees, plants, and all the other little details you would often ignore. The goal here is to be present with each step for as long as you can.

Tip #4: Mindfulness listening.

This is such a great and powerful habit to develop. Active listening through the lens of compassion will significantly enhance your relationship with yourself and with others. Most of us don't realize how disconnected we are from our bodies and feelings. And if we are disconnected from our own bodies, we can't possibly be present enough to connect with another. So, what you might realize (like I did) is that I am usually caught up in my own mind chatter as others speak to me. Here's how you can shift to being a mindful listener. Practice noticing your own thoughts as shared in the first tip. Next, make an effort when a loved one speaks to you and just listen to what they are saying. Don't carry on an inner argument or dialogue. Focus all your attention on that person. You'll be amazed at how different that interaction will be. People tend to unconsciously pick up whether we are present or not.

Tip #5: Do a body scan.

The body scan is another way to bring mindfulness into your daily routine. It can be done in a matter of minutes or as long as half an hour, depending on your lifestyle and needs. You can also choose to do it as a morning or evening ritual. It begins with you lying on your back with your palms facing up and feet slightly apart. If you're doing it outside your home, you can also do it sitting on a comfortable chair with feet resting on the floor.

Once you've settled into a comfy position, immobilize your body and then begin bringing awareness to your breath. Notice the rhythm, the experience of breathing in and exhaling out. Do not control or manipulate the breath but simply observe.

Next, I want you to notice your body: how it feels, the texture of clothing against your skin, the contours of the surface on which your body is resting, the temperature of your body, and the environment. Are you noticing any tingling, soreness, etc.? What sensations are you aware of now? Does your body feel particularly light or heavy?

Are there areas that feel hypersensitive or areas where you feel numb?

Notice that a typical body scan runs through each part of the body, paying particular attention to the way each area feels. It's advised that you move from your feet to the top of your head, i.e., toes of both feet, the ankles, lower legs, knees, thighs, pelvic region, abdomen, chest, lower back, upper back, hands, arms, neck, face and head covering as much detailed ground as you can.

Once you complete the body scan, bring your awareness back into the room and slowly open your eyes. Many videos on YouTube can also guide you through a meditative body scan with ambiance music.

A SIMPLE 5 MINUTE DAILY ACTIVITY THAT BOOSTS YOUR MENTAL HEALTH

One of the most promoted mindfulness tools is meditation. Although it doesn't work for everyone, research proves that meditation is an incredibly powerful way to boost the immune system, reduce stress, improve mental focus and clarity, among other things. It also helps curb negative self-talk and the tendency to fall into irrational thoughts. If you've tried it before and struggled to stick with it long enough, experts say it might be because you're doing it too long or focusing on the wrong objective. As a beginner, as little as one minute of mindfulness meditation can be sufficient enough to get you going. Ideally, experts recommend five minutes of mindfulness meditation. Why? Because five minutes is considered ample time to familiarize yourself with the simple act of sitting in stillness in the midst of a chaotic day or a racing mind. So, you can do this five-minute meditation in the morning, during your lunch break, pre-bedtime as you wind down, or just before sleeping.

Here's what to do:

First, you need to set a gentle five-minute timer then find a relaxed, comfortable position that works for you. You could sit in a lotus position or sit on a chair with your feet on the ground. You could also sit on the floor on a cushion. Keep your back upright but not too tight and rest your hands wherever feels comfortable. You can keep your tongue on the roof of your mouth if that feels comfortable.

The second is to bring your attention and awareness to your body. Try to notice the shape of your body, how light or heavy it feels, and just let yourself relax. Notice the sensations and relax any tension or tightness. Just breathe in and out naturally.

The third is to tune into your breath more consciously. Feel the natural flow of your breath without altering anything. Notice where it's easiest to connect with the breath. It can be your chest, throat, nostrils, or abdomen. There's no right or wrong here. It's all about connecting with yourself and remaining at ease as you focus one breath at a time.

The fourth thing is to practice compassion and kindness to yourself as you catch your mind wandering. You'll notice very often that you got distracted and are no longer focusing on breathing in and out. That's okay. As thoughts come and carry you away to something that happened in the past or what you think will happen in the future, be kind to yourself. This is natural, and we all go through this. Softly and gently redirect your attention back to the breathing.

Keep noticing your breath in silence for the entire five minutes until the timer goes. Don't worry about getting lost in thought; just keep returning to your breath. Once the gentle alarm goes off, start coming out of the meditative state and check in with your body again before bringing back your attention to the current environment.

Give yourself just one more minute to think of a positively inspiring thought such as "May I feel more grounded and calm today," and appreciate yourself for participating in this mindfulness experience and for the gift of being alive and having that breath. Now you can get up and carry on with the next activity.

THE GUIDED MEDITATION SCRIPT

I will now take you on a journey of relaxation, visual imagery, and pure visualization. You will learn to leave your problems and inner anxieties behind and will gain a new understanding and clarity of mind. Embracing instead a powerful and vibrant visualization that fills your being with wonder enabling you to understand your place within the world and all that is important. You will learn to let go of tension and impress into your mind powerful positive statements that will improve your sense of well-being.

Before we begin, please ensure you are sitting or lying down in a comfortable, well-ventilated room where you will not be disturbed for the next twenty minutes. You may read this meditation first and if it resonates with you, consider recording it with your own voice and adding some background music of a healing nature, such as Tibetan meditative music, to further enhance the experience. As you follow this guided meditation, feel free to keep your eyes closed and allow yourself to escape from the current environment and restrictions into the powerful moment presented by this meditation. Nothing else matters but the here and now. At this moment, there is nothing for you to feel concerned about. You are at peace. You will allow the tensions of the day to dissipate. You will give yourself permission to connect with the universe. Let us begin.

Close your eyes. Take a deep and slow inhale through your nose and then slowly exhale through your mouth. Repeat this a few more times, each time filling your belly completely as you breathe in and then exhale till it's completely contracted as you breathe out. As you exhale, picture any tension leaving your body as a color. Let the tension fill the airs swirling around you. If you feel angry, envision the breath as a deep red color if you can to make it vivid. Allow any and all tension to dissipate as the breath leaves your body.

Now, inhale again. Breathe in slowly through your nose for a count of four (one, two, three, four) ... Feel and see yourself breathing in a color representing peace (it can be blue, white, or any other color you like). Extend your diaphragm as you feel the air entering your lungs. Breathe in deeply to the bottom of your lungs. This time, with your lungs full of air, I want you to pause and hold the breath for a count of two (one, two) and then exhale slowly through your mouth. Inhale deeply and slowly, hold one... two... exhale slowly as you control the outflow and count one...two...three...four. Notice the color that you are inhaling and the color that you're exhaling. Continue this cycle of breathing for a few more minutes. This is rhythmic breathing. It's perfect whenever you feel tense, stressed, or nervous. Inhale calming energy, exhale and release any worries, anxieties, or physical tensions.

Inhale slow and steady to a count of four. Hold the breath for a count of two. Exhale slow and steady for a count of four.

Do this for one more minute with background music or in silence.

We carry a great deal of tension in our neck and shoulders. Raise your shoulders slowly up to your ears, hold for one...two...three, and release. Notice and acknowledge that your body is starting to feel more relaxed. Keep using your breath to relinquish any tension and feel your body begin to relax more and more.

Your arms and legs are now feeling heavier. The muscles in your back are relaxing. If there is any tension left in your shoulders, contract and tighten your muscles, hold for a count of four and then release. Feel the shoulders relax. Feel your back supported where you are now, and just enjoy the sensation of breathing and relaxing. Do this for one minute.

As you continue breathing normally without seeking to control or manipulate your body, bring your attention within. Go into your imagination and see yourself standing at the end of a hallway next to a room filled with boxes of varying sizes. Some are really small, and others are huge. This room contains boxes filled with all your problems, anxieties, worries, and regrets. Right next to you is a stone case staircase that spirals around. The steps are made from white marble. You begin to climb up the stairs supporting yourself with your fingers along the stone wall. You feel the smoothness of your stone as you touch it. It's cold and smooth. Continue to climb slowly, making your environment as vivid as you can. There are many steps spiraling up ahead of you. You feel courageous enough to keep climbing. It feels wonderful to be leaving all your problems below. And as you continue to climb, you see below you a small room. Feel a sense of relief as you climb higher, moving further away from all the clutter, chaos, and anxieties. With each step, you move towards peace and inner contentment.

You are now approaching the top step, and an inky blackness greets you. You are not afraid as you emerge onto a circular platform. You know that the sky forms the roof, and there are millions of stars twinkling in the black expanse. There is a sudden rush of freedom. Feel the sense of wonder and awe as you look toward the heavens. You are free.

In the middle of this pure, white, curved platform that you stand on is a circular flat seat slopping back into a contoured chair made out of the same marble as its surroundings. Sit and feel the coolness of the marble beneath you. It is a perfect place for reflection. Lean back and feel the stone supporting your back in all the right ways. It's as if it was carved with you in mind.

Feel how comfortable and serene it feels to be sitting here. Now, look up into the night sky. There are no clouds to mask the stars. The whole vast sky is open to you. Here you are free from the tensions of everyday life. Here you are just as perfect as the stars that are shining bright for you.

In real life, you may feel frustrated, confined, tense, and even trapped, but as you look up now into the depths of this extraordinary sky decorated with millions of stars light-years away, you feel a new sense of desire emerging within you. You feel like floating up high to meet with and become one with the universe. The desire to feel weightless, to gain a new and inspiring sense of perspective rises. You feel yourself begin to float gently out of the marble seat. You move up higher...and higher... and higher. You float up above the marble walls, and now you can see the view of the city around you. Lights that twinkle far beneath the expanse of sky. The view is magnificent. You can see for miles. The landscape lit by twinkling lights heralding the existence of those who live and share this reality with you. A cityscape that comes to life with the sprinkling of artificial lights that mirror the heavens above.

You move effortlessly, relishing in this feeling of freedom. Here you are cast afloat from the problems of daily life. It is like flying, but with no effort required. A single thought enables you to change direction at will. And you travel on. You look down. Moonlight is reflected in the rippling waters of the estuary. Gentle waves lap at the shore, and as you float out further high above the darkened waters, boats bob along the harbor walls, and the feeling here is of complete peace and tranquility. You feel invisible. There is no blame here, no regrets. Just awe at being able to see life from a whole new perspective. Traveling over the estuary, you head along the coastline scaling large cliffs, flying high above them. Thin clouds almost transparent from below are blown in from the sea, hugging the cliffs as you move higher. The clouds, wispy, fragile, and translucent, follow in your trail as you soar higher. Rising vertically now higher and higher, looking up toward the moon. Silvery grey, the moon is full. You marvel at its beauty and power, knowing how it controls the ebb and flow of the tides.

Here, suddenly, life feels less complicated. There is a sense of pureness. Of mystery and yet clarity. Life is good. Life is wonderful, and you share a sense of connection with the universe.

Breathe in deeply and then release the breath. Let go of any tension within your body. Focus on the softness of every muscle. Feel yourself free, relaxed, and free from any burden. Far below, you see low flying birds hug the surface of the water disturbed. They seem tiny and fast-moving. The water ripples gently. Sparkling stars and the light from the moon herald your way. You see the world from an enlightened viewpoint, and it is one of wonder. Here, high above the fragmented clouds, you feel a part of the world's mystery connected on every level and free from your problems. You can sense a change around you. Gradually the air becomes warmer and misty as cloud formation begins to forge together. The sky changes color. Dark muted through to light, and for a while, the sun and moon share a place in the heavens. You drop down now through the fluffy clouds and float down towards the earth's surface. You feel exalted as the sea now mirrors the changing skies—sparkling sunlight glinting across the surface and shimmers of blue. You drift down, moving on away from the water's edges still high above the city's architecture, tall concrete pillars and homes reaching up toward the sky and small private residences alone surrounded by small patches of green like a complex jigsaw of life.

Stone and irregular shapes all fitting in together in almost seamless ease. Marvel at how the man-made structures can look beautiful too. Here, you can see that life is about living and not holding onto problems. There is no place in your life anymore for anxiety that makes you feel ill. Tension headaches, depression, regrets that gnaw away at you, or the decisions that you just can't make. Here in this weightless existence, you realize that you can be free from all of the negative aspects of life, no longer shackled by an existence that holds you back. This acknowledgment is meaningful. It has the power to change your life.

As you breathe in deeply, conjure up the image of those problems and all of the boxes that you left behind. Initially, they were overwhelming, threatening in their power to hamper your life. To impact you at every turn. Now picture them reduced in size, no more threatening, just minor inconveniences that you have now scaled back in your mind. Shrink the problems smaller still. Breathe deeply again and then out. Breathing out the last of your connections to those problems and see them growing ever smaller, every minute, a fraction of their former size, and you realize your perspective was clouded before. Your judgment was off-center. Your realization of the truth in life and the importance of nature and your place in the world makes those problems seem insignificant by comparison.

Focus again on your breathing. It is time to see the problems of life as mere obstacles. It is time to look at the important things in life and to step away from any doubts, regrets, or anxieties that affect you negatively. It is time to feel contentment and to embrace pure inner peace. Drift gently now down to earth. Close your eyes and feel your descent. You are at peace with life and with yourself. Finally, you understand your part within the universe. You drift down as you're bathed in a golden light as the sun shimmers in the early morning sky. The faint warmth is comforting—a beautiful start to the day.

It is time to feel positive about your life. You have the power to do so. You are centered. You retain the feeling of peace and wonder. You are now back in your own reality. Feel yourself back in your bed, comfortable, safe, and secure. Open your eyes and stretch out your muscle. Breathe deeply to send out oxygen to your body. Realize how good you feel right now.

Keep experiencing the incredible sense of calmness and deep peace as you remember your wonderful high time above the clouds. A part of the midnight sky and then a part of the early morning transition as night became day. Understand now that your problems are such a small part of time and space and even within your own reality, understand that your problems can be dealt with quickly and clearly with clarity of mind. Breathe in deeply and keep your sense of peace and tranquility. Breathe out and noting that no tension remains. Remember that you can return to this meditation whenever you need a renewed perspective. You are at one with the universe. Namaste.

9

THE RELATIONSHIP BETWEEN SPIRITUALITY AND PERSONALITY

A lot can be said when it comes to mental health, spirituality, and religion. There's been increasing evidence showing benefits to having a healthy spiritual or religious life (depending on your preference and beliefs), but it wasn't always the case. In fact, up until the early 1990s when "religious or spiritual problems" were introduced in DSM-IV as a new diagnostic category that invited medical professionals to respect the patient's beliefs and rituals, psychiatrists who are generally less religious than their patients didn't value the role of spirituality or religion. Why? Because ever since the falling out of religion and psychiatry in the early 19th century (thanks to Charcot and his pupil Freud who associated religion with hysteria and neurosis), mental health care and all things religion were divided.

But there's no denying the fact that substantial evidence shows someone's spiritual inclinations do influence their mental health. So, is it worth taking into account? This is what we want to explore in this chapter.

A SPIRITUAL LIFE, SHOULD YOU HAVE ONE?

There's no right or wrong answer here. It all depends on your beliefs and world view. Spirituality or religion (they are not the same) can have a tremendous impact on your recovery if it aligns with your personality. But what is spirituality, and how is it different from religion?

Different people will offer different definitions for spirituality, but I choose to think of it as a way of thinking about the meaning and purpose of one's life. Spirituality is about finding your sense of worth and value in this life. It offers a worldview that suggests there is more to life than just what people experience on a sensory and physical level.

Spiritual practices include things like meditation and prayer, living by a set of rules that you establish for yourself (like how you treat people), and focusing on values such as kindness, compassion, hope, honesty, and equanimity. Spiritual people naturally prioritize mindfulness practices, which makes it easy to integrate therapies that use mindfulness. Religion, on the other hand, is linked to a particular faith, tradition, or institution. Being religious usually entails believing in the god of that particular faith. You have specific religious leaders who guide you through the shared and commonly accepted beliefs as you go through life. One can be spiritual without being religious, so this isn't a matter of forcing any particular faith upon you. It isn't even about forcing you to become a spiritual being but rather an invitation to get curious about whether your personality, well-being, and sense of purpose will be significantly enhanced by the contemplation and practice of spirituality.

For some people (including myself), awakening to my spiritual nature was part of the accelerant for my healing. I struggled for most of my life, falling in and out of depression and other mental disorders. I would undergo treatments and become "normal" for a while but then eventually fall right back into it. There was always a reason. The last big reason was my relationship gone wrong, and it just threw me a curveball that felt too big for me to handle. It wasn't until I surrendered my life to a higher awareness and reconnected with my spiritual self that treatments started working. For me, the benefits are too numerous to mention, beginning with the fact that I am alive and healthy, and I now have enough courage to share my insights on how to heal with you through this book. All that happened because I reconnected my personality with the spiritual aspect of myself.

Research has shown that those who are more spiritual or religious and use their spirituality to cope with life challenges experience many benefits to their health and well-being. If you are part of a spiritual community, you may have more support and friendships that empower you to stay positive as you go through treatment and recovery. It might be helpful to feel that connection to something bigger than yourself. Becoming spiritual can give you strength and hope, especially when you're feeling unwell. It might also help you to make sense of your experiences. All this and so much more is possible if you feel inclined to follow this path. But I must state that you are the only person who can make this choice. It cannot be forced. If you want to begin thinking or talking about your spiritual needs, find someone you trust or join a community of people whose values you share. But a few questions you can contemplate to figure out if spirituality can help you transform your life include:

1. What is important to you?
2. What gives you hope and keeps you going when things get tough?
3. Do you have a feeling of belonging and being valued? If no, would you like to?
4. What makes you feel supported?
5. Do you feel safe?
6. What makes you feel happy?

SPIRITUAL INTELLIGENCE: A CONCEPT

Spiritual intelligence (SI) is a concept that was introduced by Danah Zohar in her book *ReWriting the Corporate Brain* back in 1997. It's a term that's now widely used by some philosophers, psychologists, and developmental theorists to indicate spiritual parallels with Intelligence Quotient and Emotional Quotient. Famous author Stephen Covey also believes spiritual intelligence is essential, stating "it is the central and most fundamental of all the intelligences because it becomes the source of guidance for others."

Zohar speaks of 12 principles underlying spiritual intelligence.

1. **Self-awareness:** Knowing what I believe in and value and what deeply motivates me.
2. **Spontaneity**: Living in and being responsive in the moment.
3. **Being vision – and value-led:** Action from principles and deep beliefs and living accordingly.
4. **Holism:** Seeing larger patterns, relationships, and connections; having a sense of belonging.
5. **Compassion:** Having the quality of "feeling-with" and deep empathy.
6. **Celebration of diversity:** Valuing other people for their differences, not despite them.
7. **Field independence:** Standing against the crowd and having one's own convictions.
8. **Humility:** Having the sense of being a player in a larger drama of one's true place in the world.
9. **Tendency to ask fundamental "Why" questions**: Needing to understand things and to get to the bottom of them.
10. **Ability to reframe**: Standing back from a situation or problem and seeing the bigger picture of a wider context.
11. **Positive use of adversity:** Learning and growing from mistakes, setbacks, and suffering.
12. **Sense of vocation:** Feeling called upon to serve, to give something back.

The more we study spiritual intelligence, the more we see evidence of the relation between personality, spirituality, existential intelligence, and spiritual intelligence. Your personality is of paramount importance in the process of creating the inner motivation that triggers the innate human tendency to search for the meaning of life. In that quest, one engages that dimension of spirituality, which then activates existential intelligence to develop a system of beliefs and values and the capacity to tackle deep questions about human existence, which is usually very useful when one desires to understand the meaning of their life. The last stage is spiritual intelligence, which helps direct the right and necessary actions to implement the intended goals. There need not be any religious acceptance in all this, and that's why it's important to note that although spiritual intelligence does connect to spirituality, it does not in any way require religious precepts.

While SI can be adapted in various settings, including the workplace and within the context of how you relate to your life and others, it is important for your well-being. Research conducted in the past few years shows a correlation between SI and satisfaction with life. It is speculated that SI creates an environment that promotes inspiring self-reflection and prompts an individual to search for life's meaning. When one is more reflective and appreciative of this process of finding meaning, well-being can be enhanced, and facing difficulties in a more mindful and meditative way (trusting that you are on the right path) can help you overcome the health challenges.

LET'S TALK ABOUT PERSONAL DEVELOPMENT

What is your current understanding of personal development? Is it something you've dabbled in, or is this the first time you've heard of it? Regardless of how well versed you are on this topic; personal development is something I encourage everyone to partake in if they desire a better quality of life. Why? Because through personal development, you get to discover and develop the best versions of yourself. It helps empower and strengthen you in ways no other education can do because it's focused on understanding who you are.

For most people, personal development refers to binge-watching Tony Robbins on YouTube or saving motivational quotes on Instagram and Pinterest. But that's barely scratching the surface of what it's meant to be. Wikipedia defines personal development as activities that develop a person's capabilities and build human capital and potential, facilitate employability, and enhances the quality of life and the realization of dreams and aspirations. The way I like to approach this is simple. Personal development is about learning how to unleash my best self. I never used to care about it until I read Dr. Wayne Dyer. I immersed myself in his teachings and programs, which slowly began my journey of growth and healing. When I read the book *"You Can Heal Your Life"* by Louise Hay, I saw the light at the end of the tunnel and finally decided it was about time I gave myself the gift of a brand-new life. Sometimes I wonder how different life would be if I hadn't combined my therapy and personal development. It's hard to be sure, but I doubt I would have lasted this long without another relapse.

The tragedy of losing my Fiancé and the despair and worthlessness I was experiencing made it hard for me to believe in a bright future. Personal development and everything else I've shared so far are what helped me piece myself back into place. So why am I sharing this with you? Because I want to suggest and encourage you to take personal development seriously as you go on this quest of healing and transformation. Steer clear of thinking about it from the superficial perspective of motivational videos and instead learn to recognize the value it can bring to the different areas in your life. Namely, Mentally, Socially, Spiritually, Emotionally, and Physically. Let's take a closer look at each area of personal development.

1.Mental personal development:

This area is focused on growing and grooming your mind. There are many ways to do this, including but not limited to reading a book, listening to audiobooks/podcasts, signing up for a masterclass, or even taking free training on YouTube.

2. Physical personal development:

Did you realize that physical activity is part of your personal growth? Real healing needs to be holistic, and that's why you need to include some aspect of physical development into your routine. Consider your eating habits, sleeping and rest, as well as body movement when you plan this aspect of your growth.

3. Emotional personal development:

Emotional development will be huge in this quest of healing because, as you realized, holding back emotions is very unhelpful. In fact, engaging in activities that help you release and process your feelings in healthy ways is, in its own way, a form of sound therapy. That's why I've encouraged journaling, thought recording, and even talking to a trusted therapist in previous chapters. But you can also track your mood or put yourself through a "mental diet" where you spend a week doing everything possible to sustain an optimistic and lively attitude.

4. Social personal development:

This area of your personal development is about enhancing your communication. Think about the areas in interpersonal skills you most need help with and come up with activities that can improve it. For example, if you struggle to listen to others, then put some effort into actively listening. If you are too shy, consider taking up a course that helps you with public speaking. What social activities can you think of that would make you a better communicator?

5. Spiritual personal development:

On the topic of spiritual development, the best thing you can do is find something that brings you peace and helps you connect to your true self. That can include activities such as reading the Bible, taking nature walks, meditating, prayer and worship, etc. I have a friend who enjoys participating in Bible Study, so twice a week, he connects with members of his church to read and discuss various Bible passages. If you're not religious at all, that's perfectly fine. As I said, being spiritual has nothing to do with religion. So, for you, it might be reading something philosophical, etc.

Here's the thing. Personal development requires a plan in order for it to yield positive results. As personal development expert Jim Rohn said, "when you look at successful people, you will almost always discover a plan behind their success. It is the foundation for success." We want you to heal and transform your life successfully, which means a personal development plan is paramount. Here are the basics of a good foundation.

Step #1: Clarify your vision

When was the last time you thought about your future and the quality of life you'd like to enjoy? Usually, when battling a mental health problem, the last thing we want is to think about the future. But that's precisely where you need to start. Choose a timeframe that makes sense for you. For some, it can be ten years out, while for others, even 12 months out is a stretch. Be thoughtful and compassionate with your current state. Understand that you can always expand on your vision as you get the hang of this. So, let's imagine what you want your life to be a year from today. Think about how you feel when you wake up in the morning. What's the first thought that passes through your mind? What's the reason you're getting out of bed? How does your body feel? How serene and clear is your mind? How is your day structured now that you changed and healed yourself? What makes you feel accomplished at the end of the day? Do you have more time to spend with friends and family? How different is your morning routine? What about your work/school? What's giving you the energy to move forward? What makes you feel successful in this new reality? What goals have you been working on that gave you great satisfaction and fulfillment?

Step #2: Become aware of your strengths and areas for improvement

Now that you've exercised your mind to identify the future experience you want to create, it's time to figure out how to map this journey. Thinking from that end result, let's figure out what you've already got going for you. Always start small, where you are, with what you have. The fact that you picked up this material to heal your current condition tells me you have a lot going for you. There's enough awareness and desire to do the right thing. It also tells me there's some untapped potential and skills you can leverage to keep you moving forward.

Think for a moment about one or two talents that you've naturally excelled at since you can remember. Perhaps there's a training you took. In my case, I realized I had lots of underdeveloped skills and untapped potential. I had given up on my psychology degree because, at the time, it didn't have as great a meaning to my life as it did after going through my devastating breakup. So, I decided to lean into that and complete my degree in psychology. Now it's your turn to pick yourself up. Write down in your journal all the skills you'd like to develop or finish developing as well as the projects you'd like to start working on to move you closer to your goals.

Next, I want you to start thinking about a handful of people you can contact to be your support structure. Don't be too specific. And by the way, it's fine if you don't have all the answers. Before moving onto the next steps, write down what you feel you're naturally good at. Can you write/sing/cook/paint/code etc.? These are all powerful allies in the making of your new life.

Step #3: Build your personalized strategy

It's time to document a simple plan that you will begin implementing daily. You have clarity on the desired future, and you understand what you've got to work with and the areas you need help with. Answer the following questions: What resources do you need to start improving areas of weakness? For example, what books can you read? Which course or mastermind can you take? Do you need to go back to school?

You also need to connect with the people who can support you. Who do you trust and respect to be a mentor? Can you hire a coach or join a community of like-minded people doing what you want to do? Write down how you plan to make this connection happen.

What timeframe are you working with to implement these new changes? I recommend creating mini milestones for the different stages of your personal development journey so you can stay encouraged. Don't forget to celebrate even the tiniest of wins, as small wins always lead to massive results. For example, when you complete a course, that's a huge win even though you're not yet at that final end result.

COMBINING THE TWO IS DEFINITELY POSSIBLE

In an ideal world, you would naturally combine spirituality and personal development for optimum results. The fact is, both of these are interconnected, and a genuine personal development quest would be incomplete without incorporating spiritual practices and awareness. Why do I say this? Because the determining factor in any endeavor you partake in will always be you. So, if you are getting in your own way, there can be no real healing or lasting transformation. That's why I encourage you to create ideal conditions for yourself that allow you to combine personal development with spiritual practices.

Why combining spirituality and personal development is beneficial:

First and foremost, spirituality involves increasing your awareness and developing a belief in something bigger than yourself. Regardless of what you call this (whether you belong to a religion or not), this level of higher understanding can be very liberating and empower you to develop a level of faith in yourself that makes you an overcomer.

Personal development and any other cognitive-based therapy you take will help you uncover all the unhealthy thoughts, emotions, and habits that have been perpetuating your mental condition. They will help you identify limiting beliefs, and as you do, that higher sense of belonging and guidance will support you as you make the shift from the old you to the new you. As the negative thoughts and limiting, beliefs are released and replaced with a higher sense of faith and positive belief, you start to experience life in a new way.

The second reason these two fields work so well together is that your ability to finally regain clarity and calmness is enhanced. The more you mindfully and spiritually work on yourself from the inside out, the clearer you become about who you are, what you want, and why you want it. That increased clarity also makes you a better decision-maker and a more optimistic individual with a new outlook now that you see life through an entirely different lens. Think of it this way. If you spent all your life trapped in a cave that only had a small window through which you could see the sky, your perception of the world would be minimal and distorted. Now imagine going from that tiny perspective (the size of a window) to having the cave walls removed and seeing the entire sky for the first time. That's what we're aiming for.

The last reason I want you to consider is that this will help you become more courageous and bolder about your dreams. You will feel worthy of setting new goals and dreaming big for yourself because you feel connected to a power greater than anything you've known. And as you continue working on yourself, having a better lifestyle will feel like the most natural desire. For example, before my breakup, there were no grand dreams or visions. The goal of marrying my fiancé was as far as I could go with my small thinking and limiting beliefs. Never did I imagine that I would end up becoming an author and impacting lives through my story, study, and research on mental health. But today, I know there's far more that I can accomplish, and my best life is still ahead of me because I keep setting bigger goals. This was only possible thanks to the personal development coaching I invested in. It took me from just wanting to be healed of my mental condition to dreaming of creating something meaningful that I can be proud of. You can accomplish the same and even more.

IMPROVING YOUR MENTAL HEALTH USING THE TWO

Here are some practical techniques you can use to improve your mental health and combining spiritual and personal development practices.

#1: Meditation

This is a great way to develop yourself and become more connected with a higher level of awareness. Research shows that meditating helps improve sleep, increases pain tolerance, reduces stress, controls anxiety, enhances self-awareness, improves focus and attention span. It promotes a healthy emotional life and can be a great way to find peace and stillness.

#2: Yoga

Regular yoga (especially yoga that incorporates deep breathing and meditation) brings about greater mental clarity and calm. It increases body awareness, relieves chronic stress, and sharpens concentration. By practicing yoga, you are getting your physical development, cognitive development, and spiritual development combined.

#3. The 555 Practice

This is a morning mindfulness practice that will combine personal development and spiritual growth, and it takes only fifteen minutes. It's a mindfulness technique created by Uma Beepat, and here's how to incorporate it. First thing in the morning, commit fifteen minutes segmented in the following way. Spend five minutes in meditation and practice deep breathing. After the alarm goes off, stretch for another five minutes and finally, in the last five minutes, mentally prepare for your day and write down your intention for the day of how you want to feel, how you will show up in the world and one or two things that you want to accomplish by the end of the day.

#4: Keep a gratitude journal

Energy flows where attention goes. That means, if you invest some time daily to reflect on the events of the day and remember the moments that made you feel good, you will generate more of those feelings and eventually stabilize that state of being. I like doing mine at the end of the day when I get into bed so I can recall even the tiniest thing that made me smile. I find that elevates my mood and enables me to sleep better. This not only develops you spiritually, but research shows it has biological and mental benefits for your brain.

10

REDUCING THE SEVERITY OF YOUR
DEPRESSION & ANXIETY

D epression and anxiety can happen at the same time. In fact, many people who are depressed tend to also suffer symptoms of anxiety and vice versa. Even though these are caused by different triggers, it is common for them to overlap, making healing all that more complicated. That's why it's essential to become aware of the different ways you can reduce each of these, whether they show up singularly or together. Sometimes, one treatment isn't going to be enough, especially if you're currently in a stressful environment at work or home. So, it becomes necessary to develop tools and techniques that you can deploy in your daily life as stress triggers pop up. The goal here is to help you have as many tools and techniques as possible. Know that everything we share may not always work for every case, but it's up to you to understand your personality better so you can pick the ones that do. I like to call these coping strategies.

WHAT IS A COPING MECHANISM OR COPING STRATEGY?

It's basically a way of dealing with a problem in order to reduce stress. The more you can relieve your stress, the less severe the depression and anxiety will be. It's important to realize that not all coping mechanisms are beneficial in the long run. For example, a person may choose to use junk food as a coping mechanism, which might feel great at that moment, but in due time, that will turn into a new problem like weight issues, etc. That's why you need to be mindful of the strategies and coping mechanisms you pick. Some people go for meditation, and that's a great example of a healthy coping mechanism.

A WAY TO REDUCE ANXIETY AND DEPRESSION: COPING MECHANISMS AND STRATEGIES

When it comes to reducing anxiety and depression, you need to understand both problem-focused strategies and emotion-focused strategies. Depending on the situation at hand, you might need something to reduce stress or something to help you handle feelings of distress. If we want to effectively manage depression and anxiety, we must first realize that stress is our enemy and it is not an external issue. It's very much internal. Regardless of where you are or what's going on, if you can control your mind and stress levels, you can dampen the effects of your anxiety and depression. I know this is easier said than done, so I will share basic techniques and how to apply them. But before that, let's talk about the dark side of relying on coping mechanisms.

THE GOOD AND THE BAD

Sometimes we default to avoidance types of coping mechanisms or harmful ones that hurt us and keep us trapped in that depression and anxiety cycle. Things like smoking or using other addictive substances to ease our condition's severity only lead to more problems and are often signs of avoidance. I also see procrastination as a way of avoiding things too, and so we can also add it to this category of unhealthy coping habits. The bottom line here is that you need to exercise your power of reason and be mindful of what you choose to do when you get triggered into a downward spiral of anxiety and depression. If you want some tips of techniques to experiment with, here are several.

WHAT ARE THE 9 SIMPLE TECHNIQUES THAT I CAN DO?

The first thing you need to do is to become aware of your triggers. Once you know what triggers you, it will be easier to catch the wave before it takes you down.

So far, we have emphasized the importance of developing healthy habits and coping mechanisms. We have already mentioned things like sleep, proper nutrition, exercise, and practicing mindfulness to improve your condition. These are all highly effective strategies. I recommend incorporating them into your current plan. However, I want to take things to the next level to make sure you feel fully equipped no matter where you are or what stressful situation you find yourself in. Here are nine more techniques you can add to your self-healing kit that will improve your state and transform your current lifestyle.

#1: Deep breathing

Pause everything you're doing and give yourself some space. If you're in a room with people, try to step out to a different room or go outside and take deep, slow inhales and exhales, focusing on that breath.

Feel free to borrow the technique you learned in the guided meditation where I walked you through the rhythmic breathing practice. You can deeply and slowly inhale (one...two...three...four), filling up your lungs all the way into your belly and then hold for a count of two (one...two) then slowly exhale for a count of four (one...two...three...four). Focus on nothing but your breathing and the counting.

The first few times, you might need to do it for several minutes before you can bring back a sense of calm, but as you continue to practice this, it will get easier.

#2. Take a long nap

This might sound too simple and ineffective, but I think sleep is the best way to reset your thoughts and emotions. If you feel yourself losing control, stop everything and go to sleep for at least an hour. I also encourage you to go to bed early on the days when things feel really tough. When stressed, your body needs a lot more sleep and downtime.

#3: Practice acceptance

It's time to gain some real perspective. Instead of letting your brain and emotions get hijacked, why not get curious and question what's really going on. Is it really as bad as the voices in your head are making you believe? And even if things are bad, do you really have control over them? Sometimes that pep talk and the realization that you can't control everything is all you need to create a little more mental stability within you.

#4: Give yourself a time out

During this time out, you want to engage in something that is uplifting and naturally shifts your state. For example, if jogging and breaking a sweat usually makes you feel different, then even if you're not feeling up to it right this minute, make an effort to do a twenty-minute jog and break some sweat. You'll thank yourself later for forcing yourself to focus on something else that you enjoy instead of allowing your mind to drift and get caught up in the stress. Don't limit this to physical exercise. It can also be getting a massage, meditating, painting, coloring, poetry writing, cooking, etc. Immerse yourself for at least twenty minutes in something that takes your mind to a different level.

#5: Listen to soothing high-frequency music

If you enjoy music, it would be worthwhile to invest in spiritually uplifting music to soothe you. Research shows that the right kind of music can positively impact your brain and body chemistry. Nature sounds can also be very calming, which is why they are often incorporated into relaxation and meditation music. Have a playlist on hand wherever you go that can instantly shift your state when needed.

#6: Spend time in nature "forest bathing"

This a simple yet profoundly effective way to develop your personality and spirituality while simultaneously reducing anxiety and depression. Ever heard of forest bathing? There exists an ancient practice known as forest bath (shinrin-yoku) in Japan, which is not exercise or jogging, or hiking. It is simply being in nature and connecting with it through your senses.

Through sight, smell, touch, hearing, and tasting, you can soak yourself in nature, which bridges the gap between you and the natural world. You have to remember, our civilization is divorced from nature, and the more we advance, the harder it will become. According to a study sponsored by the Environmental Protection Agency, the average American spends 93% of his or her time indoors. This is actually detrimental to our health and well-being. That's why taking up forest bathing at least once a week is advised.

Now, I know what you're thinking. "I can't do this. I live in the city with no forest in sight." That's okay. You don't need a forest to do this. You need to find a spot (a park/garden etc.) and decide to spend an hour slowly walking and observing all the plant life and animal life around you. Make sure you have no phones, cameras, or any distracting technology. Let your body be your guide. Listen to where it wants to take you. Follow your nose and take your time. It doesn't even matter if you don't go very far. What matters is that you unlock your five senses and allow nature to enter through your ears, eyes, nose, mouth, hands, and feet. Listen to the birds singing and the breeze rustling the leaves of the trees. Observe the different greens of the leaves on the trees and how sunlight filters through the branches. Smell the fragrance of the nature around you and allow a connection and exchange of energy to form. Place your hands on the trunk of a tree. If there's a stream or river nearby, dip your fingers and toes in it. If not, find somewhere pretty and lie on the ground. Drink in the flavor of the nature around you and release your sense of joy, calmness, and oneness. You are part of this magnificent masterpiece.

There's no one-size-fits-all for doing this. Customize it to suit your needs and current situation and go where you feel most comfortable. For example, if you love the smell of water and sand, try to find a spot representing that. The effects and connection will be more powerful when you opt for environments that make you feel good.

#7: Challenge yourself to learn something new

By setting goals that challenge you, whether at work or outside (such as learning a new language or cooking a particular cuisine), you build confidence and redirect your energy. It develops your mental acuity and helps you unlock more of your potential, which aligns with both personal and spiritual development. By learning, you increase emotional resilience and arm yourself with the knowledge that makes you want to be more active instead of settling for a sedentary lifestyle. It also shifts your focus and attention from feeling sorry for yourself to empowering yourself to do something good.

#8: Help other people

Do you have a skill you can share with others online? Have you always wanted to volunteer for a particular cause? Evidence shows that people who help others through community work and volunteering become more emotionally and mentally resilient. It also takes someone's focus from their current mental problems by offering a different perspective of seeing how others are struggling (often with bigger issues). The mere act of giving your time, energy, attention, resources, and love makes you feel different and good.

I can recall a story of a member of our spiritual community who said she was having suicidal thoughts because her depression felt too unbearable but then agreed to take up just one weekend of volunteering work at a children's home. But this was no ordinary children's home. It was for kids with special needs.

Many of them were disabled and autistic. By the third and last day of her time there, she said she was a different woman. Seeing those kids who were abandoned by their parents demonstrating so much courage – the courage to try to live even when the odds were not in their favor made her question what the heck she was doing with her life. She had great parents, a wonderful upbringing, and people who loved and supported her throughout her life, even during this season of depression. Since then, she's focused on her recovery and spending as much time as possible working with disabled children. Perhaps there's a clue in there for you too.

#9: **Learn to soothe and parent yourself**

The full realization that you are responsible for yourself is one of the pivoting points of self-healing and mental well-being. You have everything you need within yourself and are worthy of a good life. Yes, life challenging and difficult situations will show up, but you are your own best coach and parent at this point. The most important relationship you will ever have is the one with yourself.

Make this a priority in your life and learn to speak to yourself with as much kindness and encouragement as you can. One important thing you can do at any moment to soothe yourself is to use the right words when you feel your anxiety increase or on days you don't want to get out of bed. Simple words like *"I know it's hard but just take it one hour at a time."* Or if that's too hard, you can say, *"I know this moment feels like hell but just take a deep breath in and keep breathing. You'll be okay [name]"* and call yourself by name. Always speak to yourself with compassion, love, and tenderness, especially when you're in a rough place.

Other soothing statements you can use on yourself:

- You are not alone.
- It's okay to feel this way; it makes sense to me.
- I love you no matter what.
- I'm sorry you're going through this.
- I know this is a difficult time for you.
- I'm here for you.
- You can count on me.

11

REGULATE YOUR EMOTIONS THROUGH GROUNDING

E motions are what we must understand and control because bad things tend to happen when they rule our minds. So how do we do this in a healthy way? That's what we'll cover next.

Understand that your emotions are good except when they aren't helping you. If an old traumatic experience stirs up emotions take you back into the past and cause you to fall into an unpleasant reactionary state, that has to be dealt with. A highly effective technique followed by almost all mental health professionals is grounding.

WHAT IS GROUNDING AND HOW CAN IT HELP?

Grounding techniques are a set of tools that can help us manage overwhelming emotions and traumatic experiences. Grounding is actually rooted in Dialectical Behavioral Therapy. It can be highly effective when feeling distressed, overwhelmed emotionally, or when something triggers a past memory and removes you from the present moment. I consider this a healthy way of getting back your sense of control.

What makes this work is the fact that you make a conscious effort to focus on some aspect of the physical world using your five senses instead of getting caught up in your chaotic internal thoughts and feelings. In so doing, grounding enables you to build a bridge back to this moment in time where your power lies.

By practicing these techniques, one is able to step away from negative thoughts or flashbacks. These techniques can also be used to stop the momentum of cognitive distortion before it gets out of hand. They are highly effective at decreasing the grip of unhelpful emotions. Different techniques will work better depending on your personality and emotional needs, so feel free to experiment with a handful and discard the ineffective ones. What you want is something that brings your focus back to the present moment, the current environment, detached from the past, and any negative mental movies. Let's look at

a few that come highly recommended by experts.

THE 5-4-3-2-1 TRICK

Before starting this exercise, pay attention to your breath. Take slow, deep breaths as you go through the following steps.

> **5:** Acknowledge FIVE things you see around you. It could be a lamp, a book, a spot on the ceiling, a cup, or anything in your immediate surrounding.

4: Acknowledge FOUR things you can touch in your immediate surrounding. It could be the pillow you're leaning on, the ground under your feet, your hair, etc.

3: Acknowledge THREE things you hear right now. This can be the sound of the air conditioner, the clock ticking, kids laughing outside, or whatever else you can hear. Try to find something outside of your body.

2: Acknowledge TWO things you can smell. If you're in the office, can you smell paper? If at home, can you smell coffee from the kitchen or your shower soap? If you can't smell anything, feel free to stand and take a brief walk to find a scent either in your current location or outside.

1: Acknowledge ONE thing you can taste. If you like, you can pay attention to your saliva or the inside of your mouth, especially if you recently drank or ate something.

PLAY THE MEMORY GAME

Activating a positive memory can help you escape unwanted negative emotions. To use this as a grounding technique, consider looking at a detailed photograph or picture of scenery that stirs up positive emotions. Do this for five to ten seconds. Then turn the picture facedown and recreate that same image in your mind in as much detail as possible.

Another way to approach this could be to find a picture with lots of objects, e.g., a busy city, the interior of a beautiful home, etc., and stare at it for ten seconds, then turn face-down and mentally list all the things you remember from that picture. I have been using this for years, and it works every time. I carry lots of inspiring photographs on my smartphone, and whenever I feel myself drift, I find a photo of somewhere exotic that makes me feel good, and then I mentally list everything that's on the picture. It takes less than a minute, and I am back in the present moment.

OTHER GROUNDING TECHNIQUES TO LOOK INTO

#1: Progressive Muscle Relaxation

This technique involves you relaxing all the muscles in your body. You can get a guided progressive muscle relaxation video on YouTube to walk you through it or simply borrow my tips. First, Tense and relax each muscle group, head to toes or vice versa. Do it, one muscle group at a time. Tense for five seconds, then let go and relax all the way, paying particular attention to the difference between tension and relaxation. As you relax, keep repeating the simple statement "relax."

#2: Recite something

You can create your own mantra or memorize a poem that you care deeply about. If you're religious, consider learning a passage from the book of Psalms that is powerful enough to refocus your attention and energy. Recite this poem, song, mantra, or Bible verse to yourself or mentally in your head. If you do it mentally, please visualize each word as you'd see it on a page. If you choose to speak the words aloud, focus on each word's shape on your lips and in your mouth.

#3: Visualize your favorite place

If you find it easy to connect with places visually, this can be a cool technique to use in seconds. Think of your favorite place. Somewhere that always makes you feel safe, loved, and at peace. It can be your childhood home, current residence, a vacation in a foreign country, or anywhere else you've been where beautiful memories were created. Use all your senses to recreate that mental image. Think of the colors, sounds, sensations, and how it felt to be there. Who were you with, if anyone? What did you do there? What made you most happy during that time?

#4: Soothe yourself through your senses

Your five senses can be a great way to bring yourself back into a calm, present state. Here are the different activities for each of your senses that can act as a soothing strategy while simultaneously promoting self-care habits.

Sense of touch can be soothed by getting a massage, soaking in a warm bath, going for a swim, soaking your feet, wrapping yourself in a cozy blanket, putting a cold compressor on your forehead, cuddling with a lover, hugging someone you like, putting on lotion on your body, playing with an animal, and stretching.

Sense of taste can be soothed by sipping your favorite herbal tea, chewing a piece of gum, eating your favorite nutritious meal mindfully, slowly sucking on hard candy.

Sense of smell can be soothed through deep "belly" breathing, lighting a scented candle, using an essential oil diffuser, shopping for your favorite flowers, using your favorite soap, shampoo, lotion, or perfume.

Sense of sight can be soothed through reading a book, watching the clouds, lighting a candle and watching the flame, a beautiful flower, watching the sunrise/sunset, looking at pictures of a loved one, past vacation, or a place you dream of visiting.

Sense of sound can be soothed through listening to uplifting music, humming or singing to yourself, playing a musical instrument, getting still and listening to the sounds of nature around you, saying positive statements to yourself, or self-encouragement.

Now I invite you to make a list that will form part of your distress kit to help you when your emotions try to kidnap your brain.

WILL ALL OF THIS WORK?

Being able to ground yourself is just as important now as when you were a child. The only difference is that you had to depend on someone else as a baby, whereas now, you need to take full responsibility for this. The more you learn to ground yourself and maintain calm in the face of chaos or a disturbing emotional experience, the more resilient and mentally healthy you will become now and in the future. This isn't just about healing your condition now. It's about giving you the tools you can continue to use for the rest of yourself to avoid any relapse.

I should remind you that not all grounding techniques will work. Different personalities will find some methods work better than others. What I've shared here is only a handful. So, if you experiment with these long enough to no avail, keep looking for and testing new ones until you find the right fit.

WHAT TO DO IF NONE OF THESE TECHNIQUES WORK:

The worst thing you can do is panic, get frustrated, or fall into negative self-talk, thinking something is wrong. There's a lot of information on the Internet with dozens of other shared ideas. Keep researching, and also check out my resource page at the back of this book for more guidance on where to find other grounding techniques.

Grounding yourself will always work, and it's a great approach to managing your emotions long-term. You just need to find the best techniques and practice them long enough.

III

WHAT NOW: TAKING THE NEXT STEPS TO RECOVER & HEAL

GOAL SETTING: MAKE IT PRACTICAL AND MEANINGFUL

L et me ask you this. How often do you begin any endeavor with a clear goal and end result in mind? I don't know if you noticed, but this book is intentionally designed to make you more vision-focused (on that ultimate result of a healthy, happy, successful life), none of which can be possible without proper goal setting.

Goal setting is touted as an essential step to becoming successful in the personal development space. But I want to show why it's also vital in your healing process whether you choose to self-heal, hire a therapist, or combine both approaches.

WHY IS GOAL SETTING SO IMPORTANT?

Think of it like this. You live in Florida and desire to drive to New York for the first time in your life. You have the end result in mind, but without a clear map of how you will get there, you might end up on the opposite side of America, frustrated and feeling like a failure. The same can be said of your quest for a new lifestyle free from the torture of mental health problems. You now have a vision of what you want your life to be like a year, two, or even three years from now.

That's your destination. What's needed now is a strong strategic plan of how to get there. This plan will include little touchpoints or milestones that can help you track progress and validate that you are on the way to that grand vision. These are the goals we want to identify and bring them to the forefront. So, when was the last time you took some time to map out your health goals or any other goal for that matter?

Why Do I Need to Set Goals?

Research shows that setting a specific goal makes us more likely to achieve the things we want. It is imperative to set clear goals when we are seeking to make significant shifts in our lives. I consider health goals the best starting point for you because it's a way for you to use this tool to turn something negative into a positive while at the same time proving to yourself how powerful you can be. By setting a goal and achieving it, you literally show yourself that you are capable of achievement. And as you keep piling on wins and hitting one milestone after the next, your self-esteem, confidence, drive, and enthusiasm increase naturally. If you want to set your life on fire and live on a good high, follow the ideas shared here, start small, take small, consistent steps toward your goal without getting distracted or discouraged, and you will permanently transform your life.

SHORT-TERM AND LONG-TERM GOALS: ARE THEY NECESSARY?

If you ask a large enough audience about goal setting, you'll come out confused. Some will swear against goal setting, while others would never go through life without clear goals. I think the reason for this divide is that many people go about goal setting superficially and half-heartedly. When you create any kind of plan, you need to commit and stay focused until you've attained it. You also need to reach for goals that are meaningful, aspirational, transformation, and measurable in some way. In that sense, setting a goal to get rich for the sake of getting rich wouldn't work out well because it fails on most of the criteria I just mentioned. Healing yourself from major depression so you can become a stable and better parent, spouse, child, or boss makes a great case and a powerful goal.

That's why I suggest you identify your big goal, which is the more long-term plan that will bring your vision into reality, as well as short-term goals that move you toward the attainment of that grand goal. For example, you have battled depression all your life and now struggle with the negative impact it has on your new relationship and current job. Despite all your attempts at containing it, things keep getting out of hand, and you need a new life. You're fed up with being a slave to emotions, the economy, etc., and always at the mercy of the next therapist, so your grand goal is to be 100% healed from depression and the tendency to relapse. That's a noble goal for yourself, your family, and those in your circle of influence. But how do you actually get to that goal? By identifying all the mini short-term goals that can enable you to move toward and eventually attain that big goal of being a healthy, successful husband so you can finally start a family of your own. Short-term goals would include like, read books on self-healing (which you're already doing, so congratulations on taking that first step), start exercising five times a week for half an hour, reduce my caffeine intake to one cup of coffee in the morning, stop drinking beers every night, etc. I think you're catching the gist of how this works. So, let's outline some strategies you can apply as you map out your short and long-term goals.

STRATEGIES FOR SETTING GOALS

Let's reflect on a few critical questions: In what ways do you want to improve your mental, emotional and physical health? Which bad habits are you ready to change? What do you wish to improve about your relationships? What skills do you want to learn? Are there any other things you've been thinking about changing in your professional life, social life, or financially that you believe will help you manifest your ideal lifestyle?

Once you have a few things in mind, pick the highly charged one that feels most pressing and directly aligned with that vision of your new life and use the questions below to fine-tune whatever came to mind. I recommend journaling this down somewhere private and easy to access.

#1: Write down all the hot ideas that came to mind as you read through the reflective questions above. Don't worry about ordering them in importance, just put them down on paper.

#2: Take what you wrote and order them in importance, looking for the one that lights a fire within and makes you want to take action now.

#3: Check to see whether you have written these in a way that makes them feel real and achievable for you. Also, make sure the statements are positive meaning, it should be what you want more of, not what you don't want. For example, if you're going to heal from anxiety disorders, instead of stating, "I want to be less anxious," you could say, "I want to be more relaxed, calm, and "clear-minded. See what I mean?

By the way, it's okay if you struggle to find what you want when starting this exercise. If you feel like you don't know what you want to set as a goal, start by doing a simple exercise called clarity through contrast. In this process, you get a piece of A4 paper and split it down the middle. On one side, label it "What I don't want," and on the other, "What I want." Begin by listing down everything you don't want. Once done, shift to the other side of the paper and find the antonym or opposite of what you wrote down. Word it in a way that makes you feel good. Now transfer the new wanted desires to your journal and proceed with step #3. Shred or burn the A4 paper. You no longer need to worry about what you don't want.

#4: Refine your desires and goals in more specific ways. For example, if you have as your top goals "to be happier," try to challenge that statement until you get something more specific. What does happiness feel and look like for you, and what actions or behavior would indicate that you are indeed becoming a happier person?

Once you are done with this, it's time to take massive action on your goals. We do that through a detailed action plan. This includes writing how you're going to measure progress, the timeframe you're giving yourself, and any other essential details. For example, if you realize your current goal needs to be broken down further into even tinier steps, this is where you map that out. I suggest goals to be 90 days or less so you can easily track progress and feel like you're moving in the direction of your vision as you review every ninety days or so. That kind of a goal might still require mini milestones broken down into weekly micro-goals. That's a great way to keep yourself on track, too. Just be sure to specify what you expect from yourself within a week and try not to make it too huge a hurdle. Now that you've broken the goals down into micro-goals, what are the next logical steps you can take today? Remember, it should be baby steps. Think of three things you could do right now to move you toward that 90-day goal, which will ultimately lead to your new lifestyle a year from now. A few more things to consider is having a vision statement written out somewhere visible so you can see it daily. I also suggest you write out your goals each morning so you can spend time immersed in this new momentum that's building at the start of your day. Last but not least, please start building a small list of the resources and people you would like to have as your support along the way.

ACHIEVE YOUR GOAL BY BEING SMART

Before moving on, I wanted to share another popular method for goal setting that you can use if you prefer a more structured approach. It's called the SMART technique. In Cognitive Behavioral therapy,

SMART (specific measurable achievable realistic and time-framed) goals are often promoted. Of course, this method may not work for everyone, but if it resonates, here's how to do it right.

S: Specific means you need to set a specific goal for yourself. If you've hired a therapist, they can help guide you through this. In essence, you want to make sure the goal is as specific as it can possibly be.

M: Measurable means you get to track progress either daily, weekly, or monthly so you can know if you're on the right and what's working. The more specific you are with your goals, the easier it is to track and measure them.

A: Achievable simply means it needs to feel like you are capable of doing it. And this can be tricky because oftentimes, battling mental health problems for long periods leaves us feeling defeated and incapable of doing anything praiseworthy. We usually lower our standards too much, leading to a cycle of low self-esteem, which is poisonous during this process.

So, while I will caution you against wishful thinking, I also want to challenge you to make your goals big enough that they excite you. You'll know it's right when you feel a little excited, and a bit scared at the same time.

R: Realistic means choosing a goal that is possible. For example, going from major depression to 100% in a week is so unrealistic. Be mindful of the timeframe, the plausibility, and your ability to commit to the end as you settle on the details of the goal.

T: Time frame involves establishing a precise amount of time that you will dedicate to this process of achieving your goal. Most people usually underestimate how much time they need to reach their destination, leading to discouragement and failure. As you decide how much time you will give yourself, remember this should be a guiding line, not a determinant. If you set 90 days for goal completion, and after that duration, you're still at it, then so be it. Carry on with no less enthusiasm and determination than when you first started. If you've done everything else outlined in this goal-setting chapter, success is inevitable as long as you don't stop along the way.

13

WHY TRACKING & SELF-EVALUATIONS ARE IMPORTANT ON YOUR HEALING JOURNEY

You've learned about SMART goal setting and the importance of measuring your progress regardless of the goal in mind. I want to emphasize this idea of tracking and measuring progress specific to your healing and recovery. As we know, things often feel stagnant, which causes many people to quit their treatment. One of the main reasons people quit their treatment is that they think it isn't improving their condition, whether it's anxiety or depression. This is a feeling you can avoid if you start to track and self-evaluate.

TRACKING AND SELF-EVALUATION, YOU NEED IT

Self-evaluation is the process of systematically observing, analyzing, and determining the value of your actions and consequent results in order to stabilize and improve it. While it can be applied toward many different aspects of your life, using this procedure in your therapy can help you manage it better and stay on track as you witness progress. It also helps to keep you accountable so you can continue to work on yourself and complete assigned homework if undergoing CBT, DBT, or ACT with a health professional. The primary purpose and why you need this is to highlight the wins, accomplishments, and good work you're doing. You have to be proud of what you're achieving week by week as you build toward your new lifestyle. Tracking and self-evaluation are beneficial to people who have a tendency of rational or analytical thinking as opposed to those that are the quantifying type. So, knowing more about your personality does help a lot. By tracking your treatment, both you and your therapist can have a baseline that can be used when things get off track.

How Can it Help Me in My Healing Journey?

Therapy is often like trying to sort out and complete a complex puzzle that you're carrying. There are many approaches that you and your therapist can apply depending on what feels right for both of you. Once you identify the final outcome, how do you get there? And better still, how do you show evidence that you're getting closer to that chosen destination? With a tracking tool, you are able to both establish where you are and where you want to go. Having a symptom analysis system could help prevent you and your therapist from feeling stuck, and it could substantially reduce ambiguity. Most therapists will have their own checklist, assessment tool, or even a mobile app that you could use, but even if you're not working with a therapist, you can develop a method of tracking progress.

THE DIFFERENT WAYS TO TRACK MY JOURNEY

The most standard approach is a written service plan with goals and objectives that you've identified. Your therapist may determine progress based on the achievement of goals with quarterly updates to those goals. You could also combine the treatment plan with rating scales and other short, standardized assessments to track symptoms over time. Certain therapists are more technologically advanced, whereby they have mobile apps that track symptoms daily and produce reports for you as well as some standardized assessments that help you know how you're doing.

Suppose you also feel the need to track habits that promote healing, such as exercise, meditation, sleep, and so on. In that case, you could additionally use mobile apps that give you daily, weekly, and monthly reports on your progress. There are other ways to keep tabs on your progress, including:

Personal journaling: For this to work, you need to do it long term and create a consistent routine. For example, you could spare five minutes each morning to write down how you're feeling. If it's the start of the day, write out how you hope the day will go and if it's at the end, write what worked and what you can feel good about. Do this for at least 12 months, and you'll have powerful resources that help you see how far you've come, mostly on the days you feel extra vulnerable.

12-hour check-ins: Think of whichever mode of communication you enjoy (writing, voice, video, etc.) and commit to recording something short every 12 hours to update yourself on how you feel. If you find that you're continually waking up in the middle of the night anxious, record that. This will enable you to become aware of triggers, patterns, and things in your life that are either promoting or hindering your recovery.

SELF-EVALUATION METHODS THAT AVOIDS BIASES

If you're going to create your own tools for self-evaluating and tracking progress, make sure there is no room for bias. Don't shortchange your recovery by cutting yourself some slack. The tools and methods you use should be easy to follow, balanced, and concise. So, aim for something straightforward, fair to your current situation, and meaningful. You could even start by testing pre-existing large-scale assessment tools and practices and use the best ones to inspire your own. The self-assessment should empower you, not deflate your self-esteem, so whether you establish your own or work with a standardized one from a therapist, use tools that remain objective and progress oriented.

14

INTO THERAPY: SHOULD I GET IT?

A lthough this book is centered on a self-healing approach, we must recognize that the psychotherapy discussed, i.e., CBT, DBT, and ACT, traditionally require a therapist. Reading books like mine and doing everything you can to practice self-care should not be diminished in importance. Many have self-healed from phobias, anxiety, and eating disorders without seeing a therapist. Still, for the most part, if you feel your condition is pretty severe, you're going to need a combination of processes to get you better.

Therefore, we must at least discuss the benefits of hiring a therapist and partaking in a more conventional treatment regimen as you learn to self-heal. Signing up for a program with a therapist doesn't contradict what is shared in this book, and it certainly doesn't make you any less responsible for your healing. It offers you a safe space and a trusted partner who you can work with and keep you accountable during this process. But a lot of people still struggle with the thought, "do I really need therapy?" After all, how many times have you heard someone bashing on therapists and how horrible therapy was? So, does it really work?

THERAPY: WHAT GOOD DOES IT DO?

While I am not convinced that everyone suffering from mental health problems needs a therapist, I believe most do. Most of us could use that little extra support no matter how great our coping strategies are or how big our distress kit might be.

Dealing with our own thoughts, feelings, and behavior isn't always easy so before you dismiss this idea, hear me out. Research has shown that verbalizing feelings can have a significant therapeutic effect on your brain. Some might think this makes you weak or that you'll come across as a wuss, but that couldn't be further from the truth.

I recently read an article of a guy who shared that he ghosted his therapist and a few weeks later started regretting the decision because things actually got worse. His main conflict was that he thought it made him look weak to his friends (as though there was something wrong with him), and that conflict made it hard for him to honor the agreement with his therapist. Unfortunately, he realized only after the fact that he was better off having that kind of a support structure in his life. It's quite sad that our society still perceives therapy as something negative, and hopefully, your friends are smart enough to see that you seeking help actually proves that you are healthy.

I have grown to see psychotherapy as a valuable tool that can help us become successful, healthy, and happy individuals. Every approach you've learned in this book can be broadly categorized as "talk thera-py," which I feel is the best when combined with self-healing. The trick, however, is to find someone you connect with. Someone you think you can trust. There are many benefits of opting for profes-sional help, including but not limited to:

- You get a whole new perspective on yourself and who you are.
- It gives you a different understanding of others and your environment.
- By sharing what's going on inside in a safe, judgment-free environment, you start releasing those strong negative emotions.
- It helps you deal with future curveballs and challenges that life will throw at you.
- You get validation that you're not crazy or broken and that you can fix whatever issues have been ailing you.
- Any physical trauma and other related physical ailments get treated as well.
- The positive effects of talking with your therapist gets internalized so that self-therapy picks up where the actual therapy leaves off.
- Being in therapy helps you improve your communication skills.
- You feel empowered and supported to make healthy choices.
- Therapy makes you feel empowered.

WHEN SHOULD I GET THERAPY?

The simple answer is that you ought to consider seeking professional help if you're struggling with emotional difficulties, if you're unable to function normally in your daily duties or when you start having mental health concerns. I don't think anyone can really tell you that you "need" therapy, but if you are experiencing the following signs, I encourage you to reach out to a professional.

#1. Your performance is significantly down whether at work or at school.

#2. Your sleep is drastically disrupted. Either you're suffering from sleeplessness or fatigue and just want to stay in bed all day.

#3. Your appetite and eating habits feel out of control. You might be stress eating and using food to dull your emotions, or it could go to the other extreme where you barely eat and end up starving your body.

#4. You've become a recluse and have difficulty maintaining any meaningful relationship. You might find yourself often in conflict with others or unable to effectively communicate.

#5. Things you used to enjoy now feel like a big burden. There's an emptiness inside that won't go away.

#6. You're becoming dependent or even addicted to alcohol or other substance or maybe even using sex as a coping mechanism.

#7. Disproportionate anger, rage, or resentment. Especially the ones that reoccur and get out of hand even with trivial things.

#8. Intrusive thoughts that seem to hijack your mind frequently.

#9. Physical health issues. If your health has taken a considerable dip, it could be a sign of underlying mental issues.

#10. Hopelessness and maybe even suicidal thoughts should be a huge alarm that you need professional help.

WHAT MAKES A THERAPIST GREAT: CHOOSING THE RIGHT ONE

A tremendous amount of research proves that healing in a patient is influenced by the therapist-patient relationship. That means choosing your therapist shouldn't be rushed or superficially done. You must find the right therapist for you. Just because a friend tells you to use their therapist doesn't mean it will work out. So how do you find a good therapist?

The first place I would start is by asking people you know and trust. This gives you an easy starting point and lots of options to conduct a thorough interview.

If you have a family doctor, that would also be a good source. If you have none of these options available, then my second suggestion would be to go online.

Conduct thorough research to find top recommended psychothera-pists in your area specializing in what you feel you need help with.

For example, if after the self-diagnosis we conducted earlier in this book you realize you're suffering from major depression, you might want to look up the best mental health professionals that specialize in that. There are also websites of national mental health professional organizations like the American Psychological Association that can help you find a therapist near you.

What makes a great therapist?

Depending on your personality and preference, your criteria may differ from mine so go with your values and what you care about. But here are some fundamentals that I think apply across the board.

1. Seek out a therapist with the right qualifications and someone who is experienced with your specific problem. Therapists often attach a lot of ambiguous initials to their names, which can be very confusing. Here are some terms to familiarize yourself with.

- PsyD stands for Doctor of Psychology.
- LMHC stands for Licensed Mental Health Counselor.
- LPC stands for Licensed Professional Counselor.
- NCC stands for National Certified Counselor.
- LCSW stands for Licensed Clinical Social Worker.
- LMFT stands for Licensed Marriage and Family Therapist.
- LCDC stands for Licensed Chemical Dependency Counselor.
- MD stands for Doctor of Medicine.

2. Choose a therapist who has been practicing in the field long enough. I think ten years is ideal.

3. Make sure the therapist has a good reputation and follows guidelines and a code of ethics. They should be licensed (registered) in the state or territory in which he or she practices. You can research to make sure they've passed their licensing test and background check.

4. A good therapist will also maintain continued education credits and stay on top of the latest research regarding the specific problem you need help with. So, ask for a professional bio if it helps you learn more about the person and their experience in the field.

5. Seek to hire someone who shows warmth, genuineness, and empathy. Typically, a therapist is willing to a brief consultation over the phone as an "interview." This is an excellent opportunity to verify their character and to see whether you're a good match.

You should feel free to interview as many therapists as you like before deciding whom to work with. The best fit should be someone you feel comfortable with, so note what you prefer in terms of gender, age group, religion, or values. There's no need to hire someone with fifty years of experience if you can't stand talking to older people and certainly no need to interview male therapists if your religion doesn't allow you to speak openly with members of the opposite sex. So, what I'm saying is be sensible about your choice and trust your gut. During the interview, you'll want to make the most of that time so you can leave feeling informed and ready to make a decision. You can adapt the questions below to ask your therapist.

- How long have you been practicing?
- Have you seen a lot of clients with similar concerns to my own?

- When was the last time you treated someone with a problem similar to mine?
- My problem is [insert yours]. How would you go about treating that?
- Do you tend to lead the session or follow my lead?
- What are your strengths as a therapist?

WHAT TO EXPECT DURING A THERAPY SESSION

The first appointment is usually nothing like follow up sessions because this is the first "intake" session you'll have where you become formally introduced and work out the logistics of this new arrangement. Your therapist will likely explain how therapy works and provide some forms for you to fill in. You'll discuss confidentiality and how the rest of the sessions will go. If you've already got information regarding payments, they will be concluded here in this first session, or it might be when you're advised on the financial aspect and how to proceed with payments.

Once the logistics are out of the way, you'll be encouraged to share your problems, the symptoms you're experiencing, the goals you have in mind, etc. That will open up the conversation around your medical history, childhood, family history, or any mental health treatment of the past. Having this information will give the therapist an overview and help them understand where to begin. If the meeting is taking place online, this process may vary, so understand this is just the standardized approach. Another factor to bear in mind is that how you foot the bill will influence this first meeting more often than not. For example, people paying through an insurance company would first go through an assessment conducted by the therapist to identify whether they meet the criteria for a mental health diagnosis (e.g., depression). So, if you're paying cash, you're likely to have a different experience. Use this first session to ask as many questions as you need to establish that rapport and to feel confident that you've made the right choice. Get clear on the nature of your relationship and establish a baseline of how things will work between you and the frequency of your meetings, and how you'll track and measure progress.

How Do I Know if It Works?

Even after going through the daunting process of interviewing and seeking out the best fit for you, that doesn't mean you will see a difference overnight. Therapy requires commitment, time, and patience on your end. Half the time, it won't be evident to you that something is improving.

I can recall when a friend of mine said, "I like my therapist, but I have no idea what he means when he says I'm making progress because, to me, it still feels like I am right where I was three months ago." And so, I asked him to walk through his private journal where he had been tracking his habits each day. We found he started the process by recording each morning, "I hate my life. I don't want to get out of bed. I wish I didn't have to go to work." Gradually, those morning sentences started shifting. The most recent morning log actually said, "I'm feeling really vulnerable today, but I think I'll be fine. Looking forward to my hour of tennis with Jim this afternoon. I will crush him today." It may not be the ideal life my friend desires, but given where he was 12 weeks ago, I'd say his therapist is spot on.

Therapy doesn't work like medication or drugs. There's no instant gratification. It's a process, which's a good thing because it resolves deep issues and permanently transforms the individual if done the right way.

So, if you're struggling with this or wondering how you'll know that it works, I encourage you to hold the long view and do what I've recommended several times – track and measure. Use the SMART goal setting method and let your therapist to help you establish the big and micro-milestones that can help you stay encouraged and know that it is working. Although therapy is a subjective process, you can still find ways of measuring your progress. If you have a great therapist, they should be able to create milestones and goals that keep evolving and adjusting as you go through treatment.

Ultimately, measuring how successful your therapy is comes down to noticing the difference in your thoughts, feelings, and behavior. Are your symptoms getting better? Do you manage your emotions a bit better than before? Are you feeling more aware and able to direct your attention and emotions?

If you went to therapy because you were dealing with anxiety issues, have they decreased in intensity? Are you able to function with your day-to-day activities without being hijacked by panic attacks? Do you have more nights where you can sleep peacefully without those middle of night panic attacks? Are you sleeping better?

You could also use a tool like the Patient Health Questionnaire (PHQ9), enabling you to monitor your symptoms. If you've got your own app or enjoy journaling like my friend, that could be a great way to track the progress. Keep in mind that it won't be a linear experience. Some weeks will still be hard. The dips or plateaus you might witness as you track do not imply that it's not working. That's why I insist on keeping the long view. Use the vision exercise we went through and keep your eyes on that one, two, or three-year vision. Be less concerned about the day-to-day temporary dips and more obsessed with that long-term vision. Above all else, learn to trust that it will work because you've decided it must work.

15

GOING FORWARDS SOMETIMES MEANS TAKING A FEW STEPS BACK

R ecovery and permanent healing, or at least a fully active lifestyle, is what we all desire. The journey to that state will come with some obstacles that you need to prepare for to avoid premature abandonment of your treatment. This last section will prepare you for the aspects that few are willing to talk about – the setbacks.

Whether you're at the early stages of your treatment or already completed your treatment and enjoying the new state of sound mental health, setbacks should not wear you down. Yes, it's discouraging when they occur, especially if you thought you were finally past that tendency to relapse. But here's the thing. We all experience some form of setback, whether minor or major, at some point in our lives. And even people without mental disorders suffer setbacks when going after their dream lifestyle. I hope you will find the information in this chapter especially encouraging so you can have it as your reminder the next time you catch yourself feeling down or about to fall into that pit of despair.

The best place to start when it comes to preparing for a setback is by understanding what it is and why it might show up.

SETBACKS AND RELAPSES: WHAT ABOUT THEM?

A setback can be defined as a moment or period when you seem to deviate or "go backward," hindering your desired outcome of being fully healthy and healed. For example, if you suffer from anxiety disorders and go a year without any panic attack, then one day a situation triggers your anxiety, and you go into a massive panic attack, that might be considered a setback.

As many of us know, a relapse is that recurring cycle of getting better and then falling back into the same problem (in my case, it was depression). With mental illness, when the condition is managed, things can feel really good, and you can feel strong and normal again, only to relapse as soon as a major event puts you under high-stress conditions. In my experience, each time I had a relapse proved worse than the previous episode. Real healing cannot just be focused on recovering from your condition; it should also focus on preventing relapse.

Why Do We Have Them?

Sometimes setbacks and relapses can occur because you change your medication or suddenly stop taking a certain drug. That's why you should always consult your psychiatrist before making any changes to prescriptions. In other instances, it can be caused by an external trigger that stresses you out beyond your ability to manage your thoughts and emotions. For example, Lucy shared her story with our online community of how she was discouraged by her setback not too long ago. Lucy had been struggling with severe anxiety disorders since she was thirteen. Her parents had taken her to several psychiatrists, and over time, it seemed to be under control. One day as she drove on the highway, she felt dizzy, and since she was currently sick with a chronic sinus infection, she immediately started panicking. She thought she would pass out, and her car would careen off the road. Somehow, she was able to get off the highway, slow down on the side of the road a few miles from home and called her mom to come to take her to the hospital. After that, it became impossible for Lucy to drive again. Each time she tried; thoughts would haunt her. She would watch the rearview mirror and imagine cars crashing into her, which got her really scared and dizzy. Feelings of disconnect would overwhelm her and eventually turn into a full-blown panic attack. It wasn't too long before she was avoiding all the highways. Of course, she realized this wasn't sustainable, especially if she wanted to keep her new job, so she sought help. She wanted to overcome her anxiety once and for all, but more importantly, she wanted to stop living with the fear of getting another episode.

Most of us can relate to Lucy's story, but the key thing to takeaway is that having a setback like her doesn't mean there's something wrong with you. The only thing you must do is liberate yourself from that fear of getting a relapse because that keeps you hostage and hinders full recovery.

What do I mean?

There are many ways to approach this. You could entertain the negative thoughts that tell you this isn't working or that you messed up. But that won't be helpful or healthy. Understand that recovery does entail having days where you fall back into irrational thoughts, negative emotions, and even habits that you know are no longer good for you. For example, if during your treatment you have a streak of days where you wake up and don't feel like life is hopeless and you actually manage to get out of bed and report to work on time, then yes, you are making progress. But suppose a few weeks in, you wake up, and your depression immediately takes over, making it impossible to get out of bed. Does that make you a failure? Absolutely not!

You are not stuck in that state. That's just the old state that is still trying to fight for your attention. Instead of assuming you've failed, and the treatment will never work, how about soothing yourself into a better feeling state? Create some bridge thoughts that can help you still face the day. For example, you could say to yourself, *"Today is going to be an off day for me, but it's okay. I know what a good day feels like, and it's okay that today I can just take things slow and pace myself. I will take it one hour at a time and just focus on getting out of bed and making myself some herbal tea. I know I'm not at my best today, but at least I am trying. I've got this."*

CAN I PREVENT IT?

Old habits die hard. There's not going to be an easy way of dealing with a relapse once it happens. But here's the thing. It is unlikely that you will experience a relapse anytime soon, so you need to release that fear at least for the next year or two. Why do I say this?

The healing process doesn't happen overnight. Even with therapy and self-care strategies for healing, you must give it time. Although no one can tell you exactly how long your recovery will take, I can assure you whatever happens in the next six to twelve months will still be part of the healing journey. So, if you stick to your new habits without fail and create a six-month streak of no episode or major issues, then one day you wake up, and it's a nightmarish day where everything seems to go wrong, that shouldn't discourage you. It's not really a relapse because it's still part of your healing.

There will be days where you will take three steps forward and days where you will take two steps back. All this is normal, and you must embrace this process. Be compassionate with yourself. Give yourself ample time to permanently heal. The more you set the right expectations, the easier it will be to avoid misinterpreting the situation and making things worse.

If, however, you really do find yourself right in the smack of a relapse, I want you to be kind and loving. Understand that what matters isn't that you never relapse or fall ill again but that you feel confident enough to pick yourself up and keep fighting the good fight. Mental health problems are like massive wars that we are fighting. They train us to become warriors. And as a warrior fighting a colossal war, some battles may knock you down. When you take a hit, you take a hit, but you never take your eye off the end objective. You know, losing one battle in the grand scheme of things is manageable as long as you never surrender. Make peace with that situation, and as quickly as you can, start getting back up!

I have trained my brain to view relapses as a hidden opportunity for further self-exploration and personal growth. Instead of perceiving myself as a failure when I catch myself falling off track, I force myself to get curious about what's happening. And on the days where it's too late for me to prevent some of my old behaviors from taking over, I usually find time afterward when I start to feel a little better to ask myself empowering questions. Remember when I shared that I used to ask myself, "why is this happening to me?" Nowadays, that irrational thought doesn't even pop up during a moment of distress. Instead, I ask questions such as "what have I learned from this?" and if it was a partic- ular trigger that I missed, I will be asking myself, "how would I like to deal with that trigger next time?" This didn't happen automatically. The small baby steps that I have taken over the years, the same ones I encourage you to take, led to this new lifestyle that I get to enjoy, and the same will be for you. To help you develop a useful framework that can alleviate the fear of a relapse, here are the most common triggers you need to become aware of, plus tips on how to avoid each.

STRESS

It's no secret, stress tops the list. Research indicates that when a stressful situation arises, people suffering from any kind of addiction tend to crave their addictive substance or activity the most. Even if you're not an addict, stress will likely trigger your mental disorder if left unchecked.

What to do: The best solution is to avoid situations that are extremely stressful until you learn how to handle your emotions. It might help to make a list of the places, people, and things that cause excessive stress in your life. For example, if you're in a toxic relationship, it might be a good idea to distance yourself or end that relationship all together so you can focus on your healing. This is part of making that all-important lifestyle change necessary for a full recovery and a better quality of life.

In some cases, you may not be able to just eliminate the extremely stressful situation, e.g., if you work for a boss that triggers you in all the wrong ways, I wouldn't necessarily suggest you quit your job because being unemployed and losing your health benefits and salary might trigger even more stress. Instead, I recommend training yourself to manage stress better. Many personal development teachers share helpful natural ways to manage stress, including Dr. Deepak Chopra. If you resonate with him, I suggest subscribing to The Chopra Well blog and YouTube channel so you can get all the free resources and meditation practices for stress management. You can also practice mindfulness and the various mindfulness techniques you've learned in this book when you are in that stressful place.

NEGATIVE EMOTIONS AND IRRATIONAL THOUGHTS

Unchecked emotions and irrational thoughts can trigger your relapse if you don't act as soon as you become aware of them. Here's the thing. No matter how much therapy and mindfulness you practice, you cannot completely eliminate negative emotions from your life.

None of us can. Negative and challenging emotions that make us uncomfortable are part of everyone's life. There will always be sadness and darkness, and negativity in the world. But that doesn't mean we are at the mercy of every negative emotion.

What to do: Learn to process your emotions and to see feelings for what they really are. Even those that are dark and often lead you into despair do not have power over you. If you can become more comfortable with the uncomfortable feelings and approach them more as an observer than a victim, they will flow in and out of your experience quite naturally. And suppose you stay calm during that temporary period of emotional disturbance instead of going into panic mode, assuming it to be a sign of impending doom. In that case, you can release them pretty quickly.

When they come, and they will - try journaling, meditating, praying, or even sitting in total silence observing the chatter and disturbance in your mind. Find a healthy way to release the negative state.

LONELINESS AND LACK OF SUPPORT

Few people talk about this aspect, but it can be a massive cause for relapse. Most of the time, the old habits and old friends will become an obstacle to our recovery. Many experts advise letting go of old friends that only help anchor in the condition and instead work on finding a new positive support group.

In the case of depression, most of us barely have real friends, so the main issue is feeling supported by people who genuinely understand you. Regardless of where you stand on that spectrum of friends (whether you have toxic or no friends at all), you need to feel supported and loved during your recovery.

What to do: If you have made the wise choice of getting therapy, make sure you stick to it until completion. Through your therapist, you can build a healthy support system, and that will create a safe space even outside the therapy room. If you're only opting for the self-healing approach, then search online or in your local area a group of like-minded people that you resonate with. If you feel trust and genuine care within your group, then you're in the right place. The people you want are friends who can uplift you and keep you account- able when you need it. Trust me, on the journey of healing, you will need people you can trust around you.

GETTING BACK ON TRACK

No matter how great and detailed your SMART goals are for your personal recovery or how prepared you are for a relapse, I can tell you it won't be easy to see the forest for the trees. You might have a distress kit full of all the right strategies and techniques for coping with your mental health disorder, but when the storm hits, it will still hurt, and you may very well find yourself face flat on the floor. What matters in such moments is the mindset you possess.

Believe it or not, your mindset will determine whether or not you recover and lead the life of your dreams. All the therapies, techniques, medication, and healing concepts in the world will be to no avail if you don't train your mindset to hold the right perspective. And if you think about it for a moment, you will realize that each time you've slipped or quit on yourself, it was because of the mindset you had. When something didn't go according to plan, you beat yourself up, engaged in unhealthy thinking and unhealthy behavior, which only made things worse. You then validated to yourself that you are, in fact, as inadequate, worthless, and as helpless as you feared. That is how you move further away from healing and deeper into misery and illness.

Now that you've read this book and increased your awareness, you can develop the kind of mindset that will lead you to that end objective of health and happiness and regain control if a setback happens. Here's how.

#1. Acknowledge that you've fallen off track.

Sometimes it's hard to recognize a setback, but if you have a healthy support system of people who care for you, they will point it out. Whether you realize it on your own or it comes from someone else, do not allow yourself that old impulsive behavior or victimhood and denial. Instead, I encourage you to be open to this new awareness. Remain receptive and objectively look at the facts being presented. Then move onto the next step.

#2. Tell yourself that it's okay.

Most research suggests that over 50% of people in recovery will experience a setback at some point in their journey even if they take every precaution. That tells me that it's normal and expected. So, in other words, you shouldn't waste your energy making a relapse or setback something horrible that should be avoided at all cost. Instead, you should be figuring out the most effective ways for you to manage a setback if and when it should arise. When it does, remind yourself that you are prepared for this.

#3. Accept full responsibility.

Aside from denial, the next worst thing you can do is blame the setback on something or someone. Sure, you were triggered, and that threw you off track but putting the blame on that trigger weakens you and steals your ability to take back control. That's why the next important thing to do is to assume responsibility for this experience. The choices you made inadvertently led you astray. This isn't to say you should now beat yourself up or justify what others did. Absolutely not! Even though others might have had a role in your difficulties, don't play the blame game. It will immobilize you and make your condition worse. What we want is to gain back control as soon as possible. So, we take full responsibility for our state and mental health and immediately start to ask high-quality empowering questions such as "what can I learn from this to make myself better?"

#4. Get help.

Trying to overcome a relapse or setback on your own is not advisable. The best and quickest way to get back on track is to call someone for support and ask for help. This can be your therapist, a counselor, or even a trusted friend. Immediately ask for some assistance even if the issue was small. Why? Because when a setback happens, the main focus should be getting back on track, and often our ego, sense of failure, or doubt can get in the way. So, we call reinforcement to help us rebuild that confidence and create a safe environment where the risk of further damage is mitigated. That will allow you the opportunity to regroup and motivate yourself again.

IT'S NOT THE END: WHAT TO REMEMBER

A question that I've been getting lately from friends is this.

"How do I get over this feeling of being a total failure after I have a relapse?"

It's a valid question and often challenging to give a simple answer because it all depends on why you have come to that conclusion in the first place. A story of a close friend comes to mind that might help you reconcile your concerns. He and I supported each other throughout our personal recovery, and we shared similar ambitions of recreating our lives. We both did tremendously well in the last few years, and he is now a thriving real estate agent working for one of the biggest companies in our city.

The last relapse almost broke him down again because he felt he had done everything in his power to get better and rebuild this new life, yet he still had a major relapse. I saw it as just a minor setback. His doctor assured him it was just a relapse. He felt different. It was catastrophic and a sign that he was never going to be anything but a complete failure. Of course, it wasn't any of those things.

What was happening here is that my friend was having a hard time coming to terms with what a mental health relapse means. So, it was up to us (his support structure) to remind him that recovery is never linear and that we all fluctuate from season to season. It's not the setback that matters but the mindset. So, I want to issue the same reassurance to you by reminding you of a few things.

First and foremost, you must avoid beating yourself up when you do have a relapse. That will only make things worse and disempower you. The second thing I want you to remember is that this too shall pass. You pulled yourself out of that pit of despair when you recovered before this setback, so this isn't an impossible mission. You can do this as many times as needed. What matters is that you've proven that you can function in life without the burden of illness that tortures you. Yes, it may take weeks or even months before you're up and running again in top form, but there's no reason for you to accept defeat. If you need to get another round of treatment, resume taking the medication prescribed by your therapist or whatever else, there's no shame in that. This is an on-going journey, and just as you will experience bumps in the road when taking care of your physical health, it's normal to have the same with your mental health.

CONCLUSION

Congratulations on sticking with this till the end. You've now learned what Cognitive Behavioral Therapy, Dialectical Behavioral Therapy, and Acceptance Commitment Therapy are, plus how they work. You also learned various ways of applying both therapy and self-care techniques to heal your mental health disorders. You should feel very proud for having the courage to take this first step. Taking a long and hard look at your destructive thought patterns and opening up your mind to new concepts that challenge your belief system and behavior is never easy. Your efforts will soon pay off.

As you continue applying what you learned, you will start to realize that people and situations don't drain or drag you down as much as they used to. Sure, you'll still face the trials and stresses of everyday life, but they won't seem like such a big deal; you'll find it easier with time to just shake things off and reset.

Best of all, you'll learn to stop taking everything so personally. You will detach from the need to value yourself based on other people's words and actions. What someone says or does or fails to do or say will no longer negatively impact your sense of worth.

All the techniques you've learned here (CBT, DBT, or ACT) will get easier as you practice them daily. Think of it like driving a car. Remember how awkward and complicated it felt the first time you sat behind the wheel? It didn't seem possible that one day you could automatically drive without giving it too much thought, and yet, if you've been doing it a while, you can probably attest to the fact that some days it feels like the car drives itself. Am I right? In just a matter of months, something as foreign as operating a machine to move from point A to B suddenly becomes second nature. But to get there, you had to invest time, money, and effort in driving lessons.

The same goes for CBT. As you make an investment in training your brain, you will reap the rewards for the rest of your life. Things that may seem hard now will become second nature, and the effort put in will be worth it when you look back from your newly rebuilt active and healthy lifestyle.

For years, therapy was considered something shameful, a taboo in some cultures. But thankfully, things have changed, and people realize taking care of your mental health is just as important and probably no different from signing up for that annual gym membership with a personal trainer. Learning how to control and regulate your emotions, stop irrational thoughts from ruling your mind, and eliminate detrimental habits from your routine is impactful to you and your entire community. The better you feel, the more you can make a difference in the world.

If you take only one thing away from this book, let it be that you now have more power over your mental health issue than you did before starting this book. You have a fully equipped distress kit with all kinds of wonderful techniques for mindfulness practices and hacks you can use to handle cognitive distortions and entire frameworks that can help with cognitive restructuring. The methods offered in CBT, DBT, and ACT can be used for the rest of your life with no harmful side effects, so don't just see this as a quick fix. Instead, approach these techniques as your allies on this recovery journey and turn them into lifelong friends that you can always lean on. Ultimately, this book has shown you that you can regain control and rebuild your life no matter how bad things have been. Realize this simple yet profound truth for yourself. The next step is to wear this new mindset of empowerment as much as you can from now on.

RESOURCES

Holland, K. (2020, September 3). Everything You Need to Know About Anxiety. Retrieved January 26, 2021, from https://www.healthline.com/health/anxiety

Higuera, V. (2020, February 11). Everything You Want to Know About Depression. Retrieved January 26, 2021, from https://www.healthline.com/health/depression

NIMH » Obsessive-Compulsive Disorder. (2021, January 28). Retrieved January 26, 2021, from https://www.nimh.nih.gov/health/topics/obsessive-compulsive-disorder-ocd/index.shtml

Why Cognitive Behavioral Therapy Is the Current Gold Standard of Psychotherapy. (2018). Retrieved January 26, 2021, from https://www.ncbi.nlm.nih.gov/pmc/articles/PMC5797481/

Psycom.net. (2019, October 21). Dialectical Behavior Therapy (DBT): Is it Right for You? Retrieved January 26, 2021, from https://www.psycom.net/what-is-dialectical-behavior-therapy/

Effectiveness of Acceptance and Commitment Therapy compared to CBT+: Preliminary results. (2018, October 1). Retrieved January 26, 2021, from https://www.sciencedirect.com/science/article/abs/pii/S0213616317301398

Effectiveness of Acceptance and Commitment Therapy on Anxiety and Depression of Razi Psychiatric Center Staff. (2018, February 15). Retrieved January 26, 2021, from https://www.ncbi.nlm.nih.gov/pmc/articles/PMC5839459/

Stanborough, R. M. J. (2020, February 4). How to Change Negative Thinking with Cognitive Restructuring. Retrieved January 26, 2021, from https://www.healthline.com/health/cognitive-restructuring

Time Management and Procrastination. (n.d.). Retrieved January 26, 2021, from https://caps.ucsc.edu/resources/time-management.html

GoodTherapy Editor Team. (n.d.). Mindfulness-Based Interventions. Retrieved January 26, 2021, from https://www.goodtherapy.org/learn-about-therapy/types/mindfulness-based-interventions

5 Simple ness Practices for Daily Life. (2018, December 13). Retrieved January 26, 2021, from https://www.mindful.org/take-a-mindful-moment-5-simple-practices-for-daily-life/

Skrzypińska, K. (2020, February 27). Does Spiritual Intelligence (SI) Exist? A Theoretical Investigation of a Tool Useful for Finding the Meaning of Life. Retrieved January 26, 2021, from https://link.

springer.com/article/10.1007/s10943-020-01005-8?error=
cookies_not_supported&code=799c0892-0deb-47eb-920f-
51f04abfedcc

M. (n.d.-a). Coping with Depression - HelpGuide.org. Retrieved
January 26, 2021, from https://www.helpguide.org/articles/
depression/coping-with-depression.htm

Neuropeak Pro. (2020, December 9). 10 Habits to Improve Your
Mood. Retrieved January 26, 2021, from https://www.neuropeakpro.
com/10-habits-to-improve-your-mood/

St.Cyr, J. L. (2019, May 22). Why Relaxation Techniques Don't Work
for Trauma & What to Do Instead. Retrieved January 26, 2021, from
https://healingwellcounseling.com/blog/trauma-survivors-why-
relaxation-techniques-dont-work-and-what-to-do-instead/

Setbacks in Mental Health Recovery Do Not Ruin Your Recovery |
HealthyPlace. (2017, February 19). Retrieved January 26, 2021, from
https://www.healthyplace.com/blogs/survivingmentalhealthstigma/
2017/02/setbacks-dont-ruin-mental-health-recovery

M. (n.d.). Finding a Therapist Who Can Help You Heal - Help-
Guide.org. Retrieved January 26, 2021, from https://www.helpguide.
org/articles/mental-health/finding-a-therapist-who-can-help-you-
heal.htm

B. (2016, August 5). How to Know if Therapy is Working. Retrieved
January 26, 2021, from https://beckinstitute.org/how-to-know-if-
therapy-is-working/

Community Mental Health Team for Older People, NSH Tayside. (n.d.). Staying Well – Relapse Prevention. Retrieved January 26, 2021, from https://www.nhstaysidecdn.scot.nhs.uk/NHSTaysideWeb/idcplg?IdcService=GET_SECURE_FILE&dDocName=PROD_233765&Rendition=web&RevisionSelectionMethod=LatestReleased&no

Flanigan, R. L. (2020, August 28). Depression & Relapse: Learning from the Setbacks. Retrieved January 26, 2021, from https://www.hopetocope.com/depression-relapse-learning-from-the-setback/

Overcoming Setbacks With Depression or Anxiety. (n.d.). Retrieved January 26, 2021, from https://www.premierhealth.com/your-health/articles/women-wisdom-wellness-/Overcoming-Setbacks-With-Depression-or-Anxiety/

BEAT ANXIETY & PANIC ATTACKS (2 IN 1)

OVERCOMING YOUR SOCIAL ANXIETY (IN RELATIONSHIPS) & DEPRESSION NATURALLY USING THERAPY (CBT & DBT & ACT), MEDITATIONS & HEALTHY LIVING

INTRODUCTION

We live in a society that conditions us into the belief that certain feelings are bad and that being positive and happy all the time is the way things should be. So, if you're a kid who doesn't fit that description (like me) or if something happens along your journey and you realize you're not happy all the time, all of a sudden, there's cause for alarm. When we feel anxious, stressed, overwhelmed, or nervous, we often get mad at ourselves for having these feelings because we believe it's wrong to feel that way. Usually, we'll tend to avoid the people, situations, or places that stir up these feelings as children. But as we grow up, we realize these feelings are EVERYWHERE! So, where does that leave us?

Transitioning into adulthood in our generation is unlike anything our parents and great-grandparents experienced. Disruptive change is real. Our world is changing in ways none of us expected, much less feel equipped to handle.

Even if you spend years getting a formal education and putting your-self into debt for a college degree, that still doesn't guarantee you'll have a great and happy life. Previous generations seemed to have a much easier time as life was slower, more pre-determined, and the economy less volatile than today. So, it was easier to predict the kind of life that awaited you if you did everything by the books. Today, it's a different story. Is it any wonder mental health has become such a hot issue in our society?

And it doesn't just affect adults. Even young teens and pre-teens find themselves trapped in a mind and body that doesn't function opti-mally. All doctors can say is "try not to worry so much "... I find that to be one of the most irritating lines anyone could tell me. And I've heard that statement far too many times for my taste. And you prob-ably picked up this book because you're fed up with something.

Perhaps you're sick and tired of going through life feeling trapped and unable to function like the friends you grew up with. You might have realized that your current lifestyle isn't sustainable. The fact that you can barely keep friends or that you'd rather drive for 12 hours than catch a thirty-minute flight because you can't handle flying isn't going to make life more comfortable as you grow older.

And given how important public speaking, social gatherings, and networking has become for a successful career, it's time to make some changes. But maybe for you, it's not even about being social. Perhaps your problem is far worse, and you're sick and tired of relying on medication and changing therapists because nothing works. Each year as the economy shifts and your debts increase, you might be feeling like you're about to lose your mind.

I don't want to come across like a know-it-all. I am aware that your story might be entirely different from the various scenarios I just shared, but here's the thing. You were attracted to this guide because, for one reason or another, you're tired of falling victim to the torturous reign of anxiety and panic attacks.

When anxiety or panic strikes for the first time, all you want to do is escape that experience. Suppose it's linked to a particular location or person. In that case, the natural inclination is to avoid that place or person altogether, especially when it happens the third or fourth time. As the problem keeps recurring in different places, you start wondering if it might be caused by you. Perhaps you are to blame. But it feels hard to own that you need help. Ultimately, there comes a day when it's you, on your couch, in the shower, or lying in bed, unable to fall asleep. For no apparent reason, full-blown anxiety attacks out of the blue, and you know for a fact that you need serious help!

Unfortunately for many of us, it takes a while before it dawns on us that this horrible experience is actually shadowing us because it's coming from within. The day you realize that is probably one of the worst days in your life because suddenly you feel completely power-less and unable to escape this invisible prison.

I've been there too.

At the age of eleven, I had my first panic attack. I couldn't figure out what was happening, but it was an overwhelming feeling that I had no control over. I honestly thought my heart was going to burst out of my chest. I tried to hide my symptoms because we were at a dinner gathering with my parents, and I didn't want to become the center of attention.

I felt dizzy, my vision was blurry, and I think for a moment there, I may have lost consciousness. Lucky for me, I was able to run outside to the backyard and just lie on the grass until I felt a little better. If I'd had my way, I would have run all the way home that evening. But I had to contain myself to avoid annoying and embarrassing my parents. Besides, what would everyone think of me? Wouldn't they call me weak? I didn't want to put myself through that kind of shame. So, I sucked it up, and it seemed to work for a while. The following months seemed fine until another event triggered my anxiety. This time, it was more potent and impossible to hide. My parents were hosting a Christmas dinner with friends and family. I had been taking piano lessons for about a year, and I wasn't too bad but nowhere ready to perform for anyone. Unfortunately, my folks saw this as an opportunity to show off their son's talents. They told everyone I was going to perform something. It was the most horrifying moment when they announced it at the dinner table. Everyone saw me as the shy kid who barely speaks, but they were eager to hear me play. I wanted the earth to open up and swallow me whole.

By the time we got to the actual performance, I was sweating, feeling nauseous, dizzy, and almost about to faint. I recall my dad sitting down and playing a quick tune to prime the audience and encourage me, then he gestured for me to join him and play. I stood up and started walking toward him, then at some point, my body froze, turned around, and ran upstairs to my room almost at its own will. I barely made it to my bed. Lying in bed, I had a full-blown panic attack which caused my mom to freak out and rush me to the hospital. In the months and years that followed, these overwhelming feelings came back sporadically. By eighteen, I seemed to hit rock bottom. I had panic attacks almost everywhere I went. My social life went down to zero. I had to quit practically every hobby I had as a kid, and the thought of growing up into a man with a career while feeling as I did almost drove me mad. I just knew I couldn't handle life as it was. I'll spare you the agonizing details of having to go through life thinking that I would never have an active and fully functional life. Doctors could never find anything wrong with me, but I knew something wasn't right. The medication I was prescribed didn't seem to solve the problem, but at least it helped me cope. So, trust me, I am well aware of how debilitating anxiety disorders can be. The main reason for creating the resources that I've built over the years for overcoming anxiety and panic is because I got to a point in my life where I'd had enough. I was sick and tired of being a victim and feeling trapped. I needed a way out.

After years of darkness and feeling trapped in a nightmarish tunnel, I finally found a way out. The documentation of techniques and solutions that I used to heal and then test others with successful outcomes is what you hold in your hand. You will be presented with proven knowledge, methods, techniques, and options for therapy programs that do not involve any use of medication.

I've seen people transform their lives when they and those around them had already lost all hope. These people believed they were doomed to live with anxiety disorders forever and thought the best case scenario was getting coping strategies that brought some temporary relief. Luckily, they were wrong. You'll read some of those triumphant stories throughout the book. Understand that I'm not suggesting this will work for every single person out there suffering from anxiety and panic disorder. However, I believe that if you are committed to this process and if you find resonance in my holistic approach to healing, you can step out of powerlessness and into your new lifestyle.

Think of this as a guidebook that will give you useful and easy to apply solutions to overcome your anxiety and panic attacks so that you can finally live the happy life you deserve. Excited? Good. Let's dive in.

I

FUNDAMENTALS ON ANXIETY, PANIC ATTACKS, AND STARTING YOUR ROAD TO OVERCOMING IT

WHY OUR NATURAL STATE IS PEACE & HAPPINESS, DESPITE THE MAJORITY OF US DRIFTING SO FAR FROM IT, AND HOW TO GET MORE IN TOUCH WITH YOUR NATURAL BEING!

What does Happiness mean to you? How do you define Peace?

I f you were to seek dictionary definitions of these two terms, you would have an intellectual earful of concepts that sound good but do nothing to transform your life.

It is futile to use someone else's definition of happiness and peace because that doesn't get you any closer to having it in your life. Most personal development students talk about peace and happiness. Many spiritual gurus teach about inner peace and happiness, but that still doesn't help the masses. There's a massive difference between knowing about something and experiencing it.

Have you ever watched a good deep-sea documentary where you saw the ocean's tide crashing against the shore with so much drama and intensity? Then as the camera ventures, a few meters down, you see a tranquil new world filled with all kinds of beautiful creatures, moving at their own pace, wholly unfazed by the action up above? This is fantastic imagery to help you understand what peace and happiness are like. You see, most of us tend to live on the surface of the waves where there's a lot of turbulence and wildness. The problem is that's the only way we know to live life. We fail to realize that there's another deeper level within us where everything is calm, blissful, and steady. This level of relaxed awareness is actually within each of us. What we need is access.

For that reason, I don't want to shove down your throat intellectual definitions that will do nothing more than entertain you for a minute. Instead, I want to invite you to reflect as you read this section of the book. Bring to mind any moments in your life, either through observation or direct experience, where you have felt happy. Think also to moments when you have felt in complete peace. That was you catching a glimpse of peace and happiness. It was you catching a whiff of your true nature. No matter how fleeting and temporary that moment, if you can bring it to mind, you can begin this process of understanding what peace and happiness mean.

Have you ever taken a moment to observe young babies playing in a park or by the beach? What's one word that comes to mind when most people think of such a scenario? I'd contend that majority would say happy, *i.e., children always look so glad.* Even when they get upset over a broken toy or falling down while running after a bunny in the yard, they quickly default back to that state we'd often refer to as happiness.

Now, let's try another scenario. You're stuck in line at the pharmacy, and the contents of your bag spills on the floor just as your phone starts ringing! I'm guessing the first impulse would probably be a stream of four-letter words that no one should hear. And even if you manage to suppress that urge to unleash your anger and frustration, we know that negative outburst isn't too far from your default setting. After all, anxiety and panic have never been associated with peace and happiness. So, what gives?

Is this happiness thing something that only young babies and the chosen few can enjoy?

The truth is actually going to feel outrageous for you. Especially if you've spent the last couple of years in deep emotional winter. Happiness is our natural state of being. Peace in mind, body, and spirit is how you were meant to experience this journey of being human!

Peace and happiness are our natural state, and most of us don't know it.

Bet you've heard of expensive beach yoga retreats that people invest a fortune in just to catch a glimpse of what peace and happiness might be like. The driving motive behind this desire to seek out happiness is actually good. Where most of us go wrong is that we assume it is something that doesn't belong to us and that we need to work hard to attain. We see it in the same light as hitting a target at work, and that's where we often fall off track. Peace and happiness are already part of our DNA. It's who we are. But even the most beautiful rose garden, when neglected and left unkempt, will develop weeds. And the weeds will choke all the beauty and cause one to wonder if there were ever rose bushes in that garden.

What I'm trying to put across is that your natural state of happiness and peace was impeded for one reason or another. The work then isn't to get something you don't have but instead restore yourself to that original natural state before your weeds took over and messed with your mind and life. When we look for circumstances to help us achieve inner peace, we end up further away from our source of happiness and only aggravate the anxiety that ails us.

HAPPINESS FROM A SCIENTIFIC APPROACH

The study of happiness has grown dramatically in the last three decades. One of the most common questions happiness investigators examine is this: How happy are people in general? In a 2007 survey, Gallup found that 52% of U.S adults who took the survey reported they were very happy. 8 out of 10 indicated they were very satisfied with their lives. Another poll done in 2013 revealed that happiness was trending downward. Only a third of the participants of this recent survey reported being very happy. Certain groups, including minorities, recent college graduates, and the disabled, revealed a decline in their happiness levels. I can only imagine what the polls would show now after being hit by a 2021 global pandemic, a crazy Trump era, and a massive unemployment rate in 2020.

It is Suffice to say, happiness is something many people are trying to understand. Few have successfully managed to get it. Happiness investigators looking to discover what makes people happy were searching to see if money, attractiveness, material possessions, satisfying relationships, or a rewarding occupation played a role in securing happiness in an individual. They still don't know with certainty. What they speculate is that age is related to happiness. Life satisfaction usually increases the older people get, but there does not appear to be gender differences in happiness (Diener, Suh, Lucas & Smith, 1999).

HOW DID WE DRIFT FAR FROM OUR NATURAL STATE?

This is a question that has no shortage of answers. You just need to look around. The addiction to technology we're all guilty of. Uncertainty of everything, including climate change, wars, sexual predators, government officials who are sometimes unfit to become heads of states, random shootings, pandemics, and the list goes on and on. I mean, unless you live in a cave, there's enough news reaching you that makes even a mentally healthy person anxious. For those already struggling with mental health disorders, especially anxiety and panic, things only get worse. It's hard not to feel angry, sad, powerless, and basically defeated by life. That is the opposite of joy and peace.

There's also plenty of research conducted by social psychologists reported in the Greater Good Magazine that suggests our happiness and peace of mind have been dwindling at incredible speeds since the 1950s, mainly due to our disconnection from nature. These studies, along with hundreds of others, point to the conclusion that we stand to benefit tremendously from nurturing a strong connection with nature. The more connected we are, the happier we are. The reverse is also true.

Some might think that this shift happened due to urbanization, but in fact, popular culture shows it has more to do with the lifestyle shift we made with the advent of technology that moved us further away from nature.

Take a personal inventory of how much time you spend watching sunsets, strolling on a park/beach, or sitting in a garden on Sunday afternoons. Now contrast that total time with the amount you spend indoors watching Netflix, on the couch, or in bed surfing the Internet or social media. You'll learn a thing or two about your current connection to the nature around you. And by that logic, the further away you feel from nature, the harder it will be to nurture the joy, power, and peace of mind you're seeking.

PANIC ATTACKS AND ANXIETY CAN OCCUR WHEN YOU DRIFT APART

After learning that your natural state is happiness and peace of mind, I hope you can already see that your anxiety issues are not meant to be with you forever. They exist because something went wrong and caused you to drift from your natural state of being. Before we can help you get back to your true self and heal the current issue, we need to understand what you're suffering from, the cause of it, and how to treat it.

Anxiety is a mental health problem that can take different forms. There is a normal level of stress that almost everyone experiences whenever there is real danger or cause for concern. For example, if you just lost your job, your brain would trigger those anxious feelings as a way to motivate you to solve the problem before next month's bills are due. That is not what this book is about. Our focus is on anxiety disorders which are a group of mental illnesses that cause constant overwhelm and fear. These excessive emotions make it difficult to function normally at work, school, home, and socially. To the degree your anxiety is left unchecked, to that degree, it will get worse. There are many types of anxiety, including generalized anxiety disorder, panic disorder, social anxiety disorder, phobia, separation anxiety, selective mutism, medication-induced anxiety, and so many others. This book's focus will remain on panic disorders, social anxiety, and general anxiety, but let's briefly define what each of the above-mentioned looks like.

- **Selective mutism:** This isn't a prevalent type of social anxiety, but some people suffer from it. Usually, it will be in young children and some teens who typically talk with their family but don't speak publicly.
- **Medication-induced anxiety:** This occurs when a person uses a particular medication or even illegal drugs, which triggers anxiety symptoms. It can also happen if one withdraws from taking a specific medicine. For example, if you've been on anti-depressants for a long time and stop taking them, it might trigger anxiety.
- **Separation anxiety:** This form of anxiety is more common in your children, but you can also find it in adults. If you often feel anxious or fearful when a person you're close to leaves your sight or if you always worry that

something terrible may happen to your loved ones, then
you're likely experiencing separation anxiety.

- **Phobias:** This isn't just about fearing a specific object or
  thing. It's more intense than that. The fear goes beyond
  what's appropriate, causing a severe biological reaction. For
  example, if you fear heights or flying, then being on a plane
  makes you sick, literally. Rock climbing even in a simulated
  closed room would cause you to faint or go into panic mode.

- **Panic disorder:** This type of anxiety is intense and will be
  our primary focus. It's when you get so fearful to the point of
  panic that you break into a sweat. Your heart pounds almost
  out of your chest, and you feel like you're having a heart
  attack. You might also get chest pains and start choking.

- **Generalized anxiety disorder:** This involves excessive
  unrealistic worry and tension with little or no reason.

- **Social anxiety disorder:** Often referred to as social
  phobia, people suffering from this are very self-conscious,
  constantly obsess about others judging them and often feel
  overwhelmed by negative emotions and worry. Being social
  is a great struggle, and they often withdraw from everyday
  social interactions.

A great question to ask would be, "what are some of the reasons I
have drifted away from my natural state of being?

Instead of seeking external causes and reasons for your anxiety, it's
time to look within. That's the only place you have control anyways.
You cannot control people, the government, the economic markets,
or the weather. So, does that mean you go through life forever help-

less? Absolutely not. Instead, you want to become more aware of some of the things you might be doing that nurtures your anxiety. Here are a few common ways we tend to drift from our natural state.

#1: We worry about the future too much.

#2: Comparing yourself to others and how they do something can cause you to drift and block happiness.

#3: Getting too caught up in your head and over-thinking everything.

#4: Holding on to resentment, anger, or regret.

#5: Negative thoughts and emotions. Allowing negative emotions to consume your mind can eventually create a permanent state of anxiety. That's why it's imperative to learn how to observe, process, and control your emotions, so they don't rule your life.

#6: False interpretation and stories that create negative meanings, such as assuming people are criticizing, judging, or ridiculing you when they are not.

#7: Guilt and shame are big ones. Feeling ashamed for making a mistake or embarrassed that you've failed at something can set off a cycle of anxiety that blows up into something serious.

#8: Fear is by far the biggest emotion that creates anxiety and other mental health disorders. Suppose it becomes a permanent state of living. In that case, it can drive you into mental instability and completely block out peace and happiness in your life.

KEEP YOUR LINES OPEN, AND GET IN TOUCH WITH YOUR NATURAL BEING

When it comes to healing and recovering your natural state of being, there's no miracle required. You live in a universe that has limitless potential for joy built into the creation process. It doesn't matter how far you've drifted from that place of peace and real happiness. You can always find your way back. This book's contents will help you get in touch with your true nature once again so you can finally have the kind of life you always dreamed of. It begins with a deep understanding of your thoughts and a clear recognition of who you really are. Yes, there's plenty of external reasons in the world to trigger stress and worry. Still, peace and happiness should never be at the mercy of conditions.

If being happy was a matter of having a perfect, problem-free life without any challenges, this whole conquest would be futile. What you need to understand is that being happy and at peace is an inner game. It's not about changing the outside world or fighting against the wrong things. Instead, it's about choosing your personal peace and happiness. It's about finding ease and training your mind to practice thoughts of minimal resistance until it becomes your natural way of reacting to conditions. Eventually, you'll become the kind of person you've always wanted to be free of the "dis-ease" that stress brings to your body.

Are you ready to choose peace and Happiness?

2

THE 3 BIGGEST MYTHS ABOUT ANXIETY DEBUNKED!

L et get something cleared up now. Anxiety disorders are real and should be treated with the same urgency as any physical disorder. Anxiety disorders are common and pervasive in the U.S. It is estimated that nearly 40 million people in the United States experience an anxiety disorder in any given year. Still, there's a lot of stigma around anxiety, and it's time to set the record straight. So here are three myths we need to debunk.

ANXIETY ISN'T A REAL ILLNESS; IT'S ALL MADE UP!

Everyone gets a little anxious from time to time. Worry over landing a job, a case of nerves before a big test, feeling nervous before a first date, or difficulty sleeping after a traumatic event are all normal. But when excessive anxiety takes over and persists in interfering with your daily thoughts and activities, it's time to seek professional help.

There's nothing ordinary about recurring nightmares, flashbacks, panic attacks that seemingly come out of the blue, or avoiding social situations because you fear being judged, embarrassed, or humiliated. The worst thing you can do is assume you are weak or try to hide the symptoms. Instead, you need to get help because it won't just go away. You can't wish it away or ignore it any more than you can a heart attack or diabetes.

The only way to treat anxiety is with medication, therapy, meditation, and other healthy lifestyle changes. So, don't let anyone make you feel like it's all in your head; it isn't!

PEOPLE WHO HAVE ANXIETY ARE WEAK, IT'S A CHOICE THAT THESE PEOPLE CHOOSE TO HAVE

Some people assume that anxiety can be switched on and off. As though it's a personal choice, but that is so far from the truth. Others think it's a way of getting attention from the people in your life. This is totally false. The fact is anxiety affects your body, mind, and behavior. It's a condition that can affect people of all ages, in all walks of life. So, we need to discard this false perception that people with anxiety are weak or broken somehow. It's one of the key reasons most people struggle in silence (mostly men). There's no shame in suffering from this mental disorder. You should approach it the same way you would bronchitis or any other health condition.

ANXIETY CAN ONLY BE TREATED THROUGH MEDICATION

Many assume that the only treatment for anxiety is medication. But as you'll discover in this book, there are many ways to heal yourself. Nowadays, medicine is perhaps the least desirable because of the side effects that follow. Although there are many cases where medication is recommended, it has to be combined with something that can address the root issue. Usually, medicine only provides a temporary remedy and a sense of relief, but to cure anxiety, one must tackle the root problem.

The most effective treatment is a particular type of therapy known as Cognitive Behavioral Therapy (CBT), based on mindfulness and changing your thinking, attitudes, behavior, and beliefs.

DO YOU KNOW WHAT MAKES YOU AFRAID?

Fear is at the root of any anxiety disorder. But what is fear, and why are we so fearful? Lots of things make us afraid. Fear is a strong emotion that can quickly rule your mind and life if left unchecked. Our brains are naturally wired to trigger anxiety-based emotions when we feel threatened or in danger. This has proved extremely useful in our survival as a species, given how tiny we are and how wild and dangerous life used to be before civilization. I'm pretty sure fear was helpful when we were hunters and gatherers trying to avoid being eaten by lions and such. Today, however, it's a different story. We are experiencing high levels of fear when there's no real or imminent threat, but our brains can't seem to tell the difference. We can get really fearful of a person, place, an event that in no way threatens our life. But because our brains are accustomed to being in constant fear, we'll react the same way our ancestors did when facing a fatal situation. Our bodies seem to react in that same way even though we are not in any real danger. There are plenty of triggers for fear in everyday life. It may not be easy to figure out each and every trigger that causes your mind and body to shift into that stressful state, so what you need to do is better manage your emotions and how you react once fear kicks in. Once you understand your fears, it becomes easy to understand your anxiety.

3

WHAT MAKES YOU ANXIOUS EVEN WHEN THERE'S NO DANGER AROUND YOU

Health professionals usually use the term "anxious" to refer to persistent fear. So, anxiety and fear are inseparable. The primary feelings (whether you are very anxious or afraid) will likely be the same, and that's why you want to become aware of the things that make you fearful and anxious.

The experience of anxiety isn't restricted to the economically deprived or politically oppressed. Anyone can suffer from it. Many tend to deny their personal anxiety or at least its intensity, sometimes even to themselves for various reasons such as the fear of rejection, avoiding embarrassment, or a sense of pride. And while it is closely related to fear, they are not one and the same.

THE DIFFERENCE BETWEEN FEAR AND ANXIETY

It's essential to understand the difference between these two states so you can diagnose your current condition. Some have referred to anxiety as "fear spread out thin," which is because, at its root, anxiety is often fueled by some kind of fear. Fear is basically a survival mechanism. It's both the psychological and emotional response to a feeling of being in danger and is most concerned with self-preservation. Anxiety, on the other hand, is a warning signal of one's increasing inability to survive.

Did you know that not all forms of anxiety are considered harmful? Many psychologists believe that periodic mild stress and anxiety can assist in increasing performance and productivity. For certain individuals, alertness and motivation are enhanced, causing them to tap into their potential even more.

So, the topic of anxiety can feel quite controversial, much like stress. There seems to be amiable and pernicious anxiety, much like how we know there is good stress and bad stress or good cholesterol and bad cholesterol.

For example, suppose you ask an athlete, a performer, or anyone else about to embark on a life-changing event. In that case, they might disclose an experience of mild anxiety on their part. The science community seems to see this as something good. However, the threat to health occurs when sustained for long periods of time and begins to take a life of its own in your mind.

Here's something you need to know about anxiety: It's not a one-size-fits-all condition whereby we can assume that specific strategies will work for everyone across the board. For example, peace and quiet or eliminating stress from your life can be useful and great advice for one person but ineffective for another. For instance, I have a friend who feels that his anxiety worsens when in a quiet, slow-paced area. When he stays alone with his thoughts, he feels less productive, isolated, and abandoned, which doesn't really help. So, his strategies for managing and healing obviously cannot include an extended period of being locked up in a room for self-contemplation.

And with that, you should also note that there are basically two types of debilitating anxiety: simple and neurotic. As the name suggests, simple anxiety is temporary emotional tension often tied to life's struggles and pressures such as paying bills, passing a final exam, or an executive who is tasked with the burden of meeting an impossible quota.

Neurotic anxiety is emotional tension that has become ingrained into your behavior, making it part of your personality. Some neurosis includes obsessive-compulsive reaction, hysteria, chronic depression, among others. Untreated neurosis can, over time, develop into psychosis. However, this generally occurs for people with the heredity disposition of mental health problems.

Another odd thing about anxiety that I realized is that your triggers might change over time. For example, I used to feel extremely anxious whenever I was at the movie theater. One day, I noticed the tension had almost dissipated because I would go to the theater and not feel as bad as I once did. The alarm that would always go off in my head somehow got disarmed as my brain realized I wasn't in any real danger when I go out to see a movie. You might notice something similar in your life whereby some trigger that used to bother you suddenly dissipates. What you don't want is to have more triggers popping up. Your relationship with anxiety is likely going to evolve as you continue on this journey of healing.

IT IS WHAT IT IS

A panic attack is an intense wave of fear characterized by its unexpectedness and debilitating immobilizing intensity. When a panic attack hits, you can't breathe, your heart feels like it's going to burst right out of your chest, and you feel like you're about to die or go mad. Most of the time, the panic attack strikes out of the blue. There's no warning or prep time. Some people can notice the trigger just before it hits. Unfortunately, I was never one of those. My triggers just weren't clear enough, so I always missed them.

While science hasn't identified the definite cause of anxiety and panic attacks, enough evidence points to various things, including environmental factors, genetic predisposition, brain chemistry, medical history, traumatic life events, and prolonged exposure to stress. Use of or withdrawal from an illicit substance can also contribute to the development of anxiety.

THE MOST COMMON CAUSES OF ANXIETY

Genes

Specific gene variants may be associated with greater levels of stress and anxiety. We are all unique human beings with different biological make-up, so you might be one of those people who might experience greater levels of anxiety than your relatives or friends for no other reason but that it's embedded in your genetic code. You could receive the exact same news, and it would trigger something in you while it does nothing to the other person. For example, I can recall when my parents told my sibling and me that we would be spending a Saturday afternoon at a family friend's home for a summer party. I immediately started feeling nervous while my sibling didn't seem to care at all. Essentially, what happens for those like us is that the genes cause chemical imbalances in the brain, leading to heightened stress levels.

What to consider if your biology is prone to stress and anxiety:

A medical professional would be able to run a series of tests to determine this. They would advise the best treatment. Some psychiatrists might recommend medication. Proceed with caution if you choose to go for that option because most of the time, the side effects of relying on medication can be quite harmful in the long run. I suggest experimenting with combinations of other treatments first unless your case is extremely severe.

Health

Pent-up stress combined with a poor diet and physical inactivity can be a great source of anxiety disorder. Do you know that? When we mistreat our bodies, we often directly impact our mental state because our biology affects our psychology and vice versa. We mistreat our bodies when we indulge in stimulants to the point of addiction. When we eat the wrong food, engage in poor sleeping habits, and avoid keeping our bodies active.

If you're in the habit of skipping meals and binge-eating crappy, over-processed junk food, you're likely not having a balanced diet. Your body and brain are missing critical nutrition to maintain optimum functioning, which could very well cause or at least contribute to an anxiety disorder's build-up.

Think for a moment about the idea of having a gene that makes you prone to anxiety. If you're mistreating your body, then you're more likely to trigger anxiety and fall ill not because of the genes per se but because of the combination of these two factors. See how this works?

So, it's not enough to say that your friend Sally sleeps as little as you and eats crap all week yet never falls sick because you don't know Sally's biological disposition. So, you might both have the same health habits, but for you, it might lead to a mental health issue.

The same is true with lacking physical exercise because activities like running, swimming, playing sports, and working out in the gym are scientifically proven to benefit the body and brain. They help in stress management and the production of feel-good hormones. Physical exercise is a great way to channel hormones like adrenaline and corti-sol, avoiding stress and anxiety.

Unhealthy mental states

Two major tenuous mental states cause emotional disturbances: Guilt and egoism.

Guilt is the sense of personal wrongdoing and being liable for punishment. By its very nature, guilt always creates psychotic tension. It might be false or true, but the psychic experience and tension are similar and real to the person in either case. True guilt results from the transgression or rejection of either some authoritative or societally established law. For instance, if you steal something from someone, you may feel a sense of guilt.

On the other hand, false or imaginary guilt comes from the failure to conform to others' expectations or judgments. For instance, if you struggled to perform well in class, perhaps peers and even the teachers would mock your performance, leading to guilt. This guilt isn't justified, but it still causes damage. Many neuroses have guilt as their central component. Often the impetus underlying false guilt is the need to win someone's approval, the need to please, or to be accepted by others.

If, as you read this, something strikes a chord in you, there might be some unchecked guilt brewing. Ask yourself the following questions:

a. What kind of guilt am I experiencing or hiding?
b. Is it really justified?
c. What is the reason behind my guilt?
d. What would be the proper way to view this situation?

If you realize you're holding on to morally justified guilt, it's time to do something about it. If it's morally unjustified, then acknowledge it for what it is, recognize that it is harming your entire life, and resolve it once and for all. You might be inclined to think that anxiety is your enemy, but the truth is, guilt and any unresolved negative emotions are the real enemies that should be dealt with. Divorce yourself from any and all guilt.

Egoism is another troublesome mental state. Usually, people suffering from egoism are so preoccupied with their personal needs they have no idea they actually suffer from it. A common trait of being egoistic is anger. There are two fundamental dimensions to consider here: Arrogance comes from feeling superior, and inadequacy that comes from feeling inferior.

A superior disposition compels a person to obsessively strive for personal attention and secure others' praise. There's a lot of exaggeration involved and a strong need for recognition. Usually, such a person is insensitive, judgmental, and even merciless when it comes to others, making them potentially volatile. We can see a lot of this behavior in our current society, especially with celebrities and athletes. Some secondary mental states that accompany this dimension of egoism include bitterness, jealousy, resentment, and envy.

An inferior disposition is actually more prevalent in our world. Most people who suffer from anxiety actually suffer from an inferiority complex, causing them to socially withdraw and feel intimidated around people. Such a person feels unworthy of personal recognition and even love. I can speak of how this personally affected me. I used to feel like nothing I did was ever good enough or right. I felt like a complete failure in life.

For some people, this is developed from childhood, maybe because of how much parents criticized them or because they struggled to understand what was being taught in school. Usually, when a person suffers from an inferiority disposition, it's because they learn to dislike themselves and believe others don't like them either. The person never quite makes the grade, regardless of how hard they may try. Secondary mental states of an inferior disposition include discouragement, emptiness, depression, loneliness, insecurity, hatred, envy, and jealousy.

Sometimes anxiety is a result of a combination of multiple factors. So, the best advice is to run a simple self-analysis first to determine how many of the common symptoms are associated with anxiety and panic attacks and if they are persistent, seek professional assistance. This book will walk you through everything you need to know so you can take the necessary steps to heal. First, let's talk about the signs and symptoms of anxiety.

HOW SHOULD I KNOW: THE SIGNS AND SYMPTOMS

#1: Excessive worry

Worrying excessively is perhaps one of the most common symptoms of anxiety disorder. This isn't just concern over an upcoming exam or an overdue project you need to hand in. I'm talking about persistent worry that you can't escape from. It's almost like being choked by an invisible and inescapable force that only you can sense.

#2: Fatigue

Most people assume that anxiety disorder is always displayed as hyperactivity in an individual, but sometimes it can be the opposite. For some individuals, chronic fatigue is how anxiety expresses itself, especially after an anxiety attack. There might be a correlation between insomnia, muscle tension, hormonal imbalances, but this is not scientifically proven yet. Most of the time, when anxiety is coupled with depression, chronic fatigue is one of the symptoms you might notice.

#3: Severe Irritability

Do you find yourself often snapping at someone over something trivial? It could be a sign of anxiety disorder. This is another ubiquitous symptom of anxiety. According to a study with over six thousand adults, more than 90% of those diagnosed with generalized anxiety disorder said they often felt highly irritable during periods when their anxiety disorder was at its worst.

#4: Social distancing and avoidance

By this, I mean you avoid any social interactions and public places. If you tend to feel anxious or fearful about upcoming social situations or if you always worry that you'll be judged, ridiculed, or scrutinized by others, then you might be experiencing anxiety disorders. Approximately 12% of American adults suffer from an anxiety disorder at some point in their lives, so this is a fairly common condition. Most of the time, one can tell they suffer from it because they struggle to interact or socialize with others causing them to avoid parties, theaters, malls, and such places. While it's not always evident that someone is suffering from this condition as the person might just seem shy, snobby, or standoffish, it is a real disease that causes a lot of torment, extreme fear, and anxiety.

#5: Problems staying focused or concentrating on a task

A study including 157 children and teens diagnosed with GAD (generalized anxiety disorder) found that more than two-thirds of them had difficulty concentrating. Another study that assessed 175 adults also found that 90% reported having trouble concentrating. Those with severe anxiety issues seem to have the greatest level of difficulty maintaining their focus. Although the evidence isn't sufficient to claim poor concentration and decrease in performance with anxiety disorder, current results show that most people suffering from it will have issues concentrating.

#6: Restlessness

Anxiety in children and teens often shows up as restlessness. You will find yourself (or the person suffering from anxiety) always feeling "on edge." Doctors usually look for this symptom when trying to make a diagnosis. So, ask yourself how calm are you on a daily basis? Are you usually feeling the uncomfortable urge to move? Do you have trouble finding your calm zone most of the time?

#7: Panic attacks

Although panic attacks are a type of anxiety, they are also signs in and of themselves that you are suffering from an anxiety disorder. Panic attacks are incredibly intense and overwhelming. They usually reach their peak within 10 minutes and rarely last more than an hour. Sometimes they happen in isolation. They are often reoccurring and make it impossible for you to do things like driving for fear that you might have one and end up in an accident. Fear is always at the root of a panic attack. To diagnose a panic attack, look out for these signs:

a. Shortness of breath

b. A racing heart

c. Tingling numbness in the hands and fingers

d. Chest pains

e. Difficulty breathing

f. Overwhelming sensation of fear or impending doom or death

g. Feeling weak, faint, or dizzy

h. Nausea or upset stomach

i. Sweating

j. Choking feeling

k. Hot or cold flashes

BE CAREFUL, THERE ISN'T JUST ONE KIND.

There is a myriad of anxiety disorders that affect millions of people in the world. That's why you first need an accurate diagnosis of what you're suffering from so you can get proper treatment. If you haven't yet seen any particular symptom or type that matches what you're currently experiencing, here are some more common disorders to consider:

#1: Anxiety Attacks: With this disorder, you suddenly feel like you're about to pass out, go crazy, die, or lose control. You can also call it a panic disorder.

#2: Concerns about your appearance: This type of disorder causes you to feel like there's something abnormal or even grotesque about your appearance even though no one else sees that defect.

For example, imagine a wife who thinks, "*I think my hair is thinning.*" That creates anxiety and intrusive thoughts. She goes in front of the mirror, touches her head, and asks her husband, who responds, "*no honey, you've got beautiful, healthy hair.*" The woman feels better for about thirty seconds until another intrusive thought enters, "*he wasn't really listening to me. He never listens to me.*" Next thing you know, she's obsessing over baldness cures as she scours the internet for a solution.

This is a trivial example, but in some cases, it can be extreme to the point that a person refuses to undress or even enter into relationships because they believe they have a defect.

#3: Performance anxiety: Another type of anxiety that many struggles with is performing or competing in front of an audience. Some call this social anxiety disorder, but it can also be more intimate than just social performance. It can also include difficulty performing with an intimate partner.

#4: Agoraphobia: With this disorder, you're always afraid something terrible might happen if you're away from home. It could be the fear of having another panic attack and appearing distraught in public. You will notice that many people suffering from panic attacks also get agoraphobia.

#5: Shy bladder syndrome: With this condition, you have trouble using a public restroom. It's considered a form of social anxiety disorder.

#6: Post-traumatic stress disorder: This condition comes from a traumatic experience that you had in the past, which still has a firm emotional grip in your daily life. It could be child abuse, death of a loved one, rape, severe injury, or torture.

As you can see, there are many forms of anxiety. The more you can quickly identify with one, the higher the chances you're suffering from that type of mental disorder. Once you know what the problem is, finding the right solution becomes plausible. Don't feel pressured to label your condition and know that research is ongoing in the medical field, so this list is by far not extensive. If you don't find that you fit 100% in any particular disorder or that you have more than one ailing you, that's okay. This isn't something to criticize or feel ashamed about. You just need a starting point so you can gather the right resources and assistance to aid your healing.

CAN I CONTROL IT?

Often when we attempt to control our anxiety, we tend to make things worse. I think it's primarily because we approach it from a place of resistance. We get mad at ourselves for activating it and, in so doing, increase the intensity of the experience. Therefore, I want to suggest that your best efforts should be in self-acceptance and self-care strategies and not "controlling or eradicating feelings of uneasiness and anxiety." The more you can develop this mindset of focusing on constructive thinking and less on being in control all the time, the easier it will be to manage and recover from anxiety disorders.

One way of doing this is to learn healthy management strategies and to undergo treatment. In so doing, you can learn specific techniques that help you manage your condition. Many of the methods you will learn in the treatment options I will be sharing in the next chapter will help you practice things like progressive muscle relaxation, mindfulness meditation, deep breathing, and so much more. All of these will aid you in reducing anxiety symptoms. Through natural remedies, lifestyle changes, and the therapy options you will learn shortly, you can find a combination of solutions that enable you to permanently heal or at the very least manage anxiety.

4

HOW YOU CAN GET BACK TO ENJOYING YOUR LIFE & WHAT REALLY MATTERS TO YOU WITHOUT ANXIETY ALWAYS GETTING IN THE WAY

The cost of allowing anxiety to rule and ruin your life is profound and far-reaching. These effects fall into three basic categories: Physical, psycho-emotional, and social. Let's briefly look at each of these. Physically, you may continuously suffer from stomach issues, heart palpitations, headaches that won't go away, muscle cramps, and various inexplicable body aches and pains. Anxiety also increases the stress hormone cortisol, which raises blood pressure and contributes overtime to heart problems, stroke, kidney disease, and sexual dysfunction.

In a 2017 Lancet study using brain scans, they measured activity in an area called the amygdala, which mounts split-second responses to danger and encodes memories of frightening events. Greater activity in the amygdala correlated with a high risk for heart disease and stroke (sourced from Harvard Health Publishing - Anxiety: What it is, what to do). We know the amygdala is overactive for people suffering from anxiety, which might drive inflammation and plaque formation, leading to heart attacks and strokes.

When it comes to psycho-emotional disorders, we find that anxiety initially decreases performance by curtailing reasoning abilities, dulling imaginative thinking, and causing general discouragement. Anxiety disorders cause us to feel disoriented, discouraged, ashamed, and depression may then follow.

Your social life also takes a massive blow because extremely anxious people tend to avoid social contact even with familiar friends to cope with their situation. Social contact usually generates feelings of uncertainty, suspicion, and uneasiness. Overall, your quality of life suffers. It becomes impossible to have functional relationships or participate in activities that you previously enjoyed. With all this news of doom and gloom, it can be hard to see a way out of this nightmare experience. But I promise you it is possible when you realize this simple truth: You have the power to heal and transform your life.

IT STARTS WITH YOU

The road to overcoming anxiety and healing your life begins with a critical decision. You must choose to face your fear. The moment you become fed up with the current condition and feel like you've reached the end of the rope, that something must change is the turning point you will need to start your recovery. Once you choose to face your fear, the next step will be to accept the responsibility of knowing yourself and owning your ability to overcome this condition.

If you are at that point and you are ready to know more about yourself and the things that are triggering your anxiety, then you are primed to heal. With the right treatment and strategy, you will be on your path to recovery. But there are so many options for treatment. How do you know which to take? There's no right or wrong answer because it depends on your personality, the intensity of your anxiety, and what feels comfortable. Listen to your gut on this, and you won't go wrong. When it comes to therapy, my preferred options are Cognitive Behavioral Therapy, Dialectical Behavioral Therapy, and Acceptance Commitment Therapy. Let's discuss each in detail so you can identify which feels right.

GIVE COGNITIVE BEHAVIORAL THERAPY (CBT) A GO

Once you successfully diagnose your anxiety, it's essential to rule out the dominant cause of it. Suppose you're suffering from anxiety because of an underlying medical condition. In that case, you need a thorough physical exam to help resolve that physical malady first. But if your anxiety stems from the causes we mentioned earlier, and the doctors say physically you are in great shape, we can wholly focus on integrating proven treatments. Consider CBT, which many people claim is the most effective treatment for almost all forms of anxiety disorders. For this form of therapy two work, there are two critical aspects to consider. First, your willingness to change, and second is your relationship with your therapist.

What is CBT?

Cognitive-behavioral therapy is a form of short-term psychotherapy that focuses on your thoughts, beliefs, and attitudes and how that affects your feelings and behavior.

It can help your find new ways to behave by changing your thought patterns. It works on the basis that the way we think and interpret life's events often affects how we feel and behave. CBT centers on identifying and changing inaccurate or distorted thinking patterns, emotional responses, and behaviors. Cognitive-behavioral therapy techniques include cognitive restructuring and behavioral changes like reducing self-defeating behaviors and developing healthy habits.

It has been well researched, and studies conducted show that it can be powerful in treating a wide range of problems, including depression, anxiety disorders, insomnia, eating disorders, alcohol, and drug use problems. A few core principles are underlying this treatment that you should know about. This is the premise by which to approach CBT.

1. Psychological problems are based in part on faulty, unhelpful ways of thinking.
2. Psychological problems are based in part on learned patterns of unhelpful behavior.
3. People suffering from psychological problems can learn better ways of coping with them, thereby relieving their symptoms and becoming more effective in their lives.

As you can tell, CBT treatment is very active and hands-on with your thinking patterns. It is goal-oriented and requires collaboration between you and your therapist with the ultimate goal of becoming your own coach and therapist once you've mastered how to get a handle on your thoughts, feelings, and behavior.

How CBT can help:

- It can help you identify the root problems causing your anxiety with clarity.
- You'll develop an awareness of your automatic thoughts.
- It will help you become aware of and challenge the underlying assumptions running your life that may be wrong.
- You'll be able to distinguish between facts and irrational thoughts.
- You will understand how past experiences can affect present feelings and beliefs.
- It will enable you to stop fearing the worst.
- You will start to see the situations in your daily life from a different perspective.
- It will give you the ability to understand other people's actions and motivations.
- You'll develop a more positive way of thinking and seeing situations.
- It will help you face your fears instead of avoiding them.
- You'll become more aware of your mood and state of mind.
- It helps you establish attainable goals.

- You will learn strategies for managing challenging moments or triggers as they arise.

The tools most used in CBT include role-playing activities, homework assignments, keeping a cognitive-behavioral diary, practicing the skills learned to promote positive behavioral change and growth, and regular one-to-one or group discussion sessions (usually it's a combination of these).

While most traditional therapy involves indefinite visits and time spent on the couch passively digging up your past, Cognitive Behavioral Therapy is timed and focuses on present thoughts and beliefs. As you go through CBT and learn to change your perception and how you see things in your life, your relationship with anxiety, and learn more about who you really are, the outcome will be a shift for the better.

THE IMPACT CBT CAN HAVE ON YOUR LIFE:

With cognitive behavior therapy, you stand to learn that while you cannot control every aspect of the world or change the past, you can, in fact, take control of how you interpret and deal with things in your environment. CBT will help you learn strategies that'll empower and aid you now and in the future, including identifying negative thoughts, goal setting, problem-solving, self-monitoring, and so much more. Let's briefly look at each of the key strategies and how they can help.

Self-monitoring:

One of the first things you'll have to do in CBT is to start monitoring yourself. That means tracking your behavior, symptoms, and experiences over time and then sharing them with your therapist. Some people like to call it diary work. Doing this will help both you and the therapist clarify what's needed so you can be on the best treatment possible. It also allows you to make adjustments where necessary. An example of this would be to keep track of the environment, any triggers, emotions, and what you're doing when a panic attack occurs.

Setting goals:

Goal setting is going to be an essential step in your recovery. If you don't set the right goal and have a target to move toward, how can you possibly know if your life is getting better? So, in CBT, your therapist can help you with goal-setting skills by teaching you how to identify the right goals for you and create short and long-term milestones. A method I like to use and recommend you take up is setting S.M.A.R.T goals. These are Specific. Measurable. Attainable. Relevant. Time-based goals. Once you have it, focus on the process and enjoy the journey till the desired outcome is achieved.

Identifying negative thoughts:

In cognitive-behavioral therapy, you will learn the importance of recognizing dominant thoughts and emotions that rule your life. As you gain this awareness, you'll start to see how thoughts, feelings, and situations can contribute to maladaptive behaviors. This process isn't necessarily easy. In fact, many people struggle with this much introspection which is why it's a good idea to do it with a health professional, so you don't fall off track or dig yourself into an inescapable hole. When done correctly, this will lead to self-discovery and insights that will liberate you from your anxiety.

Problem-solving:

Problem-solving in CBT typically involves five steps. The first is identifying the problem. The second is generating a list of possible solutions. The third is evaluating the strengths and weaknesses of each possible solution. The fourth step involves choosing a solution to implement. The fifth step is implementing the solution and sticking with it until the desired outcome is achieved.

PRACTICE MINDFULNESS WITH DIALECTICAL BEHAVIOR THERAPY (DBT)

Dialectical Behavioral Therapy is another option for helping you heal anxiety forever. It has evolved from cognitive behavioral therapy. Therefore, many of the core principles apply here. Its main goal is to teach you how to live-in-the-moment and develop healthy ways to cope with stress, regulate your emotions and improve your relationship. It focuses on mindfulness or living in the present, regulating emotions, tolerating distress, and effectively managing relationships with others.

DBT incorporates a philosophical process called dialectics. Dialectics is a Greek philosophical concept that states everything is composed of opposites and that change occurs when there is a "dialogue" between opposing forces. There are three basic assumptions to consider here:

1. All things are interconnected.
2. Change is constant and inevitable.
3. Opposites can be integrated to form a closer approximation of the truth.

So, with DBT, you and the therapist would work together to resolve the contradiction between self-acceptance and change to bring about the desired positive outcome. You would also use a technique known as validation which means your therapist will validate that your actions "make sense" within the context of your personal experiences without necessarily agreeing with that approach of solving the existing problem.

THE IMPACT DBT CAN HAVE ON YOUR LIFE:

Suppose you suffer from multiple forms of anxiety and other self-destructive behavior. In that case, this might be the right therapy for you. A unique aspect of DBT that makes it so effective is that it helps you practice self-acceptance. You learn to deal with distress and difficulties in a compassionate way instead of trying to fight or hide them. With DBT, you will learn mindfulness skills, distress tolerance, interpersonal effectiveness, and emotional regulation. Let's touch on these core strategies so you can see how they can be applied.

Core Mindfulness:

Mindfulness helps you focus on being present. It's about living in the moment and paying attention to what is happening inside you, i.e., your thoughts, feelings, sensations, and impulses. You also learn to use your senses to tune into what's happening around you. Mindfulness skills help you slow down as you learn to use healthy coping strategies amid emotional pain. It can also be used to keep you calm and avoid engaging in automatic negative thought patterns and impulsive behavior.

Distress Tolerance:

This is a powerful aspect of DBT because you learn to accept yourself and the current unpleasant situation instead of resisting it, which usually makes things worse. You will discover four techniques for handling any crisis. Distraction, improving the moment, self-soothing, and thinking of the pros and cons of not tolerating distress.

Emotional regulation:

Regulating your emotions is one of the best tools you can have as you move forward in life. You'll learn how to identify, name, and change your feelings whenever the need arises. For example, suppose you're going about your day shopping in the supermarket, and an incident occurs with the cashier that throws you off your game. In that case, you can be able to recognize what that emotion is (e.g., anger) and cope with it immediately, reducing your emotional vulnerability. That alone can help you deactivate many of the triggers that await you as you go through life and helps you have more positive emotional experiences because you can finally control what you choose to feel at any given moment regardless of external conditions.

Interpersonal Effectiveness:

Here you will learn how to nurture healthy relationships. If you struggle with being assertive and saying no when it needs to be said, this is where you develop that level of confidence to be yourself. You will learn how to become a better listener, how to communicate more effectively, and how to deal with toxic or challenging people.

ACT WITH ACCEPTANCE COMMITMENT THERAPY (ACT)

Acceptance Commitment Therapy is often referred to as the "third wave" of psychotherapy. In this context, the first wave would be the classical conditioning and operant learning-based behavioral approaches that were developed in the 1950s. Therefore, the second wave would be the more information processing type of therapy where cognitive processes and behavioral learning principles take center stage. Naturally, the third wave would be ACT. With this "third wave" of psychotherapy (which has become extremely popular for treating general anxiety disorders), the emphasis is on mindfulness, practicing empathy, compassion, and self-acceptance.

As the name implies, this form of therapy focuses on acceptance. ACT (Acceptance Commitment Therapy) suggests that increasing acceptance of your circumstance instead of resisting it can lead to increased psychological flexibility. Rather than avoid specific thoughts, emotions, or experiences, acceptance can better help you cope with things more effectively. So, using this form of treatment, you will gain insight into patterns of thinking and avoidance that have been worsening your anxiety disorder. You will also see the presence and absence of actions that fall in line with your personal values.

What stands out for me with ACT is that, unlike CBT or DBT, this form of treatment doesn't focus on reducing the frequency of unpleasant internal disturbance (e.g., cognitive distortion/irrational thoughts). Instead, it's about decreasing your need to control or eradicate these experiences while simultaneously increasing involvement in meaningful life activities, i.e., the things that are consistent with your personal values.

THE IMPACT ACT CAN HAVE IN YOUR LIFE:

There are six core principles of acceptance and commitment therapy: cognitive defusion, acceptance, observing self, contact with the present moment, values, and committed action. Let's touch on each of these.

Cognitive defusion:

Cognitive defusion is learning to detach yourself from sensations, thoughts, memories, urges, images, feelings, and thoughts that harm you. ACT teaches you how to stop fighting against and resist these unpleasant inner experiences and instead reduce their influence on you. Working with a therapist, he or she will help you see how struggling against negative thoughts is like trying to climb out of quicksand. The harder you try, the worse you make your situation. Most of the time, therapists will use metaphors that apply to your situation and then show you how to use acceptance and commitment to make things better. One of the techniques you'll be taught is how to reframe some of the thoughts that show up. For example, suppose you suffer from social anxiety disorder and usually try to cope using unhealthy strategies like drinking alcohol. In that case, you'll come to see how trying to control your anxiety is part of the problem instead of the solution.

Your therapists may also ask you to say what you're thinking and feeling. If you usually have thoughts like "Everyone thinks I'm boring," then your therapist will ask you to reframe that to "I'm having the thought that everyone thinks I am boring "... You can add the words "I have the thought..." at the beginning of every thought that isn't constructive. This gives you some detachment and reduces the impact your thoughts have so you can realize you are not your thoughts.

As you come to realize that you are neither your thoughts nor the mind, you can more naturally imagine that your feelings, thoughts, and images are just soldiers in a parade passing by but having little impact on you.

The observing self:

This is going to be a powerful tool that your therapist will teach you to utilize. It involves learning to notice that you can observe your thoughts, emotions, and environment. You will learn to see that you are in control of your thoughts and feelings. They are not dangerous, threatening, or more powerful than you. Can you imagine how liberating it will be to detach yourself from intrusive thoughts or painful emotional experiences when they attack? Nothing will ever have a strong grip on you once you take back your power and become the observer.

Acceptance:

Learning to accept unwanted experiences and things that you cannot control will significantly reduce your anxiety. It's common to find your therapist using phrases like "clean discomfort" and "dirty discomfort." Clean discomfort refers to normal feelings of anxiety when the situation calls for it, such as feeling anxious in social and performance situations. Dirty discomfort refers to what happens when anxiety is triggered by your own hyperactivity, such as becoming anxious because your anxiety is increasing. A typical exercise that many people go through involves a guided visualization where the therapist asks you to imagine that you have a switch in the back of your brain. When that switch is "ON," you will struggle and fight against any unpleasant experience, making things worse. You may become angry, sad, and anxious about the increasing anxiety. These emotions are known as secondary emotions, and they usually set up a vicious cycle. So, your therapist will ask you to switch "OFF" that button and notice what happens. As you become present and pay attention, you'll see these secondary emotions will dissipate.

Values:

Do you know who you really are and what you stand for? What is important to you in life? What has meaning in your life? Is it family? Faith? Can you identify it? Getting to know your values can help you set the right health goals and ensure you follow a treatment that ensures permanent results.

Working with an ACT therapist, you will uncover your values and identify whether you're living in integrity with those values and what adjustments need to be made. That is extremely valuable for treating anxiety because a lot of research points to low self-esteem and other value-based factors as one of the many causes that could lead to anxiety disorders.

Committed action:

As you go through the treatment, you will be asked to commit yourself to action that is in line with your values. This might cause uneasiness at first, especially if you have drifted too far from your natural state. But you must commit and implement.

One of the powerful strategies you will learn during ACT treatment is how to practice non-judgmental awareness. You'll learn to understand your emotions at a whole new level and to observe without judging yourself harshly.

Additionally, you'll also be involved in a lot of mindfulness exercises. Through mindfulness practices that run deeper than what you learn in DBT, you'll develop the tools and skills needed to maintain calm and to practice non-resistance whenever you're faced with a challenging situation or irrational thoughts.

A CHANGE IN LIFESTYLE GOES A LONG WAY

Recovering and healing from major anxiety will require a change in your current lifestyle and the habits that aren't serving you. This could mean getting back into the habit of doing things that you used to but lost interest in, or it could be learning something entirely new.

I recently watched famous actress Halley Berry talk about the training she had to undergo for six months to prepare for her role, starring alongside Keanu Reeves in John Wick 3. She said it was tough to condense into six months what would typically take regular people three years to learn, but there was no quitting and no complaining. Only showing up and getting the work done.

You don't need to be so insane about it and try to do the impossible, but in a way, you will need that same persistent mindset for a period of time (at least six months) where your only focus is sticking to the habits you know will help you transform your life. For example, if you used to exercise but gave up on it when your anxiety or depression became too intense, restarting that habit will need a lot of self-motivation. And just like Halley Berry, you need to sell yourself into this idea of training so much that you refuse to accept any thoughts of quitting, giving up, or complaining. You will need to show up for yourself each day to get the work done, no matter how uncomfortable it feels. You also need to keep trying new things, including learning new hobbies that help you express your creativity, challenge your brainpower, and so on. Now, I realize that at times even getting out of bed in the morning feels like a herculean task. And I know some days you might have dips of depression or panic attacks that completely disrupt your stamina, but I still want you to do your best even on your worst days. Why?

Because the only way to transform your life is to show yourself that you can control how you feel and behave. Your lifestyle choices can either help make things better or worse. Here are some lifestyle shifts

that are scientifically proven to work in reducing or completely eliminating anxiety disorders.

Good quality sleep: Most of us think we get enough rest, but our
society, in general, is sleep-deprived, so it's no surprise that we need
to put more effort into getting better quality sleep. If you go to bed
and spend an hour browsing social media or chatting on WhatsApp,
then try to fall asleep, your sleep quality will likely be compromised.
Anytime you are stressed and anxious, your body will naturally
require more rest and relaxation. Sleep is a great way to get the body
to rest, but you need to ensure the environment fosters good quality
rest. Unfortunately, as you may have experienced already, anxiety
makes it hard for us to find that state of good quality rest and relaxation. So even if I go to bed early (without any gadgets to distract me),
but I can't fall asleep because I am anxious for half the night; I'm still
not going to be well-rested the next morning. And since many people
suffering from anxiety tend to have insomnia, telling someone to
simply go to bed early won't cut it. So how can you start changing
your sleep habits?

Realize that it doesn't help to stay up late binge-watching Netflix or
Amazon Prime. But at the same time, you shouldn't force yourself to
go to bed too early. Learn to listen to your body. Start to practice what
experts call sleep hygiene. That means you need to create a good and
relaxing bedtime routine and then stick to it. You should also make
your bedroom as relaxing and sleep-friendly as possible. Some little
changes you could start with today include putting an end to anything
that stimulates your brain at least an hour before your bedtime—no
television, computers, coffee, cigarettes, or anything that stimulates

wakefulness. If you love drinking something after dinner, switch the coffee to herbal tea.

Exercising: Regular exercise is one of the best things you can do to reduce anxiety symptoms and promote healing. Studies conducted show that physical movement and breaking a sweat can boost your mood, improve your sleep quality, reduce tension in your body, and lower stress levels. The more you exercise, the more energy your body generates, which will benefit you in so many ways, including increasing your ability to concentrate. There are many forms of exercise depending on your preference, but I highly recommend taking some Yoga classes a few times a week. The combination of mindfulness breathing and physically moving your body has been linked to reducing anxiety symptoms. I recommend making a commitment to spend just twenty minutes daily on some form of exercise that you enjoy even a little bit. That is ample time to activate your endorphins which is the body's natural mood booster.

Good nutrition: Although there's no specific type of food you can eat to eliminate anxiety, we do know that having a healthy, well-balanced diet can help you during the recovery process. Stimulants containing caffeine and other substances that have a tendency of sending your body into hyperactivity will need to be avoided or eliminated.

Maintain a healthy eating routine and snack at regular intervals to help your body adjust and cope with the treatment and healing process. Also, consider reducing the amount of processed and junk food that you consume. Raw, simple foods will serve your body and boost your energy far more than junk foods. A diet rich in whole grains, vegetables, and fruits is a healthier option that I recommend focusing on, so here is a list of foods that have been shown to reduce anxiety.

- Foods rich in zinc such as cashews, beef, egg yolks, and oysters have been linked to lowered anxiety levels.
- Magnesium-rich foods such as leafy greens like Swiss chard and Spinach or nuts, seeds, legumes, and whole grains should be part of your daily intake.
- Foods rich in B vitamins such as avocado and almonds have also been associated with lowered anxiety levels.
- A study completed on medical students in 2011 showed that omega-3s may help reduce anxiety. Consider adding fatty fish like wild Alaskan salmon to your meal planning.

Since anxiety is thought to be correlated with a lowered antioxidant state, consider adding beans, berries, and vegetables (beets, broccoli, kale, artichokes, and asparagus) to your diet, as well as spices like turmeric and ginger, which contain antioxidant properties.

Proper hydration: Multiple studies show a correlation between dehydration and anxiety. In one 2018 survey of over 3,000 adults, those who drank more water had a lower risk of anxiety and depression than those who drank less water (source: Healthline.com). We know through firsthand experience that lack of proper hydration messes with brain functionality. The brain, which is composed mainly of water, requires a lot of it to perform optimally. So, people who drink lots of water usually feel calmer and happier. There's a lot of increased tension, a drop in focus, and mood when one doesn't hydrate enough, making anxiety levels worsen. But how do you know you're dehydrated, and how much water should you take anyway? The first signs of dehydration are thirst, a dry mouth, dark yellow urine, constipation, skin changes, including dryness, redness, or loss of turgor. You might also experience sleepiness, fatigue, confusion, headache, nausea, or even high blood pressure.

The Academy of Nutrition and Dietetics suggests that women should drink around 9 cups of water every day while men to consume around 12.5 cups. Of course, this should not be a fixed number because each body is different. Start with a fixed number and get to learn what your body thrives in. Depending on your activity levels, age, and how much water you usually take through foods like fruit and vegetables, your daily water intake may vary.

If you find water drinking to be a task too great for you, consider setting the alarm on your phone each hour to get in a cup. It's a great way to establish this as a permanent habit.

II

PRACTICAL TECHNIQUES AND YOUR PERSONAL GUIDE ON OVERCOMING YOUR ANXIETY AND PANIC ATTACKS

5

CREATE A MORNING ROUTINE TO START REDUCING ANXIETY RIGHT AT THE BEGINNING OF YOUR DAY

I t's time to get into strategies that will help you get your life back. You now have a working understanding of what happens when anxiety or panic kicks in and the leading causes. With that foundation in place, we can start taking baby steps in the right direction. This section of the book will help establish a couple of necessary pillars: your body, mind, and environment.

It should be evident by now that your body and mind are interconnected. What you feel and say to yourself impacts your body positively or negatively. The environment you spend the most time in also influences your body and mind. Therefore, the path to recovery involves being more proactive in these three aspects. But let's break them down further into bite-sized changes you can make, starting with how you approach your day.

THE IMPORTANCE OF STARTING THE DAY WITH A MORNING ROUTINE

How you start the morning determines the rest of the day. We all know how tough it can be to get the day started right, so one of the most significant shifts you can implement immediately is to create a morning routine designed to promote harmony, relaxation, and ease. Studies show that a change in morning routine for a person struggling with anxiety reduces the chances of an episode both in the morning and later in the day. It also helps increase awareness of the triggers that usually lead to an anxiety attack.

A good morning routine will bring about a sense of harmony, relaxation, and stability to your body and mind. It will give you the confidence you need to feel more in control of your emotions and, ultimately, your thoughts. Although I'm not a believer in the cookie-cutter approach or a one-size-fits-all strategy for morning routines, I want to make it as easy for you to get going as I can. That means sharing a blueprint or as many ideas as possible so you can custom make your own or imitate precisely what I share. Listen, I know it can be hard to try anything new when battling major anxiety issues, but you don't even have to think about it with what I'm sharing. Read the instructions and apply. Try whichever one feels more comfortable and discard those that don't feel right for you.

Wake up earlier

A great morning routine that sets you up for success cannot be rushed. It will take at least 60 minutes, sometimes longer. But the first shift you need to make is adjusting your bedtime so you can wake up at least 30 minutes earlier for the next week or two. In time, you'll find it easier to wake up at your perfect time, where the morning routine flows without the need to rush or skip essential things.

Morning Gratitude

When you become consciously aware that a brand new day has started for you, I encourage you to think of three things you feel grateful for. Do this even before you open your eyes. Mentally think of these three things or speak them out loud if convenient. The act of thanksgiving as the first thing you do in the morning will lift your spirits and lighten your mood. It will help you get out of bed on the right foot and keep negativity at bay.

Hydrate

We addressed the importance of drinking plenty of water. Your brain needs a lot of water to function at optimal levels, and when you sleep, you lose a lot of water naturally. So, we all wake up a little dehydrated. Add a mental disorder to that dehydration, and it's easy to see why getting up feels daunting. Yet that's what you need to do. By drinking a glass of water immediately after waking up, you hydrate the body and brain and get your juices flowing in all the right ways. What I developed over the years is the habit of drinking water with some freshly squeezed lemon first thing in the morning. Lemon water has many added benefits, but even a plain glass of water will serve just as good. The most important thing to remember is to hydrate with something natural—no coffee or even tea at this point.

Wash Up

Most people think this is obvious, but even a shower can feel like a giant task when in the midst of battling anxiety. Some might even procrastinate and skip showers, so I need you to see this as part of your morning routine. Brush teeth, floss and scrape your tongue. Take a nice hot or cold shower. In short, get yourself nice and clean. Practicing this kind of self-care and body hygiene sends a positive message to your brain and increases those feel-good hormones.

Move Your Body

I like to get my workout done before jumping into my day because I am less likely to procrastinate if I do it early in the morning. Suppose you prefer to exercise in the afternoon or later in the day. In that case, I still encourage you to do some form of body movement within the first hour. It can be a five to ten-minute stretch or yoga flow. You can also do some skipping, jumping jacks, dancing, squats, pushups, or anything that gets your blood pumping.

Journaling

Daily thought recording and capturing your emotions are going to be an essential part of your recovery. Journaling in the morning is one way you can track your recovery and take control of your day. It's a great habit to develop, especially if you want to train your mind to think thoughts that put you in a calm and comfortable state for the day ahead.

Meditate

We will be discussing mindfulness practices and mediation at length in an upcoming chapter. Still, I wanted to include it here because it is part of my morning routine. I have found meditation to be the best way for me to take command of my day. I get to slow down my body and bring myself back to a state of calm and ease. It's literally the best feeling in the world. I've been practicing this for years, so don't worry if, in the beginning, you spend all your time wandering away from one thought to another. Once you get the hang of it, I think it will play a significant role in your healing. The amount of time you spend in meditation should depend on your personality and temperament. As a beginner, even 1 minute of daily meditation is better than nothing. You could eventually build up to five minutes daily. An ideal time to strive for would be 15 minutes.

Dress to Impress Yourself

Spending all day in your pajamas or unflattering clothes, whether you work from home or not, can induce that feeling of lethargy. Even if you don't work at a formal office whereby a suit and tie are required, I want you to always dress up. Put on clothes that make you feel good. Brush your hair, and if you like, put on a little make-up (if that's your thing). Anything that makes you feel good will activate the right hormones and help you stay in the right state for most of the day. One thing to note here is that you should wear something comfortable that makes you feel great, not something that impresses others!

Read

Reading something spiritually uplifting or inspiring is one of the best-kept secrets for transforming your life and aiding your recovery. Are you a person of strong faith? Invest ten minutes each morning reading a devotional or the Bible. Do you find certain teachers, business moguls, or topics inspiring? Invest in those books and read with some tea in hand for a few minutes. Allow yourself to feed your mind with food that nourishes and promotes productivity.

These are simple things you can do. The order in which I stated them shouldn't be taken into consideration. What matters is that you integrate them into your life appropriately. Perhaps you just looked at my list and wondered how you can possibly do all these things given your current demanding schedule. In that case, here's a quick practice that can still work, and it only takes a few minutes.

THE BEST 10-MINUTE DAILY PRACTICE TO RAPIDLY REDUCE YOUR ANXIETY AT THE START OF EVERY DAY!

Suppose you seriously cannot add more than ten minutes to your morning, but you want something that will help you reduce anxiety. In that case, my best recommendation is to commit to ten-minute meditation practice. One that has been specifically designed to impact you powerfully.

The unique thing about meditating as a quick morning routine to alleviate anxiety is that you get the added bonus of improving other areas making it a holistic approach to your recovery. Both science and spirituality show that meditation will help you become more stable and focused. You will develop the ability to remain more present throughout the day and increase your sense of compassion, kindness, patience, and joy. Besides that, medication will improve your overall physical health, increase productivity, and lower stress levels. Although you could meditate anytime during the day or before going to sleep, the following guided meditation is best practiced first thing in the morning.

The scripted meditation below walks you through the step-by-step practice for calming your mind, including stabilizing your breath, letting go of unpleasant thoughts, and watching your posture.

Begin by finding a quiet and comfortable spot in your home. Settle yourself into a meditation posture. You can sit cross-legged on an elevated cushion or upright and comfortable in your favorite chair with your feet flat on the floor and your palms facing upwards and resting on your lap. Gently touch the tips of your thumb and index finger on each hand. Straighten your spine and tilt your head toward the floor to find a focus point. Make sure your shoulders and neck are relaxed. Let go of any tension in your face, neck, shoulders, and throughout your body. Half close your eyes and slightly open your mouth.

Think for a moment the main reason for entering into this mediation. Perhaps you want to address some stress or anxiety or sleeplessness or worry. Notice for a moment that you desire to take away these problems. Feel compassion for yourself rising within you as you connect with that desire of returning your mind to its natural state of peace and happiness.

You may also want to meditate so you can bring out more of your best human features. The qualities of kindness, compassion, generosity, patience, and living a life not just to benefit yourself but also help everyone you encounter. Even if it is done through the simple act of smiling at a stranger. Bring that clarity of intention as you enter deeper into this meditation.

Now, bring your attention to your breath. Focus on the breath coming in and out of your nostrils. Notice how cool it is as it comes in and how warm it feels as it goes out. Move your attention to your abdomen. Notice how it rises and falls as you deeply inhale and exhale. If thoughts, bodily sensations, plans, flashbacks, or anything else grabs your attention and you find yourself distracted from focusing on your breathing, that's okay. As soon as you catch yourself, just come back to observing your breathing. Allow these thoughts and sensations to drift by you. And do not feel bad or judge the experience. Mind-wandering is perfectly normal as you learn to meditate. The more you focus on your breathing, the easier it will be for the thoughts and sensations to disappear naturally, just like clouds passing through the sky. Keep focusing on your breathing for a few minutes in silence.

Now, steer your awareness from your breath to your mind. There's still no need to push away your thoughts, and you also don't need to draw them in for examination. But try and notice that there's a part of your mind that's detached from the perceptions coming from your senses. Your eyes, ears, nose, taste, and touch feed you information, but there's more to you than that. There's also a part of your mind that can simply watch and embrace or release thoughts. Notice that this part of your mind isn't the perceptions or the thoughts themselves. Allow this awareness to permeate and fill your attention. Connect with that aspect of yourself naturally... without force, without the need to make anything happen. There's no right or wrong.

As you come closer to experiencing the fullness of your awareness, focus on the space between the thoughts. In the same way, there are gaps between musical notes, so too there exists gaps between thoughts when no thought is present. And you can experience your mind's conscious nature itself. See if you can bring your focus into these gaps and examine what your mind is without them. If you can, gradually expand the gaps between your thoughts so that the thoughts become fewer and fewer, and the intervals of pure awareness get bigger.

Now we can come out of the mediation. Allow your senses to arise again. Notice your senses being reactivated. Feeling sight, taste, smell, touch, and sound activating. Notice any difference in how you feel. Are you feeling closer to the present moment? Are you feeling calmer? Are you more at ease and at peace? Feel that connection to that deeper part of yourself, beneath the thoughts and perceptions to pure awareness. In the same way that physical exercise gradually makes the body healthier, you've just exercised your mind in a way that gradually makes it calmer and happier.

Feel good now and be proud of yourself because you just invested ten minutes in a practice that will help you cultivate your best human qualities and gradually move toward your best self who is kinder, calmer, more compassionate, and able to forge deep, meaningful connections with others.

MORE PRACTICES THAT YOU CAN ADD TO YOUR MORNING ROUTINE

#1: Avoid checking your phone first thing in the morning:

Most people open their eyes and reach for their phone even before getting out of bed. They get bombarded with messages, emails, and the temptation to scroll through social media to catch what they missed while sleeping. For people dealing with anxiety, this is a recipe for disaster.

If you charge your phone by your bed or use it as an alarm clock, you'll likely end up consumed by the alerts and news that await you. Before you know it, you're sucked in, and a quick scroll turns into the 20 minutes you had for self-care. I recommend charging your phone as far away from your bed as possible. Make sure it is not within reach. If you can leave all your gadgets outside your bedroom area, that's even better. Smartphones have transformed the way we communicate, and that's great. But they have also become a massive source of anxiety for everyone. Adding a new rule to detach from your phone the night before and allowing the first minutes of the day to be a distraction and phone-free time can significantly impact your mood and how calm you feel during your self-care morning routine. This is especially necessary if you have a demanding career or if you usually wake up, check your phone, and already feel anxious for the day ahead.

#2: Do some morning visualization and set clear intentions for your day:

It might seem too simple, but trust me, setting an intention of how you want to feel on this brand new day can help you maintain a calm state. And if you don't want to stretch it by affirming the whole day, then just make an intention for how you want to feel in the morning. Sit for a few minutes, either after breakfast or before leaving the house, and spend a few minutes visualizing how you want your morning or day to go. Set an intentional tone and feel yourself moving through the day in that calm, focused, and empowered state. Consider recalling a memory that evokes the kind of feeling you want to have in this new day. For example, I usually sit for a few minutes before leaving for the office and remember a fond memory of me on the peak of a mountain overlooking the summit. I had gone hiking up a mountain with some friends, and it was an incredible experience. I can vividly recall the details of the scenery, how peaceful and powerful

I felt. The sounds of nature that surrounded me made it seem like I was floating about everything else. I felt so proud and accomplished and unstoppable after making that long and challenging trek to the top. Now I bring that memory to life each morning, and it does wonders to my confidence and sense of empowerment. Now it's your turn. Can you think of a specific memory that brings out similar emotions? Allow yourself to soak in that memory and build that same intention into each new day, even if you're spending the day in an office building.

#3: Add some essential oils to your shower:

A soothing shower in the morning is essential if you want to have a great morning. But I want you to take it a step further and invest in some soothing essential oils that you can add to your shower. It is the perfect antidote to anxiety because essential oils are known to calm down the senses and release tension in the body. It adds that much-needed feeling of self-care in the morning routine. Think of it as a personalized spa experience. Oils like lavender, chamomile, frankincense contain properties that promote a sense of ease, so pick a smell that resonates with you and make this part of your morning shower. You could even have a particular essential oil for the morning shower to get you invigorated and ready to take on the day and then a special one for the evening that enables you to unwind and prepare for a peaceful sleep. While using essential oils in the shower, make sure to practice some deep breathing. Take slow deep breaths and enjoy tuning into your sense of smell. Through this simple practice, you will be activating lots of positive practices all at the same time, including personal hygiene and self-care practices as well as mindfulness practices through deep breathing.

MAKING THOSE MORNING ROUTINES STICK EFFECTIVELY

The hardest part of making your morning routine stick is to figure out what works best for you. It's not merely a question of willpower or discipline. It's also about asking yourself what you genuinely enjoy and what aligns with your current lifestyle. For example, if you have young children, it's rather challenging to carve out an hour in the morning for your self-care and morning ritual. If you have a long commute to work, it's also challenging to do many of the things gurus claim must be done in the morning for optimal performance. So, the first thing I would do is look at your lifestyle, the daily demands that you need to meet, and then ask yourself, "what do I enjoy doing, and how much time can I commit for myself each morning?" So, if you only have 20 minutes for your morning routine, that's perfectly okay. I prefer having 20 minutes daily doing something that makes me feel good instead of waking up at 4 am in the morning and cut my sleep short just to have a full hour of activities I don't particularly enjoy. Especially if I'm doing it because a guru told me it works. See where I'm going with this?

Everything I shared in this chapter may or may not be enjoyable for you. It's upon you to take that initiative, personalize what feels right for you, and then do it consistently. If you only have twenty minutes, mix and match a bit of reading with some light stretches and meditation. If you enjoy the idea of a nice shower with essential oils, then add that as well.

To make your routine stick, you will need to experiment with a few suggestions until you figure out the best fit for you.

A good starting place might be taking notice of your biggest stressors and problems that trigger your anxiety, then consider morning activities that might help alleviate them. If, for example, you get anxious as soon as you think about the day ahead and all the things you have to do, then consider journaling first thing in the morning, write down a simple plan of execution for the day, do some light visualization, and set your intention for the day.

Make it as easy as possible, so you stick with this new morning ritual. The first few weeks of your new routine matter the most because this is when the habit forms. Experts recommend writing down the main activities and sticking them around the house (on the mirror, fridge, laptop) where you can easily see them so they can stay top of mind.

You can also use your alarm as a reminder. For example, if you've committed to a 30 minute virtual workout at 7.30 am, then your alarm should go off at 7.25am, alerting you to be ready in five minutes. After a few days, you'll find your body clock will start getting into the rhythm, and you may not need an alarm. The same goes for drinking water at various points during the day. Use that smartphone for something other than social media and internet surfing!

You should also set clear and specific goals with your morning routine and try to do the same activities at the same time each day. For example, instead of saying I will work out every morning before breakfast, decide what time you will work out, how long the workout will last, and which activity it will be. You can also prepare the night before little reminders and triggers to get you into a particular habit. If you enjoy having some tea before showering and you'd like to use that time to journal, place your diary right next to the teapot the night before. This will enable each activity to serve as a cue for the next one. In time, the habit will form. It will flow naturally as long as you enjoy integrating that activity into your life.

If you are seeing a therapist or have a support group, that's also a great way to receive the encouragement you need to stick with your routine. Let your support team know what you are doing and allow them to become accountability partners checking up on you regularly to make sure you're not cheating your way out of recovery.

EXAMPLES OF GREAT MORNING ROUTINES THAT ARE EASY TO ADAPT:

Kristy's nutritious breakfast combined with mindful eating:

Kristy realized that emphasizing a nutritious breakfast and practicing mindfulness helped create a calm and productive morning. She says that she sits and mindfully eats a nutritious breakfast as part of a calm start to the day. Kristy shares that she feels energized and more stable mentally and physically when she includes healthy fats, protein, and slow-releasing carbs into her breakfast meal choice.

How to make your breakfast nutritious and enjoyable:

Consider smoked salmon on seeded whole grain bread, a good source of vitamin D and Omega-3 fatty acids. You can also opt for eggs with spinach to boost essential amino acids that help your brain produce dopamine and serotonin. If you're a fruit lover, berry chia puddings are a great nutritious option. You could also go for almonds and yogurt with probiotics. Are you a porridge fan? How about having some oats with banana and nut butter, or alternatively, you could go for oatcakes topped with avocado. For a vegan option, consider adding turmeric to your tofu. Regardless of your breakfast choice, make sure you eat mindfully.

Julie's mindful morning self-care routine:

Julie's routine begins with a mindful appreciation routine, a mindful shower, some stretches, and a quick meditation. With the mindful appreciation, Julie spends five minutes upon waking up to reflect on one thing she's happily anticipating. Some days, that one thing is hopping back to bed at the end of the day! So, it's not about something extraordinary. Instead, it's the act of simple gratitude first thing in the morning. You could feel thankful that you have a bed and a home, a healthy body, or even the fact that despite your current challenges, you are still alive.

Energetically, that positive appreciation feeling sets a mood for the rest of the morning. Julie also says she enjoys using her sense of smell to invigorate her. Her morning ritual includes a calming shower gel and a specifically chosen scent that she applies to her body. That scent has the power to transform her mood instantly. By taking a warm shower, practicing mindfulness while in the shower, and then investing a few minutes in oiling her entire body with a pleasurable aroma, Julie can encourage, invigorate and motivate herself into a good feeling state.

Consider experimenting with scents like peppermint, lavender, pine, myrrh, or rose, depending on your personal taste. Think about how you would like to feel all day, and then pick a scent that matches that feeling. For example, if you want to feel calm and relaxed, myrrh or lavender is recommended.

6

THE ALMOST UNKNOWN HEALING POWER OF BREATHWORK AND COLD-WATER THERAPY FOR OBLITERATING YOUR ANXIETY

W e've discussed therapy and the different forms known to effectively deal with anxiety and panic attacks. Getting into treatment and combining that with other lifestyle changes that promote health and wellbeing could be the key to healing your life forever. Unfortunately, therapy comes with a significant drawback. If you don't have health insurance or the finances to foot the bill, it's not a plausible solution. For many people, the thought of paying for a therapist only exacerbates their anxiety because of the costs involved. So, what can you do if you're not in a position to invest in a therapist?

This book has already introduced you to the main psychotherapeutic treatments the therapist would guide you through. Combine that knowledge with what you're about to learn in this chapter, and you should already notice a difference in your condition. And by the way, what I am about to share can be viewed as a form of therapy, except this one is 100% free.

Breathwork and how to use it as your meditation practice:

Ever heard of the term breathwork? It's a general term used to refer to any breathing technique or exercise that emphasizes using your breath to improve your mental, physical and spiritual state. Most practices take about twenty minutes to an hour of sustained rhythmic breathing.

Many therapy forms incorporate breathwork, each with its own unique approach. Some are easy to do at home, while others will require a practitioner to guide you. Breathwork is inspired by Eastern practices like Tai Chi and yoga, which, as you know, really help the body utilize the breath to bring about radical transformation. In breathwork, the main emphasis should be to raise your self-awareness. It can take the form of talk therapy, breathing exercises, art, music, and bodywork.

As a form of therapy, breathwork has shown positive results when treating anxiety which is why you're going to learn how to incorporate breathwork into your daily routine. There are many forms of breathwork therapy, most of which are founded on similar principles. The best ones include:

Biodynamic Breathwork

The biodynamic breath and trauma release system integrates six elements: breath, movement, sound, touch, emotion, and meditation. The purpose of this is to release tension, support natural healing, and restructure internal systems. Through this approach, balance is restored to your entire system. Treatment includes exercises like deep, connected breathing, revisiting ingrained memories and sensations. It can also include music or sound therapy, whole body shaking, vocalization, and dance therapy.

Holotropic Breathwork

This form of breathwork is concerned with achieving wholeness of mind, body, and spirit. Evocative music and occasional bodywork are used as you perform specific breathing exercises while lying down. In this particular breathwork, you would also create mandalas related to your breathwork experience immediately after the breathing exercises. That will help you integrate what you learn about yourself during the session.

While there are several other forms, let's discuss some breathwork exercises that you can do immediately.

- *Box breathing.* That involves taking slow, deep breathes to the count of four, holding your breath for another count of four, and then slowly exhaling for a count of four.
- *Continuous circular breathing.* That involves using full deep breaths in and out continuously. You don't need to hold your breath at any point. Instead, you want to create a circular rhythm that symbolizes the circle of breath.
- *Immersion in water.* That involves immersing yourself in water and either breathing deeply above the surface of the water or with the aid of a snorkel.
- *20 connected breaths.* That involves breathing in and out 20 times. Here, you would take four sets of four short breaths

and one deep breath. The breathing should be done through the nose unless you're unable due to specific medical reasons.

WHY PRACTICE DEEP BREATHING OR BREATHWORK?

There are many benefits of practicing this form of therapy. Studies show that even a few deep breaths can lower blood pressure and cortisol levels and increase parasympathetic tone. Take your deep breathing to the next level by incorporating breathwork. You get a whole new level of benefits, including mood elevation, decreased stress and anxiety, increased self-awareness, and an overall feeling of joy and happiness.

It's important to note here that while I recommend doing this with a combination of meditation, it shouldn't substitute your morning routine meditation because they are, in essence, different practices with different objectives. So, when you practice your deep breathing exercise as you meditate, make it intentionally geared toward the breathwork technique and not as a way of stilling the mind, as is usually the case with regular meditation.

USING COLD WATER DURING BATH TIME

Besides breathwork, there's another little-known (and also free) therapy known as hydrotherapy. It is a simple remedy that you can do immediately and receive great benefits. Hydrotherapy involves using cold water on your body to help it heal and feel better.

There was a time when we spent a lot of time outdoors. We were continually in contact with nature and directly influenced by changing climate and weather patterns. Although nowadays we barely leave the house save for going to work in an enclosed office or to run grocery errands and such, we can still benefit from some of the insights gained by the experts who found healing properties in natural remedy. One such natural treatment is the use of water. Applying different temperatures to our skin can change our physiology and mood. Did you know that?

Taking a cold swim or doing a "plunge" in a spa with such facilities has shown that the body responds positively. Sure, it's shocking at first, but the cold causes blood circulation to improve in a matter of minutes. The cold shocks the blood vessels, causing vasoconstriction, making the blood move from the surface of your body to the core as a means to conserve heat. This movement brings nutrition and oxygen to the area where circulation is low. It also helps gently detoxify the area. When combined with warm water, the blood vessels vasodilate, bringing blood back to the surface, creating a holistic experience for your entire body. Plenty of medical research has supported the combination of hot and cold baths showing a decrease in stress hormones like cortisol. Evidence also indicates that water bathing helps the balance of the feel-good neurotransmitter serotonin.

Since we know anxiety may cause an increase in blood pressure and inflammation, it's easy to see how a cold shower can help calm your entire nervous system down and promote the release of endorphins in your brain.

When doing this form of therapy at home, I recommend starting with a few minutes at a time, especially if you've never taken cold baths. Consider creating a few rounds of hot and cold and then finishing up the shower with lukewarm water.

DO THEY REALLY WORK?

Breathwork and hydrotherapy have been successful at treating anxiety, but again, it all depends on your particular situation.

A French study suggests patients with anxiety can benefit from the mechanisms of hydrotherapy. Balneotherapy (using water baths for healing) was compared to paroxetine (Paxil), a leading SSRI medication. 237 patients with GAD (generalized anxiety disorder) were assigned randomly to balneotherapy and 120 to the medication. The balneotherapy consisted of weekly medical visits and daily bath treatments using natural mineral water for twenty-one days. How? The patients were immersed in a bubble bath (37 degrees Celsius for ten minutes) then a shower with a firm massage-like pressure targeting the abdomen area along the spine, neck, and arm region for 3 minutes. Finally, the legs, neck and scapular, and spine area would be massaged underwater for another ten minutes. At the end of the duration, both groups showed improvement with a clear superior result for the group that did the water therapy. Remission and sustained response rates were also significantly higher for the hydrotherapy group than the drug group (Dubois et al., 2010).

Regular cold showers can boost your immune system, increase your feel-good hormones and invigorate your brain. That creates the calm state necessary to take back control of your day when anxiety takes over. Breathwork, especially when combined with meditation, is powerful. If done consistently, it will not only increase your awareness, but you will also feel more stable and capable of maintaining an anxiety-free state.

How cold showers and breathwork made an ordinary man seem superhuman:

The famous daredevil and Guinness World Record holder Wim Hof (famously known as the Iceman) has devised a method known as the Wim Hof method (wimhofmethod.com) that combines breathwork and cold showers. He believes anyone can use this method to bring about significant benefits to your entire body. The idea behind it is to combine cold water therapy, breathing, and commitment. Hof believes he has been able to achieve his crazy feats of survival (climbing Kilimanjaro wearing only shorts and shoes, running a half marathon above the Arctic Circle barefoot, and being submerged in an ice bath for 1hr 52 minutes 42 seconds) thanks to his combination of meditation, breathing exercises and exposure to cold as a means of controlling the body's autonomous response systems. By leveraging these simple techniques, you could beat the stress and anxiety that ails you and accelerate your recovery. All you have to do is learn simple breathing techniques (the ones mentioned in this chapter), train yourself to handle some cold water or ice baths and commit to doing it. If you're skeptical about this, give it a try for seven days only. The worst that can happen is that nothing changes. The upside, however, is that you find a simple way to transform your life forever without adding on the cost of buying pricey health supplements or hiring an expensive therapist.

7

WHY YOUR DIET & LIFESTYLE PLAYS A CRITICAL ROLE IN YOUR JOURNEY OF OVERCOMING YOUR ANXIETY DISORDER

Before science became as advanced as we know it today, diet and lifestyle weren't considered necessary in the context of health. I mean, do you know there was a time when cigarette smoking was advertised on television as something good? I know. It's horrifying, but before the 1950s, there wasn't good evidence showing that cigarette smoking was bad for you. So, it wouldn't be uncommon to find ads with doctors endorsing it to the public. Much of this was because our understanding of the human body was minimal.

Today, however, we've made some headway and learned that ciga-rettes lead to lung cancer, and caffeine doesn't make you smarter! Okay, why am I sharing all this with you? Because it's crucial to develop a proper understanding of how your body works and the impact of your lifestyle choices on your health. In your case, the knowledge you need to get is the connection between your psychological and biological processes. Or stated simply, how your physical body affects your emotional and mental state.

Many people don't realize that there's a link between the physical state and the mental state. It would be impossible to attain permanent healing if we skip over this part, so pay close attention as we uncover the real reason behind the changes I have been recommending with your nutrition and lifestyle.

MIND SHIFT: THINKING OF YOUR PHYSICAL AND MENTAL HEALTH AS ONE

When we realize that we are suffering from a mental disorder, the first and most recommended solution is typically medication, therapy, or some quick fix instead of emphasizing understanding the mind-body connection. That's why I want to invite you to make this shift for yourself, as it is the only way to permanently eradicate the suffering you've had to endure to this point.

What is the connection? The mind - a manifest functioning of the brain - and the other body systems interact in ways critical for health, illness, and wellbeing (Ray, 2004, p.29). Our bodies are intelligent and alive. So whatever signals and messages the brain sends out, the body will respond accordingly. Depending on the dominant thoughts that we allow to set up camp in our minds, corresponding signals that alter our brains will be released to the rest of the body, which will change our biology. That will, in turn, send corresponding feedback to validate the initial message. In no time, you have a feedback loop that solidifies as your normal state. So, if you're stuck in anxious or intrusive thoughts, your brain will release the appropriate hormones and fire neurons that alert the rest of the body that something is wrong.

Blood pressure and heart rate will rise. The body will go into that fight or flight mode, and your physical state will reflect that you experienced anxiety. As the body continues to remain in this distressed state, more corresponding emotions and thoughts will fill your mind. That will elevate your anxiety levels and cause you to feel sick to your stomach. This vicious cycle becomes almost impossible to break, especially if sustained for prolonged periods. The food you consume will also help to exacerbate your state and continue to reinforce your anxiety. Poor mental health leads to poor physical health just as much as poor physical fitness leads to poor mental health. Sometimes it is a chicken and egg situation whereby it's impossible to state which came first. If you suffered from a severe chronic illness as a child or chronic pain due to an accident, that might have activated the disorder. Due to continued poor diet and self-neglect, the disorder grew into a life of its own. It took up residence in your mind and continued to cause damage long after that particular physical condition healed.

As you can see, the starting point might be hard to pinpoint, so don't let that become a priority. What matters is that you are here now and ready to reclaim both your mental and physical health. How do you do this?

A good starting point is with your nutrition. Most people assume getting fit is about working out for hours each day. The truth is, you can get fit and significantly improve your physical health by adjusting your diet first. Then as the diet helps the biology shift, the physiology and psychology will shift too.

A HEALTHY GUT CAN HELP YOU HAVE A HEALTHY MIND

The diet you choose over the next few months will hinder or accelerate your healing. I want you to start viewing your food as medicine and fuel for your body. In Traditional Chinese Medicine, Ayurvedic Medicine, and Native American culture, food has always been an essential aspect of treating illness and maintaining health. An increasing number of studies provide evidence for the curative and preventive properties of certain foods. For example, Green tea is a good source of antioxidants, ginger may be an effective treatment for nausea, and garlic is often used for various things, including to lower cholesterol.

Research from Harvard says food choices can make the difference between feeling worse and feeling more stable. Do you know which foods are actually pro healing? Here are six things you need to drop and five that you need to incorporate into your diet starting now.

#1. Alcohol:

Alcohol is a depressant. More specifically, it depresses the working order of your nervous system, making it challenging to think, reason, understand things or even control your motor function. Oh, and did I mention, your central nervous system processes emotions. So, what happens when you have one too many? Everything goes out of what. Your kidney and liver get overworked, your brain decreases in functionality, and your emotions feel out of control.

#2. Artificial Sweeteners:

Aspartame, the common ingredient found in products like diet soda, blocks the production of serotonin. That can lead to headaches, insomnia mood swings, among other issues.

#3. Caffeine:

Even a modest amount of caffeine can excavate your anxiety and even contribute to depression. One study found that moderate and high coffee drinkers scored higher on the depression scale among healthy college students than others. Let's also not forget the disruptive effect that caffeine has on sleep. And if you have disturbed sleep, I can assure you, anxiety levels will skyrocket. If you want to aid your healing, this is something you need to avoid at all costs. And I don't just mean coffee. Consider eliminating energy drinks and soda as they too contain plenty of caffeine.

#4. Hydrogenated oil:

Think of fried chicken, fried cheese sticks, fried calamari, french fries, and basically any fried junk food that you usually fall back on when you feel overwhelmed by emotions. Unfortunately, eating this kind of food actually makes things worse in the long run. Saturated fats like the ones found in deli meats, high-fat dairy, and butter can create a lot of damage to your body if they clog your arteries and impede proper blood flow to the brain. I know this sounds super harsh, but the reality is, eating deep-fried foods digs you deeper into anxiety and other mental health disorders.

#5. High sodium foods:

Remember how experts touted fat-free foods as the go-to solution for weight loss? It turns out many of the products endorsed as fat-free contain high levels of sodium. All that extra salt is actually bad for your emotions because it disrupts aspects of your neurological system. Not only can this mess with your mental health, but it can also mess with your immune system response and create an experience of fatigue, bloating, and fluid retention. Foods with high sodium include savory snacks like pretzels, crackers, popcorn and chips, burritos and tacos, cheese, chicken, cold cuts and cured meats, eggs, omelets, and pizza.

#6. Processed foods:

Want to know the perfect storm when it comes to messing up your physical and mental health? Processed foods. They're high in sodium and pave the way for an inflammatory response in the body. An article in Psychiatric Times shared that inflammation has a direct effect on the brain and behavior. It can negatively affect the areas of the brain responsible for motivation and motor activity and the areas that control anxiety and alarm. Before you get disheartened, let me state that you don't need to cut out all processed foods. Examples of processed foods that experts agree can work for someone looking to eat healthier include yogurt, sauerkraut, chickpeas, canned beans, granola, veggie burgers, unsweetened almond milk, organic jelly, fortified cereals, freeze-dried fruit, pickles, and dark chocolate.

9 BEST FOODS FOR REDUCING ANXIETY:

#1. Fatty Fish: Salmon, mackerel, sardines, trout, and herring are among the top favorite fatty fish that should become part of your diet as they are rich in omega-3. Why does omega-3 matter? There's plenty of evidence that links this fatty acid to improved cognitive function and mental health. Omega 3 rich foods that contain alpha-linolenic acid (ALA) provide two important fatty acids, namely: eicosapentaenoic acid (EPA) and docosahexaenoic acid (DHA). Both EPA and DHA regulate neurotransmitters, reduce inflammation and promote healthy brain function. A small study on twenty-four people with substance abuse problems found that the EPA and DHA supplementation reduced anxiety levels. This isn't conclusive research, but it should be enough to convince you of the great benefits that await you. Please note that omega-3 is not identical to omega-6, so don't substitute one for the other. With omega-6, you should only take it in small, moderate quantities.

#2. Pumpkin seeds: A study carried out on 100 female high school students found that zinc deficiency may negatively affect mood. That's why pumpkin seeds are great for your diet. Pumpkin seeds are an excellent source of potassium which helps regulate electrolyte balance and manage blood pressure. It also contains Zinc, which is essential for brain and development, all of which help reduce stress and anxiety symptoms.

#3. Dark chocolate: For most people, dark chocolate's bitter flavor profile is off-putting, but most research indicates it's worth getting used to having a bit of dark chocolate frequently. A 2019 survey-based study published in the journal Depression & Anxiety suggests that people who eat dark chocolate often are less likely to report depressive symptoms. Although depression isn't the same as anxiety, the two share similarities and often go hand in hand. This research is far from conclusive, but I'd say it's worth a try. Consider adding small amounts to your morning cereal or tea.

#4. Turmeric: This is a spice commonly used in India and Southeast Asia. Turmeric contains an active ingredient called curcumin, which has properties that lower anxiety due to its anti-inflammatory properties. One study found that an increase of curcumin in the diet also increased DHA and reduced anxiety. If you're not a fan of pungent spices, don't worry, turmeric has a minimal flavor and can be added to almost any food as well as smoothies.

#5. Yogurt: Go for plain greek yogurt as much as possible, especially the one with at least five strains of active culture and rich in probiotics. The right kind of yogurt is said to be great for alleviating stress and stabilizing your mood.

#6. Kiwi: One of my favorite fruits of all time and apparently promoted by experts as an excellent fruit for reducing stress and anxiety. Studies indicate that the combination of vitamins C and E plus folate may help reduce oxidative stress. It may also help in the production of serotonin in your brain, which will promote a sense of well-being and happiness. Besides, have you seen how beautiful and colorful kiwis are on the inside? Instant mood booster if it's on your breakfast bowl.

#7. Chamomile: A great routine to add to your nighttime ritual is winding up your day with a nice cup of warm, soothing chamomile tea. A 2016 clinical trial with results published in the journal phytomedicine suggests that those who drank tea over a long-term period significantly reduced severe GAD (generalized anxiety disorder) symptoms. Perhaps it's linked to the fact that it enhances your sleepiness, ensuring you get good quality sleep which, as we know, directly impacts mental health, especially anxiety.

#8. Green tea: Are you a fan of herbal tea? More specifically, green tea? If not, it's time to stock up. Green tea contains an amino acid called theanine which has anti-anxiety and calming effects. Some experts claim it increases the production of serotonin and dopamine. This can be an excellent substitute for coffee, soda, or even alcohol.

#9. Avocado: There's no doubt that when it comes to avocado, you can't have too much of this superfood. It's packed with all kinds of excellent nutrients, including vitamin B6 and magnesium, which help with serotonin production. You can find lots of avocado-based recipes for breakfast, lunch, and dinner on YouTube and Google.

MOVING YOUR BODY HELPS INCREASE HAPPY HORMONES

You've heard me talk about diet and the importance of eating the right food because food affects your mental state just as much as it affects your physical condition. Now let's add another critical component to your recovery plan: exercise.

Most people only value exercise when they need to lose a few pounds before beach season kicks in. But if you want to transform your life and enjoy holistic health, some form of regular exercising will have to become your new norm. Research has found that your diet, fitness level, and the amount of stress you're exposed to directly influence your panic disorder and anxiety. By exercising your body regularly, you can help reduce anxiety and even the frequency and intensity of panic attacks. I also find exercise to be an excellent way for me to release mental and physical tension. Why does exercise work?

- Because exercise releases feel-good endorphins and other natural brain chemicals that enhance your sense of wellbeing.
- While exercising, you actually take your mind off worrisome thoughts and emotions, which cuts that cycle of negative thinking.
- It's a great coping strategy. Doing something positive to distract yourself when having a tough day (like Yoga, Pilates, Endurance training, or cross-training) is much better than binge-eating or alcohol. It gives you a win-win situation where you come out feeling good, help your body get fit, and keeps intrusive thoughts at bay.
- Exercise also increases your confidence levels. Think about it. Doesn't it feel good to set a goal of working out daily for 20 minutes and then actually showing yourself that you can commit and get it done?

I often have forced myself to start my workout routine, and it felt almost impossible to get my body moving. Still, fifteen minutes into it, I felt so glad that I began the workout. By the time the week was over, I was so proud to see tick marks of success on my journal, demonstrating I was still on my workout streak. It made me feel like I can do anything else I set my mind to. These mini-goals are great for boosting confidence. And of course, there's the added bonus of having a better-shaped body, which makes us feel good.

Do you need to join a gym or jog to work out your body?

You absolutely don't need a gym membership or train with weights or even jog outdoors if none of these things apply to you. A gym membership is great for the person who needs that feeling of community and support, and social interaction. But if you feel better working out in the comfort of your apartment, then, by all means, do that!

If you're a complete beginner, you could start with something as simple as regular power walks, light jogging outdoors, playing football, basketball, or any other fitness activity that gets your heart pumping and your body sweating. If none of these appeals to you, consider Pilates, power yoga, Zumba, kickboxing, or Latin dance lessons.

The most important thing is that you enjoy the activity you're doing and create your own plan of action that you can stick to.

What are the best anti-anxiety workouts?

- Running
- Power walks
- Dancing
- Tennis

- Swimming
- Biking
- Yoga

TOP FOUR EXERCISES YOU CAN TRY AT HOME

#1: Tai Chi:

This is a soft martial art that includes fluid movements along with core control. You will focus on posture, breathing, and visualization in this workout, making it great for de-stressing and feeling rooted in your body.

#2: High-Intensity home workout:

When you go on YouTube, you can find dozens of free high-intensity workout routines that you can do from the comfort of your bedroom or living area. An article from Science Daily shares some interesting findings on the effect of high-intensity exercises in relation to reducing anxiety. A new study by researchers at the University of Missouri-Columbia shows that relatively high-intensity training is superior in reducing stress and anxiety. Moreover, the researchers found that high-intensity exercise primarily benefits women. The older you are, the more you'll notice the positive impact on your physical and mental state (sourced from Sciencedaily.com "High-Intensity Exercise Best Way To Reduce Anxiety, University of Missouri Study Finds).

So, if Tai chi is a bit too chilled for you, or if you just want to mix things up a bit, try doing high-intensity workouts a few times a week.

#3: Aerobics:

Regular aerobic exercising (swimming, cycling, running) is associated with better psychological health. According to recent studies, whether it's a single session or a long-term program for aerobics exercises, you can improve your psychological state. How long is enough to reap some rewards of aerobic exercises? As little as ten minutes but experts encourage you to consistently stick to the exercise regimen for at least 10 weeks for maximum benefit. YouTube is filled with tons of free aerobics workouts that you can follow along. Check out HASfit on YouTube for free workouts and workout programs if you're confused about where to start. All you need is a mat for comfort and a stretch band. If you enjoy indoor running, swimming, or cycling, consider joining a club near you to make it easy for you to do it daily.

#4: Yoga:

This list wouldn't be complete without some yoga which has become the go-to exercise for people wanting to channel their inner Zen and at the same time burn some calories. The nature of yoga focused on deep breathing, reconnecting with your body, and getting grounded within yourself. This is great for someone suffering from anxiety because it enables you to tap into your inner strength and to show yourself that you have the power to do amazing things with your body. And if you can change your body, surely you can change your thoughts. The fact is yoga works every single time! Unless you quit on yourself.

Studies show that yoga classes can help you reduce anxiety, anger, depression, and even neurotic symptoms. According to a Harvard

Medical School Article (Yoga for anxiety and depression), research suggests that yoga modulates stress response systems. That, in turn, decreases psychological arousal (e.g., reducing the heart rate, lowering blood pressure, and easing respiration). Substantial evidence is building up to demonstrate that yoga practice is a relatively low-risk, high-yield approach to improving overall health. And the best part is it's easy to do, and you can find free yoga sessions online or join a virtual or physical yoga class. All you need is a yoga mat and a nice set of lungs for intentional breathing!

Bonus:

Once you decide what exercises you will commit to, create a customized plan that's easy to follow. Don't overcomplicate things and keep your workout program as simple and as enjoyable as you possibly can. Be flexible with the program. If you usually get bored quickly, create a variety of exercises that you can keep changing up week after week so you can stick to your workout goals. Make your goals attainable and celebrate the small wins. Instead of striving for perfection, focus on progress and excellence. If you stop during an exercise or don't complete a set in any workout, don't assume that means failure. Instead, recognize that you are on a journey that won't always be easy. The most important thing is that you pick yourself up and go at it again with vigor and enthusiasm, trusting that each move is getting you closer to that healthy version of yourself.

A GOOD NIGHT'S SLEEP DOES MORE THAN YOU THINK

By now, you may have realized we are establishing the lifestyle changes that will enable you to transform your health and life. These things all build upon each other. Without the right nutrition, you won't have the energy or stamina to workout daily. And without sleep, it doesn't matter how good your diet is or how much you kill yourself in the gym; it will all fall apart. Poor sleep directly impacts your mental health. You cannot reduce or heal anxiety disorders without proper sleep. Your mood, cognitive functions, and overall health depend on you to work appropriately. So, one of the first things you need to work on (I mean starting tonight) is to adjust your sleeping habits. You need restorative sleep to maintain a balanced brain. Sleep quality and length do matter; let no one tell you differently. Research shows that sleep-deprived individuals have a stronger tendency to classify neutral images as negative. That means ordinary experiences that you encounter on a daily basis will seem more menacing and contribute to your anxiety.

Falling asleep and getting good quality sleep is often a challenge when battling anxiety disorders. So, what can you do?

#1: Avoid stimulants later in the day:

If you can cut out all stimulants, that would be the best solution, but I know it might be difficult for some. So instead, I want you to have a limit after which you will consume no stimulants. I recommend setting a curfew for yourself depending on your lifestyle and work schedule but roughly six to eight hours before bedtime. So, if your bedtime is 10pm, then you shouldn't consume any stimulants after 4 pm latest.

#2: Try this 3-minute relaxation technique:

Lie flat and comfortably on your bed. Focus your attention on your breathing. Take a few deep breaths, exhaling slowly. Mentally scan your body. Take notice of any areas that feel tense and cramped. Gently loosen them. Let go of as much tension as you can. Rotate your head in a gentle and smooth circular motion once or twice if it feels good. Roll your shoulders forward and backward several times. Let all of your muscles completely relax. Recall a pleasant thought, event, or place. It can be as recent as today or something that happened in the past. Notice how your body feels as you soak in this good memory. Take deep breaths and exhale slowly.

#3: Create an ideal sleep environment:

That includes ensuring your smartphone and any technology that distracts you are out of reach. Try keeping your phone as far away from your sleeping area as possible. It's also important to shut out all light from your bedroom. This is especially useful if you have trouble falling asleep. Also, remember to minimize noise and keep the room temperature cool enough to be under a blanket. Suppose there's a particular scent that helps you relax or fall asleep. In that case, you can spray it or light a candle as you get ready for bed so it can aid you in this relaxation and sleeping process.

#4: Create a calming sleep routine:

It's just as important to have a routine for your bedtime as it is in the morning because it helps you wind down and fall asleep faster. Certain activities are too stimulating and bad for your anxiety when done too close to your bedtime. This includes social media browsing, alcohol and coffee consumption, and even high-intensity workouts. Although exercise is good for you, doing it just before bed will make it hard to fall asleep.

Although there's no perfect sleep routine, a few things you may want to consider include:

a. setting the alarm sixty minutes before bedtime to indicate to your brain that it's time to unwind and let go of a hectic day. Once that alarm goes off, don't snooze or ignore it. Do not keep binge-watching television or chatting with friends. Instead, move into your personalized unwind routine.
b. Make yourself some relaxing herbal tea like chamomile and sit with a book for a few minutes or listen to some soothing music.
c. Guided meditation for relaxation and sleep can be great at this point if that resonates.
d. Wash up before bed. If you like baths or a hot shower before sleeping, you can do that. Otherwise, some dental hygiene and a gentle facewash are sufficient. As you wash up, practice some mindfulness and notice the sensation of your teeth as you brush and how the water feels in your hands and face.

e. Set the mood in your bedroom. Whether you have a partner or not, it's good to select the right mood, including dim lighting and cool temperature, to send the signal to your body that you're ready for sleep.

f. Do you like essential oils and aromatherapy? Then add fragrances like lavender and cedarwood to your routine by placing a diffuser in your bedroom or using a few drops of essential oil on your pillow before bed. If you like baths, consider scenting it with a few drops of your favorite essential oil.

g. Think peaceful thoughts. Instead of fixating on worrisome thoughts of things that haven't yet happened or things that have already passed, try focusing on something that makes you feel good. This would be an excellent time to practice some evening gratitude, visualizing a restful scene where you would enjoy falling asleep and basically using your imagination to aid you into relaxation instead of allowing it to run wild. You need to tame your mind and teach your imagination to go where you want it to go, especially in the evening. Do you enjoy quiet beaches? Why not visualize yourself walking barefoot on a beautiful beach with waves brushing against the shore and the sand on your feet. Practice breathing slowly and peacefully as you relax in this chosen environment.

h. Do a body scan as soon as you hit the bed. Once you get into bed, your brain will probably start drifting and thinking about a million things. Bring it to your body and do a body scan as you relax your muscles. Here's a simple exercise to try. Slowly tense one group of muscles. Hold the tension to the count of five, then release slowly as you exhale. Relax to the count of ten, then move to the next muscle group. Begin from the toes all the way up to your head, one muscle group at a time, and think of nothing else.

i. Read something spiritually uplifting and joyful. Now is not the time to read the news or thriller novels. You don't want to stimulate your brain or nervous system, so instead, I encourage you to find something spiritual, philosophical, or comical to read. If you are a person of faith, then read a passage from the Bible. If you enjoy fairytales, comics or jokes, then read that and if you enjoy ancient thinkers, then read a page from Aristotle if that's your thing.

What happens when you just can't sleep no matter what you try?

On those nights when nothing works, don't force it. Practice acceptance. Use the power of validation and positive self-talk to make this experience okay too. Instead of getting upset over the fact that you've been lying there for three hours and nothing happened, you can say to yourself, "I'm still awake now, but sooner or later, I will have to fall asleep. Even if it's not this night, the fact that I will be a little tired in the morning means I'll probably fall asleep right away tomorrow night." One thing I would advise when it comes to insomnia, I find it better to wake up and do some quiet activity instead of lying there in frustration. I will pick a book and read if it's too late or too early in the morning to do something else.

CUT DOWN THE STRESSORS!

Stress and anxiety go hand in hand, but they aren't the same. Stress is any strain on your brain or physical body. Since all biological experiences impact your psychology, a stressed-out body or brain will mess with your mental health. While treating anxiety and panic attacks, stress can make the process more difficult, especially if you have a stressful lifestyle. When combined, stress and anxiety can make your life feel like a living hell. So, we need to do everything possible to reduce, manage or, if possible, eliminate the things that cause you to get stressed.

Of course, if you tell me you hate your boss and your job and that it's the number one cause for stress in your life right now, that's a doozy. It's not exactly smart to eliminate this stress by quitting your job because you open up a host of reasons to be anxious and fearful, like facing unemployment, running out of rent money, etc. So, there are some cases where you need to exercise stress management. One thing you can do to manage work stress is to implement the changes already discussed, i.e., get a healthy diet, limit caffeine and alcohol, exercise, meditate, and get enough sleep. But sometimes, your anxiety is triggered while at work, even if you're practicing this new lifestyle shift. In that case, you need a way out. Here are a few things you can instantly do at work to bring your stress levels down.

#1. Listen to your favorite song:

There's always that one song that can take you from dystopia to utopia in a matter of minutes. That song should always be on your smartphone for those days when everyone at work seems to push your buttons. Step away from the room for a few minutes, find somewhere with some fresh air (a terrace, the rooftop, outside the office building), and plug-in your earphones for a few minutes. Breathe deeply, dance to the beat, sing aloud if it's safe, and just allow yourself to be elsewhere for those three minutes. Playing music has a positive effect on the brain and body. It can lower blood pressure, reduce cortisol, and if you pick the right jam, it will fill you with boundless joy and happiness in no time.

#2: Do some belly breathing:

Breathing from your diaphragm can help reduce the amount of work your body needs to do to breathe. At work, you can do this by sitting in a comfortable chair with your head, neck and shoulders relaxed and your knees bent. Put one hand under your rib cage and one hand over your heart. Inhale and exhale through your nose, noticing how or if your stomach and chest move as you breathe. Focus on breathing more through your belly instead of your chest. Notice the movement (the rise and fall of your abdomen) and the corresponding sensations within your body. Try to keep your chest as still as possible for this type of breathing. You can do this for as little as five minutes, and you will feel the full effect if you go up to ten minutes.

#3: Chew gum:

This is an easy and quick fix that can help calm you down in almost any situation, whether at work or home. One study showed that people who chew gum had a greater sense of wellbeing and lower stress levels. This might be due to the fact that chewing gum causes brain waves similar to those of relaxed people, and it promotes blood flow to the brain.

#4: Learn to say no:

Sometimes the thing causing you to stress is out of your control, or worse still, it's unnecessary added pressure. If you like people-pleasing, it will be hard to reduce your anxiety because you'll keep piling on things to do for others, making your life more difficult. If you find yourself taking on more than you can handle, it's time to learn how to say no. Be selective about what you take on, and remember, no is a full sentence. You don't have to justify yourself or feel guilty, especially when you already know you have many responsibilities. Learning to say no can significantly reduce or help you manage your stress levels.

8

BEDTIME: MORE THAN CREATING A ROUTINE

According to Harvard Medical School, sleep difficulties affect more than 50% of adult patients with a generalized anxiety disorder. It will impact teenagers and children as well. One sleep laboratory study found that youngsters with an anxiety disorder took longer to fall asleep and slept less deeply when compared with a control group of healthy children. Insomnia is also considered a risk factor for developing an anxiety disorder and may even prevent recovery. So, if you thought sleep was a trivial matter or that creating calming sleep routines was just nice to have, think again. In this chapter, I want to awaken you to the benefits of getting proper rest and sell you on the fact that you need to do everything in your power to improve your current sleep pattern. Let's start with some simple facts about how sleeping well keeps you healthy.

SLEEP AND ITS HOLISTIC BOOST TO YOUR HEALTH

Research has shown that sleep is just as important as eating and exercise for anyone who wants to enjoy a healthy, vibrant lifestyle. Poor sleep is linked to increased body weight, depression, increased inflammation, low concentration levels, mood disorders, low productivity levels, increased stress, and increased risk of heart disease and stroke. What's more, even a small loss of sleep has been shown to impair immune function.

In a sizeable 2-week study that monitored the development of the common cold (participants were given nasal drops with the cold virus). The study found that those who slept less than 7 hours were almost three times more likely to develop a cold than those who slept 8 hours or more. So, sleep runs deeper than just aiding in your mental health. Consider for a moment how often you get colds. If you frequently fall sick, switching up your sleep time and getting adequate hours for your body type can help, especially during the colder months. Besides all these side effects of being sleep deprived, there are many other ways your body will benefit from good sleep.

Sharper brain and optimum cognitive functioning:

When operating with little to no sleep, you'll struggle to focus, learn, or recall details. Why? Because sleep plays a big part in both learning and memory. Without proper sleep, taking in new information is very troublesome. Your reflexes also slow down when sleep-deprived, so by increasing sleep time, you get to improve how your brain and body function and assimilates information.

Stronger immune system:

The immune system is a complex network that's spread out throughout your body. It provides multiple lines of defense against illness. When functioning optimally, the immune system will maintain that delicate balance needed to keep you feeling and looking healthy. When a threat or injury arises, it triggers inflammation, fatigue, fever, and pain. We need the immune system to be strong enough to fight any and all potential threats. We also need it to be well regulated so that the body isn't always in attack mode, as that isn't ideal either. That's where sleep comes in.

Getting sufficient hours of high-quality sleep enables your body to create the right atmosphere for a well-balanced immune system that is efficient, responsive when needed, and less prone to allergic reactions. As the body sleeps, certain components of the immune system get revved up. For example, there's an increased production of cytokines associated with inflammation. This activity appears to be driven both by sleep and circadian rhythm (the body's 24-hour internal clock).

Although experts aren't entirely sure why the immune system works best during sleep time, it is believed that this system works best when physical and mental performance are at a minimum. As breathing and muscle activity slows down, there's more energy for the immune system to perform its tasks. Also, we know that melatonin (a sleep-promoting hormone) is adept at counteracting the stress that can come from inflammation during sleep.

Mood booster:

Another benefit of sleep is natural emotion regulation which also boosts your mood. It stabilizes your emotions and makes it easier for you to handle and process your feelings. If something unpleasant or unexpected happens, you're more likely to remain calm and optimistic when you're well-rested.

BEDTIME ROUTINE TO HELP YOU GET A GOOD NIGHT'S SLEEP

In the previous chapter, you learned that a good night's sleep can do wonders for your mental health. That's why I emphasized the importance of creating a calming sleep routine. In case you are wondering where to begin or what specific things you can do to promote high-quality sleep, here are more tips proven to work.

Reduce blue light exposure after sunset:

You have an internal clock often referred to as the circadian rhythm, which regulates hormones like melatonin. Melatonin is essential in helping you relax and get deep sleep. Blue light, usually found in electronic devices like smartphones and computers, is the worst for the emission of this type of light. It tricks your brain into thinking it's still daytime. And unfortunately, that inhibits your ability to feel sleepy. You can do a few things if you must use these gadgets, including installing an app that blocks blue light on your smartphone and laptop. You can also wear glasses that block blue light. Since television and bright lights also contribute to the delay of melatonin release, you may want to stop watching TV and turn off bright lights two hours before bedtime.

Create a set time to sleep and wake up:

Consistency with your sleep and waking times can help you align with your circadian rhythm and promote better quality sleep. Irregular sleep patterns lead to poor sleep and confuse your circadian rhythm. In fact, it's not enough to go to bed early some days and later on others. The idea that you can sleep late on weekends only is actually bad for your health. If possible, try to wake up naturally at a similar time every day that aligns with your lifestyle. You don't need to be an early bird. What you need is to understand your best wake-up time and maintain it.

Avoid late-night meals:

Eating late at night may negatively impact your sleep and the natural release of HGH and melatonin. That's not to say you should never snack at night. A study found that a high carb meal eaten four hours before bed helped people sleep faster, while another discovered that a low carb diet also improved sleep. So, what does that mean for you? That there's no right or wrong. Find what works best for your body, and you will know based on how well you sleep. As a general rule of thumb, late-night snacking should be as light on your digestive system as possible, and there shouldn't be any stimulants consumed in the process.

Don't drink liquids before bed:

Hydrating with plenty of water throughout the day is terrific. But you don't want to wait till bedtime to gobble down the last six glasses that you missed during the day. Why? Because that interrupted sleep that will ensue (thanks to the frequent peeing that will be involved) will affect sleep quality.

Everyone is different, so some people might be okay with a glass or two of water just before jumping into bed. Maybe even a few cups of herbal tea half an hour before bed won't create any interference, but if you realize you pee a lot, I suggest no drinks one to two hours before sleep time. You should also pee right before jumping into bed to reduce the chance of waking up in the middle of the night.

WOULD YOUR ROOM SET UP AFFECT THE WAY YOU SLEEP?

The answer is absolutely yes. Various studies indicate that external noise, often from traffic, can cause poor sleep and long-term health issues. One study on women's bedroom environment showed that 50% of the participants noticed improved sleep quality when noise and light diminished. As such, it's imperative to make some adjustments to the current state of your sleeping quarters.

A great place to start is with your curtains, the lighting system, and the room temperature. These are simple, quick fixes you can do regardless of your location, and they will impact your sleep. See if you can minimize external noise and light. Get some dimly lit lampshades instead of the bright overhead bedroom lights. Make sure your bedroom is as quiet, relaxing, and clean as it can be. I have a friend who completely blocked out the windows in his bedroom by covering them up with wooden blocks. That kept out all light and noise, so even though he lives in a rather noisy apartment building, his bedroom is completely peaceful and Zen-like.

Not a fan of completely darkening your room?

Consider purchasing room-darkening blinds, shades, or drapes that allow you to go totally dark in the evening but still have some sunshine during the day.

CONTROL YOURSELF IN THE THINGS TO DO AND NOT TO DO IN BED

Given how tricky this topic of sleep is for us, we need to increase our discipline around bedtime rituals and get honest about what we can and cannot control. What happens in the bedroom is entirely under your control. The neighbors, streetcars, or whatever else happens outside your home will never be in your control, so if you get frustrated by the noisy neighbors who seem to enjoy cranking on the music till the wee hours of the night in the middle of the week, consider what you can do in your sleeping space to eliminate more of that noise.

Take a moment not to consider the quality and quantity of your sleep. But how easy has it been for you to fall asleep in the last few months? Do you often wake up in the middle of the night and struggle to fall back asleep? Are there any distractions in your room that might be affecting your sleep?

What you want to eliminate from the bedroom:

Don't feed in bed:

If you can avoid eating anything before bed, that is ideal. But suppose you had a long day and got home late, so you need a snack before jumping into bed. In that case, eat standing by the kitchen counter and make sure it isn't something fatty. Whole grain bread with some peanut butter spread ought to ease those hunger pangs and enable you to sleep well. What you must never do is carry your food to the bedroom. Not only is this poor hygiene because you're likely to start attracting all kinds of bugs into your bed, but it's also a very unhealthy habit to get into. All food should be left in the living quarters unless there's a medical reason causing you to feed in bed.

The television:

If your television is in your bedroom, it's time to exile it to the living room. Watching some tv, whether it's comedy or horror, has adverse effects on your sleep. Sleep specialist W. Christopher Winter, MD, says that the glowy effect of the screen actually stimulates our brain and inhibits the secretion of melatonin. Regardless of how comforting you find watching an episode of *Friends* before sleeping, stop watching an hour before sleep and do it elsewhere - not in the bedroom.

Avoid having intensely negative discussions in the bedroom:

For many married couples of those in a committed relationship, the only chance for connecting with your loved one is at the end of the busy day (more specifically in bed). If there's a pending discussion, a disagreement, or something intense that must be discussed, I urge you to pause it until the next morning. If it cannot wait, then have a discussion before both of you are lying in bed trying to fall asleep. Do not engage in negative talk, trying to hash things out right before sleep. Instead, I want you to make your bedroom area a sanctuary. The place where only positive vibes are allowed. Intimacy, romance, cuddling, and encouragement should be the only activities going on under the sheets. All else should be off-limits once you get under the sheets. Besides, most arguments dissipate when a couple "sleeps on it" because we all tend to be more rational and calmer in the morning.

Don't sleep with the family pet:

Yes, I know how much you love your pet and how comforting it is to have it lying next to you. But suppose you're struggling with insomnia or severe sleep deprivation. In that case, you really want to consider giving your pet a new bed. Pets can sometimes make it hard for us to sleep because they can create sleep disruption as they move, twitch, and breathe. We can find ourselves waking up several times in one night, which is really bad for recovery. You don't necessarily need to get them out of the bedroom but just let them sleep in their own space so you can have more freedom to get a full night's sleep.

The last tip I want to give that is entirely within your control is to train yourself into the habit of using the bedroom purely for sleep and intimacy. Condition your brain to refuse anything else. That includes working on your laptop while in bed, browsing Instagram and Facebook, or even talking on the phone. When you get under the sheets, it should be either to sleep, which should happen within that first half-hour or to make love with your partner, which will ultimately enable you to relax and sleep. This is all part of your sleep hygiene. By including the tips shared in your evening routine, you are more likely to see significant changes in your sleep quality and quantity.

9

THE WILDLY EFFECTIVE, YET SURPRISINGLY SIMPLE, METHOD FOR STOPPING PANIC ATTACKS IN THEIR TRACKS (AND WAYS TO REDUCE THEIR FREQUENCY!)

D on't panic! How many times have you heard that? If only it were that easy. Panic attacks suck, but you know what sucks even more? That feeling of powerlessness, knowing that you can't control or stop anything. Now, I know everyone experiences their own version of panic attack disorders, but what if you could learn some simple and healthy coping techniques that could actually help you stop the attacks before they cause any significant damage?

Plan an Escape Route and Develop Coping Techniques Before Panic Attacks:

Trying to control a panic attack or avoid it entirely before recovery is at 100% is futile, in my opinion. In fact, I think even after your treatment and recovery, you should never worry about not getting another attack. Instead, focus on healthy strategies to immediately help you alleviate an attack's symptoms long before maturity.

A metaphor I like to use is this: If you're running a race carrying a boiled egg on a small spoon that must get to the finish line, I wouldn't worry so much about dropping the egg. Instead, I would focus on what needs to happen so that whenever the egg drops, I can easily pick it up without damaging it and continue my race to the end.

The same is true for your healing and overall mental wellbeing. You don't have to be perfect to declare yourself healed. But you do need to know exactly what to do as soon as the first sign of an anxiety or panic attack rears its ugly head. That demands a carefully thought out plan which includes healthy coping mechanisms.

KNOW YOURSELF AND YOUR TRIGGERS:

The more you know yourself and how you react to certain stimuli or situations, the easier it becomes to identify those triggers. For example, you might realize that your morning rush often generates a lot of anxiety. What does that tell you? The morning ritual has to be transformed into something that produces calm and ease. The more control you have with your morning, the less likely you will spiral downward and activate an attack. By integrating things like mindfulness meditation, yoga, journaling, and so on into your morning routine, you will see that internal shift that will bring out the desired change in your mental state.

Another thing you need to do is learn to recognize your symptoms. That involves knowing how your body feels and identifying your thought processes as anxiety begins to build. So, think for a moment about the sensations and biological cues that typically overwhelm your system right as the stress gains momentum. Do you usually start shaking, or does your stomach fill up with butterflies? Perhaps for you, it's a tightening on your stomach and a sense of "lack of air" as your breath quickens and shortens. It's very possible that even before the physical symptoms, there are psychological warning signs that pop up, like intrusive thoughts which trigger that feeling of nervousness. The more you can catch any of these psychological and biological signals, the easier it becomes to end the anxiety before it blows up into an actual attack.

Now I want to share some healthy coping strategies that you will need to practice when in a relaxed state. I suggest doing them daily so they can stick and become the natural impulse when you get triggered.

Deep breathing:

As soon as those overwhelming emotions kick in, the first step should be to distance yourself from that environment. You don't need to make any drastic physical changes, but you need to distance yourself mentally, and the best way to do that is through deep breathing.

Take long, deep breaths and mentally count to ten (backwards). Inhale through the nose and out through the mouth. If you lose count, start again from ten moving toward one. That will distract you from the heat of the moment, reconnect you to your breath (which is a powerful anchoring technique). By pumping more blood into the brain, you'll tend to feel less tense and more balanced.

Sometimes, the breathwork isn't enough to pause the panic attack, so try one of the other techniques.

Get grounded:

A great grounding technique is about tuning into yourself and finding a stabilizing point. See if you can close your eyes for five seconds, then reopen and connect with 4 things that you can see in that immediate surrounding. Can you mentally name the 4 objects or something that you see? Great. Next, I want you to touch 3 things (a table, the wall, a curtain, or anything else), smell two things, and taste 1 thing in your immediate vicinity. If you happen to be at your cubicle, then touch the surfaces next to you, including your own body parts, open up a book and smell that and just focus on tasting the insides of your mouth. Of course, I prefer you go outside for more variety but do the best where you are under current circumstances. What matters in this grounding exercise is that you force your mind to connect with your external senses.

Ice yourself:

Ice packs work for many people, so consider keeping some ice packs in the freezer, especially if you get those nighttime panic attacks. A friend of mine usually has two small and two big ice packs ready to go. When he feels panic coming, he puts the small ones in his hands and the large ones either on his lower back or belly. When he has difficulty breathing, he will usually grab an ice pack and rub it from the middle of his chest down to the bottom of his belly very slowly until his heart rate starts to mellow. You might want to try this out as well.

Carry some lavender essential oil or a scented handkerchief:

Lavender is considered a powerful soothing agent. Sometimes, it might be all you need to stop growing anxiety. Many studies show that lavender can help relieve stress. If you get the oil, try holding it under your nose and inhaling gently or dabbing a little onto your handkerchief to smell. The best kind is the natural essential oil, as that is the safest to inhale. You can also apply a little on your wrists, almost like perfume, rub them together and inhale throughout the day as needed.

Not a fan of lavender? Try out chamomile, lemon, orange, or bergamot and see if they work for you

Repeat a mantra:

A mantra is a word, phrase, or sound that you repeat until you gain some sense of calmness and focus. Internally repeating a mantra can really help you put a stop to an oncoming panic attack. It doesn't have to be something grandiose as long as the mantra resonates with you deeply. If you're a person of faith, you could quote a verse from the Bible or even say a simple phrase like "This too shall pass." If you enjoy Sanskrit mantras, you could find one that makes you feel good such as "Sat. Chit. Ananda."

The main objective is to gently repeat the mantra and to bring all your focus on the feeling generated by that calming, soothing repetition until your physical state slows down and your breathing and muscles relax.

HOW SIMPLE IS THIS SIMPLE METHOD?

Panic attacks usually feel like you're literally choking to death. You may feel like you're hyperventilating or experiencing shortness of breath. The best way to get through an attack is by simply focusing on your breath and doing this simple breathing exercise.

Start by breathing slowly and purposefully to counteract that shallow breathing that's attempting to enhance the attack. If comfortable, place your hands on your belly and fill it with the breath. As you inhale, feel, and connect with this rising sensation as the belly expands. As you exhale, the abdomen will contract inward. Follow this movement and drain it of every bit of air. You could also count each breath. For example, count to four as you inhale, hold for three, then count to four as you exhale. Keep all your focus here. Center yourself in this movement and focus on that slow inhale and slow exhale. Do this until you feel a shift and your body and mind feel soothed. It's a simple exercise, but there is great power in mindfulness breathing. If you can stay in it for as little as seven minutes without allowing yourself to drift anywhere else, you will bring yourself back to a calm state and chase away that attack naturally.

7 ADDITIONAL SIMPLE TIPS TO REDUCE YOUR ANXIETY (AND PANIC ATTACK) WHENEVER IT FLARES UP, NO MATTER WHERE YOU ARE

#1: Close your eyes:

Sometimes the panic attack or anxiety is exacerbated by the stimuli in your environment, making it harder for you to focus on your breath, so consider closing your eyes if it's safe enough. Allow those external stimuli to fade into the distance and bring your attention back to the breath. Then follow the simple breathing technique shared earlier.

#2: Engage in light exercise:

This may not apply to all situations, but if you generally enjoy exercising, it might be good to engage in some light workout as you feel the anxiety building. Pause what you're doing and take a ten-minute power walk, skip rope, dance, do some power yoga or bike for a few minutes, allowing your mind to focus entirely on the physical effort you're making and giving your body the chance to break a sweat.

#3: Remind yourself that this is not the end:

Often when we are getting an anxiety attack, we feel like the world is coming to an end or as though it will last forever. When those thoughts start creeping in, remind yourself that this too shall pass.

#4: Focus on an object:

When the mind is racing, it's hard to control your anxiety or even focus on your coping techniques. I like to use an object to curb the distressing signals, feelings, and emotions until I feel centered. I carry around a family heirloom that I use as my object of attention whenever necessary. Still, you can choose any item that captures your interest. It can be a plant in your office, a candle, seashell, a smooth stone, or any object with enough depth to grab your attention. Think about the purpose of the item, the shape, and maybe even its origin.

#5: Switch to a less anxiety-filled task:

Sometimes the easiest way to avoid getting an anxiety attack is to remove yourself from the current task and do something that takes your mind off your worries. It is especially true if you recognize the task at hand is one that triggers your anxiety.

I am not advocating procrastination here. Just give yourself a break and do something enjoyable until your mind returns to a calmer state. Then reframe your perception about the task that's triggering your anxiety. Only when it feels okay do I suggest jumping back into the task with lots of breaks in between.

#6: Fact check your thoughts:

Some, in fact, many of the thoughts that come up when you're about to get an anxiety attack are distorted and harmful to your mental well-being. Consider pausing and doing a self-analysis of the thoughts driving you to believe that something is wrong. You might be surprised to realize that the thoughts are triggering anxiety even though it's unnecessary. For example, if you find yourself thinking, "I'm going to die, "... It's a good idea to question that thought. Ask yourself, "Am I really going to die? Is there a bomb, dangerous animal, or anything in my vicinity that is actually threatening my life?"

I used to be bullied by this thought for almost 2 decades of my life. Eventually, I realized it would show up right before an attack manifested. So, I decided to fact-check it whenever my mind went there. Ultimately, the thought would come. It wouldn't freak me out so much because I had developed this new understanding about myself and how much I fear dying. Then I also learned to make peace with the fact that everyone will die. If mine is today, then I'm at peace with that. But there sure as heck better be an entirely justifiable reason for why I would be thinking that when I'm in a supermarket grocery shopping!

#7: Listen to your favorite song or watch a funny clip:

This works really well for some people, especially if you have a special connection with music or if you've had a childhood program that instantly changes your mental state.

I encourage you to have a playlist at hand that can be your go-to technique as soon as you sense the tension building. Music is known to have many healing properties, so go ahead and give yourself a five-minute music party in your office cubicle and watch the tension melt away.

10

LONG-TERM STRATEGIES TO HELP YOU REDUCE & OVERCOME YOUR ANXIETY ONCE AND FOR ALL, NOT JUST FOR A FEW WEEKS

I f you want to truly transform your life and overcome anxiety, you need to play the long game. Techniques and instant fixes are great, but nothing beats having the confidence that you are genuinely healed. That requires making some lifestyle changes, educating yourself on what anxiety is, how it manifests in your life, and what you can do to permanently heal. So far, you've been learning about the facts around this mental disorder. Now you need to personalize that education so you can implement it.

LONG-TERM HEALING STARTS WITH LEARNING:

Do you consider yourself a lifelong learner? If learning has a negative connotation in your life, you will need to shift that belief system because your continued education on mental health and wellbeing will become your saving grace. To understand more about your body and how you function, you will need to educate yourself on how your mind and body work and how your psychological states influence your biological states. Although this book has given you a beginner's crash course, it should not be the end but merely the first step toward further learning. There are many ways to obtain this knowledge. Google is one of the best resources at your fingertips but make sure to learn from trusted websites like mentalhealth.gov, goodtherapy.org or ask your physician for resources and referrals.

Since everyone experiences anxiety in their own unique way, you will need to educate yourself on how your anxiety shows up and what triggers it. Once you can clearly identify both symptoms and triggers, you'll be able to create the right treatment regimen and even identify the right talk therapy should you choose to go down that route. Using your mind to bring back a calm state when anxiety and panic start to show up will require a lot of discipline, so you need to start investing in the necessary resources and develop the practices mentioned earlier. But even with gained knowledge, you might still find yourself completely blanking out whenever it's a severe episode. After all, it can be hard to keep your head straight when your mind and body go into a "death is imminent" state. So, although I want you to use all the other techniques and mindset strategies already explained, here are some specific thoughts you can unleash, especially when panic strikes.

Thought reframes that can help you curb negative thinking.

First, say to yourself, "whatever happens, it's okay. I choose to not feel anxiety. Having the symptom is bad enough. I don't need to add oil to the fire. Been there, done that. I choose not to fear this. And I choose to accept myself and the current situation just as it is."

Second, if the symptom is still persisting, grab your phone and call a friend or therapist. Let them know what's happening. If you have an ongoing treatment regimen that you created for yourself, you can also switch to that. The most important thing is to avoid freaking out, judging yourself harshly, or making yourself feel wrong for feeling as you do.

RELAXATION TECHNIQUES ARE YOUR NEW BEST FRIEND

Relation techniques are great for helping you prevent anxiety and panic attacks. The examples I will be sharing are scientifically proven to slow down your heart rate, lower blood pressure, slow down your breathing, reduce tension, and even boost your confidence. If you also feel like you need to work on your emotions especially intense ones like anger, these exercises may help.

#1: Progressive muscle relaxation:

Experts often refer to this technique as Jacobson relaxation, so don't freak out if you hear that terminology from your doctor. With this technique, you will need to sit or preferably lie down for the best results. What you need is to tighten and relax various muscle groups to stimulate feelings of relaxation and calmness. When doing this exercise, remember to know your boundaries. Do not over-strain your muscles, especially during contraction. Keep your breaths slow and steady as you move from one muscle group to the next. It's best to practice this for a couple of weeks when you're feeling good (you can get into the habit of practicing as soon as you jump into bed and first thing in the morning) so that you can get the hang of it. This technique will be more effective during an anxiety attack only if it has been practiced long enough. There are eight main steps to follow:

- One. Choose a comfortable room with minimal distractions where you can either lie or sit down.
- Two. Start by contracting the muscles in the foot for 5 seconds and releasing the contraction over a ten-second count. Your focus should be to relieve the tension in that particular body part, so notice and feel the muscles relax. If you usually get cramps, splay out the toes instead of curling them inwards. The effect is the same.
- Three. Contract and relax the muscles of the lower legs for the same amount of time.
- Four. Contract and relax the muscles at the hips and buttocks section (this is more impactful if lying down).
- Five. Now do the same on the muscles of the stomach and chest.
- Six. After exercising the torso, contract and relax the shoulders.
- Seven. Next, concentrate on the face muscles. To do this, you can squeeze your eyes shut and clench the jaw for 5 seconds, then slowly release for 10 seconds.
- Eight. The last step is to relax the hands. Make a fist on each hand, hold that contraction for 5 seconds, and then slowly release for 10 seconds.

If you need to use a timer to keep pace with the seconds, that's okay, or you can just count mentally.

Sometimes people use this technique in combination with some of the other methods you'll see below. If that works for you, feel free to experiment.

#2: Deep breathing exercises:

We've emphasized breathing several times in this book but only because of its transformative powers. Use it as a relaxation and meditative technique, and you will experience exhilarating calmness and ease. The whole exercise involves slow deep, and even breaths. That's it! You can do them anytime, anywhere. A particular type of controlled breathing that you can practice today is box breathing.

- One. Start by breathing in through the nose for a count of 2-4 seconds.
- Two. Hold your breath for a count of 2-4 seconds.
- Three. Breath out for a count of 2-4 seconds.
- Four. Hold your breath again for another count of 2-4 seconds.
- Repeat as necessary.

#3: Autogenic training:

Use this relaxation technique to stimulate both psychological and physical calmness. Autogenic training involves slowing and controlling your breath while teaching your body to respond to verbal instructions. For example, you can focus on a particular part of your body and intentionally bring the sensation of warmth and relaxation. You will start to feel a shift and a deep sense of ease coming over you. It's often done with a practitioner, but once you learn the techniques, you can also experiment independently. Here's how.

- One. Sit upright, reclined, or lie down in a position that feels most comfortable for you.
- Two. Begin to introduce verbally some of the sensations you wish to experience and repeat these cues silently. For example, I am completely calm (say it verbally once). My left arm is heavy (repeat this six times). I am completely calm (say it once). My left arm is warm (repeat six times). I am completely calm (say once). My heart beats calmly and regularly (six times). I am completely calm (say once). My heart beats calmly and regularly (six times). I am completely calm (say once). My breathing is calm and regular... it breathes me (six times). I am completely calm (say once).
- Three. Come out of the relaxation by verbally stating, " Arms firm - Breathe deeply - Open eyes." Then follow those instructions.

You can rotate different sensations as you practice this technique. You can induce heaviness, warmth, heart practice (calling attention to the heartbeat, breathing practice (focus on breath), abdominal practice (focus on abdominal sensations), and head practice (focus on the coolness of the forehead).

#4: Biofeedback-assisted relaxation:

Biofeedback-assisted relaxation involves using electronic devices to measure different bodily functions such as skin temperature, pulse rate, or tension in the muscles. The purpose is to help you control or relax a specific part of your body. This technique requires you to attach sensors to the specific part of your body as you relax that muscle group and then monitor and take measurements. This feedback helps you to know which areas to relax and where to focus on most. In most cases, this type of technique is done in a specialist therapy clinic, but you could purchase a portable machine if you want to test it at home. I do, however, caution you to check with your professional healthcare giver before investing in the equipment to ensure they are safe to use and that your body can handle such an experiment.

#5: Guided imagery:

This relaxation technique involves replacing negative or stressful feelings by visualizing pleasant and calming scenarios that trigger corresponding sensations. Suppose you're naturally good at daydreaming or imagining things. In that case, this should be easy to practice, but if all you see when you close your eyes is a never-ending abyss of frightful darkness, then consider either getting some guided meditations or asking your therapist to assist you in guided imagery. Here are three simple steps to test on your own.

- One. Lie down (or sit) in a comfortable position and close your eyes.
- Two. Bring to mind a relaxing environment either from

your memory or something you saw in a movie that you genuinely enjoyed. The best would be to draw from firsthand experience as that would enable you to recall the sensations and elements of that environment. Engage your five senses and notice what you see, smell, hear, taste, and touch.

- Three. Sustain this visualization as long as needed to feel the shift within and remember to take deep breaths as you focus on enhancing the calmness that this exercise brings.

LIFESTYLE CHANGE PLAYS A BIG ROLE IN BATTLING ANXIETY

Deepak Chopra teaches that anxiety is the most common pandemic in our civilization, and it comes about because we anticipate pain in the future. What that implies for us is that the more we train our minds to be present, the easier it will be to manage anxiety. But there's more to this than being present. We also need to deeply assess current habits and lifestyle as these might make our anxiety worse regardless of how much effort we put into being more mindful. Although the standard advice is to seek treatment immediately, let's not overlook the importance of leading a healthy and holistic lifestyle. That also includes having a good work-life balance. Lifestyle includes exercise, nutrition, relationships, time in nature, stress management, recreation, and relaxation, service to others, and spiritual or religious development. We will dive deeper into each of these areas in section three of this book but for now, take a moment to look at these areas as things stand. Do you feel like you're leading a healthy lifestyle? Are all areas thriving? What would you like to shift?

LONG-TERM STRATEGIES COMES WITH LONG-TERM GOALS

If you want your recovery to be enjoyable and successful, you'll need to set some long-term goals that support your healing strategies. Working with a good therapist usually means you also receive guidance on setting goals, but if you're planning on doing this without a therapist, here is an excellent goal-setting formula that will enable you to track progress. It's known as S.M.A.R.T, which is an acronym for **S**pecific **M**easurable **A**ttainable **R**ealistic **T**ime-bound goal setting technique.

To make this practical, think of a desirable objective that you'd like to experience. For example, you might choose to start with a goal of making seven new friends this year if you struggle with social anxiety. That goal is specific (you chose seven friends). It is measurable, attainable, realistic, and time-bound (you decided to do this within 12 months). An unrealistic goal would be never to get a panic attack again. That black and white thinking sets you up for failure. It creates unnecessary pressure because even after healing and recovery, you may periodically experience some symptoms and then handle them before they get out of hand. So instead of creating goals that add pressure and build up your stress in negative ways, use this technique on a goal that you know will thrill you.

First, I want you to identify that goal. What would you like to change concerning your anxiety? Write this in your journal or Google doc and be specific. If you have multiple goals, spread them out so that you have short, medium, and long-term goals that all align. By the way, if you feel a little anxious about the goal, maybe even scared, that's perfectly normal. Right now, is your time to use your imagination productively. Get creative with it, and don't worry about how to do it just yet.

The second step, once the goal/s is clear, is to break it up into digestible chunks. You know you won't be able to go from point A to B in an instant, so we need some mini-milestones along the way. Let me illustrate this with Jenny's story.

Jenny has lived with anxiety since she was sixteen. She always had problems performing well on tests, and despite generally being a good student, panic was the typical reaction during any test or performance check. As she entered the workforce and responsibilities mounted, she experienced everything from a general anxiety disorder when interacting with her manager to full-on panic attacks. The more pressure increased, the more frequent the attacks became.

After seeking some professional guidance, Jenny was finally ready to work on herself and signed up for a talk therapy treatment. But she didn't just leave it at that. Jenny also decided to give herself the feeling of control by creating a S.M.A.R.T goal to ensure she takes back control of her life. The main desirable objective for Jenny was to reduce the frequency and intensity of her attacks. She wanted to get to the point where it doesn't just catch her off guard. So, to make it specific, she went after the frequency and intensity of her panic attack. In order to make this measurable, she decided to track her mood and journal daily. At different points of the day, she would pause for a minute to rate her anxiety level on a scale from 0-10 (with 10 being full-on panic). She committed to these exercises three times a day and diligently recorded the answers on her phone. This was to continue for twelve months at the end of which Jenny wanted to have gradually lowered the frequency down by at least half, which meant, if within the first month she was having an attack twice a week, by the end of the year, she desired it to be once a week. That felt very realistic and attainable for her.

As you can see, by creating some structure around her treatment plan, setting a goal that felt attainable, and tracking the progress, anxiety became more manageable for Jenny. The best part is, although the first twelve months didn't show much improvement, by the end of the second year, she was down to one attack a month. As she continues with this goal-setting process, she reached a point where a whole month recorded no ratings of 10 and no attacks.

That's the journey ahead. It takes courage and requires a commitment. Breaking it down into daily steps really helps, so if Jenny's approach resonates, feel free to borrow it.

The third thing you must do before implementing your daily activities to move toward the objective is to identify the obstacles that might get in the way. There will always be challenges to overcome. If you can identify them and prepare for those obstacles, you will likely handle them without too much strain. For example, if you noticed in Jenny's story, she committed to a 1-minute check-in three times a day and recorded everything on her smartphone. That came from her realization that she hates carrying around journals but doesn't mind voice recording little notes from her phone. She also chose a daily recording system that created minimum resistance for her ensuring she would stay consistent. What obstacles stand in the way of your goal? Is it something technical? Can you find some workarounds?

Another thing I want to note here is that consistency is key. Whatever goal you're working toward, make sure those activities are scheduled so you can create a routine for yourself. For example, if you need to exercise, do it at the same time every day or every week. If you're thought recording like Jenny, do it at the same time each day. Set the alarm to remind you if needed.

WHY MOTIVATION IS NECESSARY

Sometimes even getting out of bed feels impossible. How can you possibly set and achieve goals if taking a shower is a feat of willpower that you seem to be lacking? It's true that mental disorders usually decrease interest in many of the activities we'd otherwise partake in. For example, someone with a social anxiety disorder might set a goal of making seven new friends within twelve months. Still, if she never keeps the commitment of meeting new people, it doesn't matter how perfectly planned her S.M.A.R.T goals are. Lack of motivation can be a huge hindrance to reaching your goals, so if the thought of taking action seems overwhelming, pause for a moment. Breathe deeply and acknowledge that this feels huge for you. Remind yourself that it's not about being perfect or getting it right all the time. Instead, it's about taking small baby steps forward no matter how much you stumble.

Have you ever watched an infant learn how to walk? There is nothing graceful about it, but it is adorable, and we all cheer and commend that baby for each tiny step. It would be best if you parented yourself in this season by acknowledging each small step forward. If the goal is to exercise three times a week at your local gym for forty-five minutes and you only manage thirty minutes a day, that's better than missing your workout. If the squat exercise requires 20 reps and you push all the way to 15 reps, don't think you're a failure. Be grateful and proud that you can do 15 and move on to the program's next exercise. Tomorrow, you'll manage to do 16 reps, and before you know it, 20 reps won't make you feel like passing out. The key to finding that motivation for things that feel impossible is to connect with your why.

Why are you choosing to do this? And why do you think there's so much resistance? Is it because you want to avoid discomfort? Do you doubt yourself? Have you lost hope about healing? The more you can understand the negative driving emotion, the easier it gets to reverse that emotion because you could even give yourself a pep talk. For example, if you feel like you've tried everything, but nothing works, then you could say to yourself, "*I've never really tried it in this order before or using this technique. Besides, it doesn't matter that it hasn't worked the last ten times because I only need it to work once, and I'll be on my way to recovery.*" Sometimes a pep talk and a reminder of why you want to heal is all you need to bring in some motivation.

Meet Dave and Lucy

Dave, a 37-year old manager, had a difficult time at work. He had started his career with plenty of ambition and planned to be one of the greatest in his field. So far, things seemed to be on the right track, but about nine months ago, Dave felt as though he was running out of air while attending a meeting. His heart rate significantly increased; his throat and mouth dried up, and he began to sweat profusely. Although it was a chilly day with clouds covering the sky, he felt as though someone was considerably raising the room's temperature. It felt like sitting in a Sauna while fully clothed. *"Who in their right mind would increase the temperature in the board room, and why was everyone else seemingly calm and normal?"* Dave wondered.

As he tried to pay attention to the presentation, Dave's mind kept wandering and worrying about what he was experiencing and how he could excuse himself from the meeting without raising any concerns. He feared what his colleagues and boss would think. Dave really wanted to protect the seemingly perfect image they had of him. After all, he had spent years working hard on that image, and yet here he sat feeling as though he was about to pass out or, worse yet, die.

After that traumatizing moment, Dave started dreading meetings, especially since he hadn't realized he was experiencing anxiety (more specifically, that he had gotten a panic attack). Each week he would try to come up with some lame excuse so he wouldn't have to go back and face that experience again. Things only got worse after that as he started passing up opportunities to give presentations for fear of messing up or reactivating that same feeling. It wasn't too long before people noticed, and his career started to suffer. He missed a couple of promotions, and suddenly, it dawned on him that he was falling off track.

Dave kept everything to himself for months. He constantly worried over how he felt, which built into a generalized anxiety disorder. His confidence tanked. From the moment he would open his eyes, Dave was stressed and anxious. His wife and friends advised him to "just get over it." They told him he was simply worrying too much, and although they meant well, none of it helped.

On the other hand, Lucy was only 28 when she got convinced that she was very sick. She felt a whole range of strange sensations on a daily basis and couldn't figure out why. Her physician didn't seem to know either. "You're in good health, Lucy. Go home and stop worrying so much" was the usual answer after every hospital visit. Over and over, she heard the same answer. Lucy decided to get a second opinion at the hospital, and still, nothing new was uncovered. A few times, Lucy ended up calling an ambulance because she was convinced her heart was giving up on her. It was at this point that the doctors finally diagnosed her with anxiety. The doctor tending to her said she was too stressed and needed to relax more. Lucy was prescribed anti-depressants, but she refused to take them because she felt it wouldn't help since she wasn't suffering from depression.

The uncertainty of not knowing what was ailing her or how to treat this problem that she knew was there kept her continuously anxious, which only made things worse. Fortunately, Lucy was a fighter, so she decided to go on her own quest and seek answers elsewhere. That's when she turned to the Internet, where she found stories of people who were sick and displaying the same symptoms she had.

Discovering that she wasn't alone and definitely not crazy was a huge relief. But that didn't help her get better. Each week the anxiety was spiking aggressively. Her "illness" was all Lucy could think about, and it started to weigh heavily on her physical health and relationships. Her boyfriend tried to reassure and support her, but nothing was working anymore. The panic attacks were increasing in frequency and intensity. She would have dinner with her boyfriend at times, and out of the blue, she would feel like she's dying, unable to move. Lucy's life got utterly out of hand and more like a circus freak show as everything started crumbling before her. Things she used to enjoy doing, like driving, hiking, and weekend picnics, became impossible.

The consequences of anxiety seriously limited both Dave and Lucy. They tried to cope and even hide it for a while, but eventually, it took a toll on their life. Thanks to the Internet, they connected with me through content and teachings and learned all the book's techniques. Although it was hard to start on the recovery path, one of the ways each of these individuals was able to commit to their treatment path and goals was due to the fact that I encouraged them to reconnect with their "why." For Dave, his big why was healing for his family. As a husband and father, he felt it was paramount that he got his life back on track. Even when it wasn't comfortable, the motivation needed to make an effort was derived from his love and dedication to his family.

On the other hand, Lucy struggled a lot to feel motivated enough to execute her health goals. Some days she struggled to get out of her pajamas. She often had a long list of reasons why not to take action. Then she realized that unless she found a way out of this, she would always be stuck. She desired to start her own business and get married to her boyfriend. None of that would happen unless she completed her treatment and committed to achieving her health goals. As she connected her desires of business and marriage to the daily work of mental healing, motivation grew, and she realized that she could take small steps daily to heal from her anxiety.

Now, there's probably a negative voice in you that might say, "*Sure, but my case is different. I'm probably never going to get better. This won't work for me. It never does. I've already tried so many times.*" Let me remind you that it's okay to have that voice of doubt as it's just trying to protect you. What you must do is compassionately override that suggestion. See it for what it really is - a friendly warning. Your anxiety is actually caused in part by that overly cautious voice of doubt, so once you hear it out, acknowledge that you're not fighting its ideas but merely exploring other possibilities. I mean, what if it does work this time? What if you are not ready to heal? What if your desire to have [fill in the blank] is the big why that was missing from your life. Perhaps now is the time. I believe it's your time. Do you?

11

HOW TO FIND A THERAPIST BEST SUITED TO YOUR NEEDS & ONE THAT WILL ACTUALLY HELP YOU! (IF YOU NEED ONE, OF COURSE!)

Anxiety disorders can be treated by a wide range of health professionals, including psychologists, psychiatrists, clinical social workers, and psychiatric nurses. But how do you know which is the right one for you? And does everyone need to see a therapist?

First, let me clarify that not everyone needs a therapist to heal from anxiety disorders, but most do. Given that each case is unique and different, I will leave that choice in your capable hands because only you know where you stand and how practical it is for you to do this on your own without professional guidance. On the off chance that you do, in fact, decide to invest in a therapist, here are a few things to consider.

#**1:** You need to choose a therapist who is right for you. That includes picking the gender, age, and appearance you most resonate with. I'm not saying to look for models or attractive therapists but instead find someone who makes you feel calm, safe, understood, and someone you enjoy being with. After all, this is a relationship that you'll have to commit to. So, if you realize you work best with male or female doctors in general, go for that.

#2: Choose someone who values you as a person and treats you as an equal. There has to be that human connection and empathy going on at all times; otherwise, it won't end well.

#3: Pick a therapist who is relatable, easily accessible, and someone you believe will help you grow and act as the much-needed guide. Finding that "right fit" in this case is very important because this is someone who is qualified medically to walk with you through this challenge and someone who will help you transform from this current you to the new you that you long for. You can think of it as a caterpillar becoming a butterfly. That process isn't going to be easy, but with the right guide, it will take place successfully, and life will never be the same. Does your therapist give you the feeling that he or she is the right person for this quest? If the answer isn't a resounding yes, then you need to keep searching.

THE CONNECTION IS EVERYTHING.

When choosing your therapist, the first and most important thing is to feel a connection between you and them. There has to be some rapport and trust established before you commit to the treatment. A good way for you to feel safe enough to do this is to identify your preferences and match them with your potential therapists. So, don't be afraid to interview as many as will agree. Get to know the person either via a phone call or in-person before making your decision. During the interview, you'll need to have a set of questions to ensure you get the most out of the interaction. Here are a few:

- Are you specialized in treating anxiety disorders?
- How do you approach treating a case like mine?
- How long do you estimate it would take before I can expect to feel better?
- What do you generally do if a patient doesn't feel any better within your typical time frame?
- How can I help in my recovery?
- Why did you choose to become a therapist?
- What credentials and training do you have?
- Are you now, or have you ever been in therapy?
- Do you follow any particular faith (this is especially useful if religion and spirituality matter to you)?

AGREED ON ONE GOAL AND METHOD

Once you've chosen your ideal therapist, the next order of business is to establish a close alliance founded on an agreed-upon vision with corresponding S.M.A.R.T goals for the two of you to collaborate toward. You must be on the same page when it comes to your ultimate objective. A good therapist will desire to agree on how the therapy will progress and how you can work together to meet your goals. It's up to you, however, to show up ready to participate. If you already have your goals identified and know which treatment you prefer, then only work with a therapist who gets that. Alternatively, go for one with whom you feel a connection, and together you can set the right goal and choose the suitable method of treatment.

When it comes to treatment techniques, there are numerous ways to healing mental disorders. Some common types include:

- **Cognitive or cognitive-behavioral therapy:** This is a form of talk therapy that focuses on making connections between thoughts, behavior, and feelings.
- **Client-centered therapy:** This is a non-directive form of talk therapy that emphasizes positive unconditional regard.
- **Existential therapy:** This technique focuses on your free will and self-determination rather than the symptoms.
- **Psychoanalytic or psychodynamic therapy:** This form of treatment focuses on getting in touch with and working through painful feelings in the unconscious mind.
- **Gestalt therapy:** This technique focuses on the "here and now" experiences.

It is essential to consider which treatment resonates with you based on the approach and focus that you want. For example, if you believe there's an unconscious motivation for your anxiety, you might want to see someone who can offer psychodynamic treatment therapy. If you're going to work on your family and not just on your anxiety issues, then perhaps a family-oriented systems therapist might be best. If what you care about is to change thought patterns because you think doing that will change your life, then cognitive therapy treatment will probably be best. If you have no idea what orientation you prefer, discuss it with your therapist either during the interview process or in the first therapy session so you can both agree on the method that feels best for you.

DO CREDENTIALS MATTER?

The formal education that a therapist has is essential, but more integral to your successful treatment is whether you trust him or her. How safe and understood do you feel? Is your therapist continually learning and improving on their knowledge and the latest research regarding your specific disorder? These are the things that will directly impact your treatment and relationship. Just so we are clear, I'm not stating you shouldn't check their license and credentials. Do that for sure but at the same time, listen to your intuition. It shouldn't be enough to settle for a therapist just because they have thirty years of experience and work with celebrities.

MEETING FOR THE FIRST TIME, HERE'S WHAT TO EXPECT

The first meeting with your therapist will be similar to your doctor appointments. It usually involves signing forms, sitting in the waiting room, and waiting for someone to call your name. Of course, if it's a home practice, the experience might be a bit more casual. Some of the forms you'll likely fill include insurance information, medical history (including any current medications), a record release form, a questionnaire about your symptoms, therapist-patient services agreement, and

HIPPA forms. In some cases, you might fill out some of this paperwork before your first session.

What does the first session entail?

The first session is usually different from future visits as this is the first time you sit in-person to know each other and get an idea of how to proceed. Future visits typically follow a more systematic approach focusing on the treatment itself, but a lot of ground has to be covered in this first one. Your therapist will likely ask you what your symptoms are, what brought you to therapy, and other questions regarding your childhood, education, relationships, and life in general.

This is also where you can discuss objectives, treatment options, and the length of your treatment. If there are certain protocols to be employed, he or she will let you know but feel free to raise any concerns and get clarity about how this relationship will work.

Depending on your issue and the chosen method, treatment can last a few sessions, several weeks, or several years. It might be a good idea to agree on a particular timeframe, and you can even ask for the therapist's opinion on how long they think it will take before you feel better but understand that there is no set answer. Every patient is different, so at best, you're getting an estimate. But at least it gives you a target and focal point.

If you are paying through insurance, the length of treatment matters even more because some insurance companies only cover a set number of sessions in a given year, so you'll both need to factor in that restriction as you formulate a plan of action.

The last thing I want you to confirm during this first session is to agree upon the method that will be employed to treat your anxiety. Given how diverse therapy can be, you both must agree on an approach based on the options I shared earlier. Your therapist should feel confident and experienced enough to guide you through that specific method. If they lack experience or training in that particular method, I advise you to find someone else because you might not get the best results by forcing it to work.

III

MAKING THE NEW
LIFESTYLE LAST

WILL EVERY STEP IN THE GUIDE
WORK FOR ME?

You've made it to the last section of the book, where personalizing and implementing your chosen recovery path is the main focus. There's been a lot of information, strategies, and suggestions on approaching and managing your anxiety. We even discussed the possibility of working with a therapist and how to choose a good one.

One thing you need to realize is that you and I respond differently. Therefore, one treatment may work better for you than me. And if you choose to go with a particular treatment and it doesn't yield the results you desire, try adding another. Create combinations that make sense to you because it's okay if the standard rules of recovery fail to apply to your particular case. What matters is that you stick to your healing program and tweak as necessary until the objective is reached. I also want you to remember a couple of important factors as you go through the treatment process.

The first and most important is that your intention must be to work with anxiety, not against it. Steven Hayes, a professor of Clinical Psychology at the University of Nevada in Reno and a man who has experienced his fair share of panic attacks, says we should always be more self-compassionate and accepting during this process. Hayes is the founder of Acceptance Commitment Therapy (ACT), which focuses on acceptance and neutral, non-judgmental observation of negative thoughts. Through this non-resistance, we can more easily come into the present moment and refrain from seeing anxiety as the enemy. The more you make anxiety the enemy, the more your body will wage war essentially against itself. So, whenever the urge arises to make yourself wrong or broken, pause and bring some compassion into the moment. Recognize that an aspect of you is genuinely and chronically afraid, and the right thing to do isn't to deny or push it away, but instead, to bring it close and treat it with some dignity.

You need to remember that you need to spend more time doing things that feel good for you. Do you know what you enjoy? What naturally releases those feel-good hormones? It would help if you got obsessed with this self-discovery because those are the small details that will make your treatment and recovery enjoyable and ultimately successful. I will give you a full outline of how to make a lifestyle shift, but unless the actual activities are fun and feel right for you, they won't be sustainable or produce great results. So, if your thing is yoga or Pilates, that should become your main workout.

DID I CHOOSE THE RIGHT ONE?

Perhaps you might be asking yourself that about many things, including whether this book has been worth the investment. It's normal to need that extra reassurance that you are on the right track and that you've made the right choice. By reading this far into this book, I can already tell you're good at making the right choices because you now have insights that were perhaps missing or unclear before starting this book. And if you've also signed up for a treatment or finally chosen to work with a therapist, that too is what's right for you. If you sometimes start questioning whether it's working during the recovery, consider going through your journal or just thinking back to how things were a few months or years prior.

The recovery period is different for everyone. It might take you several months or years before you feel completely comfortable in your own skin and more aware and in control of your emotions. That doesn't mean things aren't changing in the interim. Each day is a step toward that final objective, and mini-milestones will add up and create a snowball effect. For example, if, thanks to reading this book, you now start your personalized morning and bedtime routine, that's already a sign of recovery. As long as you keep moving forward, you will see progress and results.

If, as a result of reading this book, you feel courageous enough to start facing your fears, feelings and if you feel a sense of hope growing within, then you've already begun making the shift. And the fact that you even got this book, to start with, is a clear example that you have started loving and investing in yourself.

WORKING IT OUT!

It's important to give yourself the necessary time your mind and body need to make the changes permanent. Even if you were to sign up for talk therapy, the shortest sessions for less severe disorders require several weeks and at least eight sessions. That should help you realize that you need to give yourself ample time and that vein fact, the more complex your disorder, the more patience you will need to exercise. Don't put undue pressure on your body to move faster than it can. As long as you track and see tiny bits of improvements, remind yourself that you are healing.

Michelle shares how she learned to develop self-compassion and patience for her healing as it took twelve years to make a significant shift. She was first diagnosed with panic attack disorder which grew into social anxiety, agoraphobia, and severe clinical depression. At her lowest, she was isolated from everyone and started developing suicidal thoughts. All hope was gone, and she just didn't believe there was a way out. Yet twelve years later, she says she barely recognizes herself when she looks in the mirror as she is an entirely different woman. All that unhelpful panic has been eliminated from her life. She loves spending time with friends and family, runs her own business, and enjoys traveling a lot. Michelle now has hobbies, takes holidays, and loves to try new experiences.

A key lesson from Michelle is her realization that panic, anxiety, and depression can be great teachers. They force us to have the courage that we never realized was inside us, and they require us to develop greater compassion, empathy, acceptance, and patience first for ourselves and then for others. But one cannot heal or recover from anxiety unless they are willing to face and feel their own feelings allowing them time to process. That "time" is critical because that's also when healing occurs. According to Michelle, avoidance, and impatience actually keeps the fear cycle alive. That inhibits any progress.

So, one thing you can't afford to do is get impatient or set unrealistic expectations on your healing. Just like Michelle, you are to see your recovery as a quest of self-discovery and self-love. Don't just read this book to tick a box or to satisfy your curiosity. Commit fully without conditions or apprehension, trusting that healing will become inevitable by allowing your body and mind permission to process those painful and dark emotions. You need to develop this self-belief in your powerful ability to restore your quality of life to where you desire it to be so that as you continue on your treatment, it shouldn't be a question of whether or not it will work but instead a declaration that in due time, new success is inevitable.

13

TRULY ACCEPTING YOUR ANXIOUS THOUGHTS & EMOTIONS CAN ACTUALLY HELP YOU DEAL WITH THEM MUCH MORE EFFECTIVELY (TRUE ACCEPTANCE IS DIFFERENT TO WHAT YOU THINK)

A 13th-century poet called Rumi famously compared emotions (joy, depression, etc.) to unexpected visitors. His advice was to let them in laughing. It makes sense, but that's easier said than done. We usually hide, deny or suppress our emotions, especially the negative ones. We're inclined to bury intense feelings like anger and resentment and to suppress or deny loneliness. In a cultural age that's pro-positivity, the pressure to be "happy" and "positive" all the time can be overwhelming to some of us. Most of us try to mask or camouflage what we're feeling, and unfortunately, that only worsens our condition. Think about how many people would be comfortable walking into their office and openly share with colleagues that they are currently battling a mental disorder. Chances are, very few would feel confident enough to share this openly. There's a lot of stigma and shame attached to mental health disorders; therefore, accepting one's condition and those negative emotions becomes challenging. Yet, the invitation is to find a way to practice acceptance and to shift the way we think of anxiety disorder in the first place.

Most people assume acceptance is about making it okay to be sick and powerless. That it's about resigning yourself to a life of dysfunction and constant fear. That's not acceptance; that's defeat!

True acceptance involves being present with the emotion and your current state of discomfort and anxiety without judgment. It's not about denying that you have the problem or even believing that there's no hope for you. Instead, it's about acknowledging that you are still alive, and, despite the current situation, you can and will get better. So, you sit with your feelings and take them for what they are - negative feelings! But as with all emotions and uncomfortable states, they too shall pass, and you will be stronger and better for having lived through that experience.

A few years ago, when Brett Ford (a psychology professor at the University of Toronto) was still a doctoral student at the University of California, Berkeley, she and three fellow Berkeley researchers devised a three-part study in which they were attempting to analyze Acceptance and why it works. Their findings were published in the Journal of Personality and Social Psychology. According to their findings, the magic of acceptance lies in its blunting effect on emotional reactions to stressful events. In other words, accepting dark emotions like rage, anxiety, or hopelessness won't bring you down or amplify the emotional experience. It also won't make you happy (at least not directly), so it leaves you at this neutral place which might be better for your mental health.

THE NEGATIVE EFFECTS OF ANXIETY AND PANIC ATTACKS

Anxiety disorders of any kind are imagination gone evil which triggers chronic fear and stress. Nothing good can arise from such a state. When it comes to the impact living with such a disorder has in your life, the list is long and affects more than just your ability to interact with others. Let's talk about some of the far-reaching effects chronic anxiety and panic attacks can have on you.

Low immune system:

Have you noticed that when you're stressed and anxious, it's easier to "catch something"? That's because when anxiety builds up, your immune system shuts down. After all, the body is under duress. That makes it hard for the body to fight illness and viral infection, so you become very vulnerable to anything in the air.

Weight gain:

Most of us eat more when stressed and anxious, so it's no surprise that our weight will fluctuate as things worsen. There's also the fact that your brain floods your body with hormones of adrenalin and cortisol, which causes most of us to seek out sweet comfort foods like ice cream, cake, and chocolate. However, the rise and subsequent drop in blood sugar levels will lead to a constant craving for salty and sugary foods again. This unending roller coaster can easily lead to weight gain and even obesity if left unchecked.

Gastrointestinal disorders:

The more anxiety builds up, the harder it is to keep your stomach calm. For many of us, the first symptom that something is building is usually butterflies in the stomach. Constant worry and anxiety attacks can create chronic digestion issues and excretory problems (stomach pains, bloating, abdominal cramping, diarrhea, irritable bowel syndrome, vomiting, etc.).

Respiratory issues:

When you get anxious, your breathing becomes short, shallow, and rapid. Your breathing pattern becomes erratic, and you typically experience dizziness, tingling sensations, and at times numbness of the hands and feet. Some people even pass out due to this imbalance between the inhaled oxygen and exhaled carbon dioxide. But even if you don't pass out, this experience of shortness of breath is very uncomfortable. For those with pre-existing respiratory problems like Asthma, the condition might actually worsen. Patients suffering from inflamed airways or chronic obstructive pulmonary disease (COPD) will usually end up in the ER whenever they get a panic attack or anxiety build-up because their system cannot handle that imbalance. So, it becomes even more necessary to keep anxiety and stress in check when one has respiratory problems.

Heart Disease:

Heart palpitations and rapid breathing patterns are common during a panic attack. Unfortunately, as they continue to persist and increase in frequency, this heightened state can cause high blood pressure and coronary problems such as heart disease or heart attack.

Memory loss:

Most people suffering from chronic anxiety report having issues remembering things. They just seem to forget important information, appointments, and so on. That's because generalized anxiety disorder can sometimes impact your short-term memory. If this happens regularly or you realize you're having trouble recalling or keeping up with your hectic schedule, it might be a side effect of the anxiety. Unfortunately, forgetting things might impact your performance at work or school, making you feel more anxious, causing you to fall deeper into that pit of despair.

FACE IT HEAD ON. AVOIDANCE IS NOT THE ANSWER!

There's a culprit that few of us like to discuss because it tends to stir up wrong feelings and agitate the very thing we are trying to cure, but it must be said. Have you ever heard of avoidance coping? Avoidance coping is changing your behavior to avoid thinking about, feeling, or doing something difficult. For example, Have you ever said "No" to an invitation from someone you care about (friend or family member) even though you did want to go to that event/party and show your support? Still, you chickened out because you knew there wouldn't be anyone else there that you would get along with, and the thought of being judged by strangers made you feel anxious? Or perhaps you've had a tense moment at the office with a co-worker. But instead of having that difficult conversation to resolve the issue and voice your frustration, you spend all week going out of your way to avoid them.

You might even ask for a different shift if possible just to avoid seeing or thinking about them. Here's one more that I have been guilty of several times in the past. I used to believe that my relationships were doomed because of my anxiety. And each time I would get into a relationship, it never ended well and didn't last very long. The main reason for my broken relationships always hinged on some unresolved conflict that I didn't want to have. I felt like I just didn't have the stomach to do it, so instead of sticking around to try and work things out, I would often send a text or leave a voice message telling the other person it was over, and I wished them well. More times than not, it would cause my ex to have an emotional outburst which only made me feel worse. At first, I struggled to realize that I was the one with the issue. I couldn't see that I was using avoidance behaviors, so as you read this, you might want to take a moment and reflect on your relationships and how you approach stress. Do you often procrastinate when something feels hard? Do you avoid discussing or facing issues? Make some notes of events or situations where you have used avoidance coping and then realize that something needs to shift.

Avoidance coping is extremely unhealthy for us and, in fact, only exacerbates anxiety. Sure, it feels good to avoid thinking about or doing something at that moment, but the consequences are usually far more stressful. Relying on this as a strategy for stress relief can get out of hand and create more stress. So, what I want you to do is ditch this coping mechanism and instead form healthy habits that build resilience.

What you need to do is to take small steps toward making changes to your behavior. Here's a simple step you can take.

The next time you realize you've just chosen to avoid facing a situation because you're worried about triggering your anxiety, pause and look at your options. You can choose to implement active coping options instead of that harmful avoidance coping strategy. There are two types of active coping options you could choose from: Active-behavioral coping, which addresses the problem directly. Active-cognitive coping which involves changing how you think about the stressor.

So, think about the issue at hand and see if you can reframe your thoughts and identify resources you didn't realize. Perhaps you can recognize hidden benefits in the situation that you didn't notice at first glance. Is it possible to approach the problem from a mental standpoint that doesn't include avoidance? Are there strategies you can actively use that involve doing something different to affect your situation positively?

Going back to the earlier examples that I shared of different scenarios, instead of merely saying "No" to the invitation for fear of being judged by others, let your friend/family member know that you are nervous about attending that party or event. Please share that you would want to support them, but the thought of being left alone in a place where you wouldn't know anyone else causes significant discomfort. Ask the person if they can help make things easier by introducing you to a few of the other attendees or if they could give you some specific practical tasks that would make you feel less alone and more at ease.

When it comes to conflict with a co-worker, rather than avoid them, make a plan to talk with the person and acknowledge that you feel anxious. You could even let them know that this isn't easy for you at the start of the discussion. As part of your plan, please decide on a neutral place to talk that makes you feel at ease and, if needed, enlist the help of another (boss or colleague) to be a mediator, depending on how serious the issue is. I would also suggest including a self-care plan to reward yourself (treat yourself to something nice) after successfully doing this bold thing of facing your fear.

In my case, when I realized that I was guilty of avoidance coping, I started identifying the situations where that occurred. I would immediately turn to my journal to write out what I did and how I would like to do things differently. In some cases, I realized that I still had the chance to take some action and make things right. Then it would be up to me to follow up with some effort. But even when I wasn't able to "fix" my error, I still wrote down my emotions and how I would do things differently. This gave me that sense of relief and the ability to face my fears, albeit on paper. So instead of escaping things, I gradually got better and faced them head-on.

TEARS OF HOPE

In 1998 a movement known as positive psychology (PP) was launched, and it quickly gained momentum in contemporary psychology. As with everything else, there's been a maturity of sorts as people seek out something more holistic that doesn't just focus on being positive all the time. That's where the second wave of positive psychology comes into play as it promises to be more balanced and inclusive. In theory, PP 2.0 recognizes that it is scientifically and experientially indefensible to only focus on positive emotions, positive traits, and positive institutions. This is a very good thing for us, you know why? Because for people dealing with mental disorders, this idea of being positive all the time only makes things worse. We can't just switch off anxiety, and we certainly can't feel happy when we're not. So, where does that leave us?

This second wave aims to give us an answer. Essentially it makes it okay for us to acknowledge and even embrace our dark and undesirable feelings. So instead of sitting on the couch loathing yourself for having dark intrusive thoughts that make you want to crawl into a hole in the ground, PP 2.0 says it's okay. Just sit with your dark, uncomfortable emotions and cry if you must but remind yourself that it's okay. You are okay. Nothing is wrong with you for having negative emotions. Observe how your mind will just pick up negative emotions and serve them to you on a platter. Realize that while you may not have access to happy utopia-like thoughts and emotions, it's still on the menu, and eventually, you might catch a glimpse of that too. But for now, you'll just accept yourself as you are and feel proud for noticing and becoming aware of these disturbing emotions. Think back to the setting that might have landed you in this undesirable place. Is it lack of sleep? Were you thinking about a setback or troubling experience that happened? Is it too much stress? Are you struggling in some way? Usually, there's a trigger that causes this negative state to kick into high gear. The more you can identify those triggers, the better. But even if you can't recall what triggered you, the fact that you're here sitting with your negativity and feeling uncomfortable is good enough to start practicing PP 2.0. How does one do this?

How to handle negative emotions without resisting them:

Remember, what you resist persists. We want you to have a healthy way of facing and processing the negative emotions and intrusive thoughts that come. To do that, we're going to employ a mnemonic technique gaining worldwide popularity for its effectiveness.

A researcher named Ceri Sims published the mnemonic "TEARS HOPE" in a journal titled "Second Wave Positive Psychology Coaching with Difficult Emotions" that you can implement anytime negative emotions show up. Here's how this method works.

T (Teach and Learn): This is about enhancing your self-awareness and knowledge of your mind-body connection. The purpose is to learn how your body and mind respond to stress and why you have panic attacks. There's always a driving reason behind it, and it's essential to understand it.

E (Express and enable sensory and embodied experiences): Be curious and remain conscious of all that your body is experiencing. Notice all sensations and be okay with whatever is showing up without judgment or resistance. *For example, when my heart rate increases and my stomach tightens up in knots, I simply deepen my breath, stop whatever I'm doing, and repeat to myself that it's okay. Whatever is coming, I will sit my body and just ride the wave. It creates great comfort for my brain.*

A (Accept and befriend): The intention here is to accept whatever emotions or sensations you're having—practice self-compassion and tolerance for that frustration and discomfort.

R (Re-appraise and reframe): This is where you use your preferred method of therapeutic technique to help you see the broad perspective of things. You want to reframe your thoughts and shift your view about the events that are taking place. Cognitive-behavioral approaches can be great for this step.

S (Social support): This is where you engage in a practice that will enable you to find calmness and practice loving kindness. You could do a loving-kindness meditation which will expand your sense of connectedness with yourself and others.

H (Hedonic well-being or Happiness): This is where you shift your focus to happy memories, success stories, and all the positive aspects of your life. Why? Because research shows, it's highly beneficial to keep a 3:1 ratio of positive vs. negative emotions. Practically speaking, you would need to increase the amount of time you spend authentically feeling good. So, when you do catch that good feeling, make sure you ride it as long as possible.

O (Observe): This is where you practice non-judgment in your life. Again, meditation and other mindfulness practices can be integrated here.

P (Physiology): This is where you integrate breathing techniques, relaxation, and self-care exercises.

E (Eudaimonia): This is an ancient Greek term that can be loosely translated to mean human flourishing and happiness. In this context, its purpose is to encourage you to have goals that you're moving toward. Goals that thrill and excite you and enable you to lead a more authentic life that fulfills you.

Turn the Negative to Positive (I was able to do it, now it's your turn):

Anxiety by itself is neither good nor bad, in my opinion. It's mainly the relationship we have with it that determines how it impacts our lifestyles. To prove this, I want to share a story from a fellow community member named Rosie.

As a child, Rosie was very outgoing. She studied ballet and tap dance, joined the school chorus, and even performed in school plays. The spotlight was something Rosie enjoyed, and it suited her. Other kids would complain of pre-show jitters whenever they were getting ready for a big performance, and Rosie never understood why. Feeling nervous was foreign to her. One day, something changed. Suddenly, like the flip of a switch, Rosie found herself feeling tense, scared, and afraid to speak in front of her classmates (there were only 20 kids in the room). What happened? She experienced a key triggering event that activated her anxiety. In February 2001, a classmate vomited all over her while they were riding the school bus. Like any other child, she was grossed out! Although she felt humiliated and unable to control the incident, she didn't think much of it until the next day when she felt frightened to get on the bus or even go to school. The thought of seeing her friend's face after that event made her completely nauseous, and for the next three days, she never left home. Her parents tried to be understanding and let her take some time to process her emotions. She kept insisting that going to school would make her fall ill, so they let her have it easy until finally, they forced her to go back. Once she returned, things weren't normal anymore. She began to see her school guidance counselor to avoid any situation that made her nervous. These visits became so frequent that her parents were alerted, and Rosie was advised to start seeing the school psychologist. Her parents did their best to support and encourage her. Each visit brought no improvement despite her willingness to show up, so the doctor suggested medication. The parents stubbornly refused as they were concerned this would only lead to long-term addiction and further harm to their little girl.

Daily life continued to prove challenging for Rosie. Not long after, she dropped all her extra-curriculum activities and became invisible during class activities. Her engagement level both at home and school dropped significantly. At this point, the parents decided to hire a therapist to help keep the anxiety at bay. The treatment suggested by the therapist seemed to help Rosie maintain her classes, but her social life never recovered. Rosie became a recluse and spent most of her late teenage years grappling with bouts of depression and moving from one therapist to the next. By the time she was in her twenties, her parents had invested a fortune in her well-being and finally found a therapist who was able to teach Rosie some healthy coping mechanisms including, nighttime rituals that included meditation, daily journal, and thought tracking and practicing non-judgment. Rosie says her mother has been a strong influence in her recovery because she never gave up hope and always encouraged her.

Over the years, her anxiety evolved and included obsessive-compulsive behavior, agoraphobia, social anxiety, and bouts of depression. Rosie got to a point where she would only leave the house to go to school and the hospital. The idea of flying, riding buses, or socializing devastated her. Even as a college graduate, she spent each day agonizing over things that normal girls would scoff at and spent all her free time locked up in her room or crying in her mother's lap. Eventually, she did make an effort to conquer her fears and anxiety, and once she found my materials and joined our supportive community, she's been able to reclaim her life. The last posting, she did was actually during her second cross-Atlantic journey, which didn't require any medication (although she still likes to carry some Xanax just in case). It has been 14 years since that trigger moment, and while Rosie's journey hasn't been a bed of roses, she is living proof that it is possible to take back control of your life. It took several therapists, lots of experimentation, and effort on her part, not to mention family support. And she feels confident that the next 14 years will be full of adventure and freedom.

I feel the same way, and my relationship with anxiety has changed tremendously. I cannot say that I will never have another panic attack, but I can assure you, I will handle whatever comes. I have made peace with the fact that the present moment and my emotions are all I can ultimately control. So, I leave the future where it is and trust that I have enough tools, healing coping strategies, and a solid belief in myself to handle anything, including another anxiety attack. Thus far, my streak of anxiety-free days continues to reign, and I savor every minute of it!

WOULD YOU LIKE A NEW WAY OF LOOKING AT ANXIETY, SO YOU COME OUT FEELING EMPOWERED?

Consider viewing it as a protective mechanism. See it as a message from your brain and body. Notice when it shows up and try to understand the signals and messages being sent. Stress and fear, which often trigger anxiety, are both protection mechanisms. Like a fight or flight instinct, anxiety might be your body letting you know that you're in the proximity of danger. Whether that danger is emotional or physical, real or imagined, the signals are accurate, and you should never ignore or judge them as bad. The way you choose to view your anxiety will determine how quickly you can heal. See it as a villain, and you're basically at war with your own body. Instead of making it the bad guy, see if you can "team-up" to resolve the underlying and real problem.

14

WHAT' SPIRITUAL GREATS' LIKE THE BUDDHA CAN TEACH YOU ABOUT HEALING YOUR ANXIETY (WITHOUT HAVING TO BE RELIGIOUS OR SPIRITUAL, IF YOU DON'T WANT TO BE!)

For a long time, I thought mental illness was something experienced by those who were broken somehow. Of course, that tells you a lot about how I viewed myself. Through personal education and increasing my awareness of faith, religion, and spirituality, I've come to realize that many people learn to live with and even overcome mental health disorders. Sometimes, those people are highly respected religious and spiritual leaders. That's why I include this as one of the last chapters in the book. Buddhism is in many ways connected to almost any spiritual or religious practice I can think of, which makes it ideal whether you want to add it to an existing tradition or as a standalone practice.

Perhaps you've never considered spirituality or religion to be of value. Maybe you gave it up because you felt it wrong to claim to be a person of faith, all the while battling with a mental illness. I met a woman who told me she felt so sinful about her depression diagnosis and figured she should as well quit going to church every week because God doesn't like sinners.

I don't know where you stand when it comes to faith, church, religion, or even spirituality, and quite frankly, it doesn't matter. What does matter is that you develop a personal belief in yourself and your ability to heal. How you reach there will be unique to you. But I hope you can pick a few inspiring and insightful lessons from reading about how global figures like the Buddha and lesser-known individuals like Jude Demers have found peace through Buddhism.

Who is Jude Demers? She's a practicing Buddhist who lives with mental illness. Demers says, "Buddhism is known as the science of the mind." I like that definition because it puts us squarely in the arena of personal discovery. By practicing Buddhism not as a religion but as a lifestyle, you become the "scientist" of your own mind and life, experimenting to see what works for you. As you develop and train your mind, inner peace becomes a reality. That's what we're here to discover - how to find peace. We know that as your mind finds peace, your anxiety and fears will dissolve into nothingness. So, where does one begin?

FINDING YOUR PEACE WITHIN

Peace can be defined in a myriad of ways, depending on your source. I am going to broadly define it as the state you experience when what you say, think, feel, and do are in alignment. That can only happen when you become true to yourself and start leading an authentic life. Most people are shocked when I tell them to stop looking for a magic switch that will take away all discomfort, negative feelings, unpleasant situations, and stress in life. Peace will not be yours because you live in a perfect world; it can only be yours when you become a master of your mind.

The more you can align with your values and live in accordance with that, the easier it will be to start making this shift. Peace is dynamic, and it requires courage if you want to live peacefully on a daily, weekly, and monthly basis.

The main form of mental training is meditation. Scientific studies show that meditation can reduce anxiety when practiced over time as you will learn to see negative thoughts and emotions from a different perspective. Instead of letting thoughts nag and steal your peace, you can learn to recognize and release unproductive thoughts. By the way, you don't have to sit in a lotus position for hours each day to practice meditation. Deep breathing, yoga, and chanting are all powerful ways of practicing meditation and mindfulness. Whichever method works to get you to that state of nirvana (the mental state of peace and happiness) is what you should consider implementing.

Here's the thing. You've spent a significant amount of time living in the reality of negative thinking and feeling. The turbulence you experience is real. Practicing meditation in Buddhism isn't about denying that instead of transcending from that viewpoint to a new and more liberating one. If you're more of a religious person, you can also use meditation as a form of prayer to receive the same benefits.

From a Buddhist perspective, the root cause of all suffering is that we don't take enough time through prayer and meditation to come to know ourselves, i.e., our true nature and our enlightened "Buddha" mind. Let's see if we can help you take a step in the right direction by the end of this chapter.

TRANSCENDING FEAR BY UNCOVERING THE SOURCE

One of the great teachings one can learn from Buddhism is that our suffering and fears generally stem from our impermanence and the impermanence of all things. Think about it for a moment. There's so much fear around death, losing our loved ones, losing our precious material possessions, and so on. We're afraid to lose our job or a stock market trade or an ongoing war, and most of all, we're so scared that we will fail. That fear of failure stems from a belief of being unworthy and not good enough. Despite the fears that torment your mind, uncovering the source is the fastest way to tame that voice of anxiety.

You can discover its source through the path of self-inquiry (intro-spection) or the practice of looking within, which is often part of Buddhism. For instance, suppose fear of death is at the source of your anxiety. Having enough courage to look at it boldly, you'd soon realize that there's another healthier way of thinking about death. You could ask yourself the question, "If everything dies and changes, then what is really true? Is there something behind the appearances? Is there something I can depend on that does survive death?"

If you could spend time in contemplation of these types of questions, you'd notice a shift in the way you view everything. Letting go of this fear will seem more natural because you will see avoidance of the natural cycle of life is actually working against your very nature. As you discover the truth about this particular fear, healing would occur. In essence, what we need to do to activate healing in our minds is to observe with mindfulness, be fully present with whatever is there, and accept. That is where transformation takes place.

THE DIALOGUE IN YOUR HEAD DOES NOT DEFINE YOU

Have you noticed there's ongoing chatter 24/7 in your mind? If you have, what tone does it possess? Is it empowering or disempowering? I remember when I first became aware of my inner dialogue. It was frightening to me that all that negative self-talk was carrying on without my conscious knowledge.

I would walk into a restaurant or coffee shop and find the darkest, most secluded spot, walk to my seat all the while, noticing the people who were staring at me like I was some lost weirdo. All that harsh judgment that seemingly sat on the faces of strangers was actually brewed within my mind first through my inner dialogue. The story I was telling myself was what my ego believed. *I'm a failure at everything. People think I'm stupid and weird. I'm stuck with this sickness. I will never be successful or find love.* On and on it went. What did I do? Nothing, because I didn't have enough awareness to realize that it was just a story. Many of us have lived the "story" of being mentally ill for so long; we don't even know it's a made-up story. You could just as easily start telling the story of "*I am healthy and healed,*" but your ego would just scoff and say you're ridiculous because it's so accustomed to telling the story of sickness. I bet throughout this book you've had many moments where that inner dialogue took over and discouraged you or said things like, "*this can't work for you; you already tried these strategies before. What a waste of money buying this book!*"

That inner dialogue has been the blueprint that your ego lives by, and unless you do something to change that story, no amount of medication, talk therapy, or lifestyle changes will give you the life of your dreams. Automatic inner dialogue is a real thing, and it's time you pay attention to what you're telling yourself. A friend of mine told me how he recently caught himself replaying a scene in his mind of getting rejected at a job interview for something he felt so qualified for. There was a little voice in the back of his head saying, "*you'll never get the job; you're not skilled enough.*" That discouraging process caused him so much anxiety and mental exhaustion. He would have triggered a full-blown panic attack if he hadn't been quick enough to catch his inner speech.

Sometimes the inner dialogue isn't even directed at you. It might be focused on judging other people, commenting on what's going on, arguing internally with you know or don't know, and so much more. These activities can quickly become triggers for your anxiety and panic attacks.

Buddhism has teachings on how to deal with this inner dialogue. It involves coming to a place of self-observation to perceive with awareness and clarity these conversations and realize that we are not our thoughts. The true self (who you really are) is not the ego or the mind where this inner dialogue is taking place. Through increased self-awareness, you can learn to detach from all the mind's mental processes and activities and simply observe.

How to start turning your inner conversation into more constructive thoughts:

- Become aware of the conversation you're having and calmly try to observe (like an investigator or a director of a movie) the activity in your mind.
- Strive to keep your attention on what's going on inside your head. You might keep getting distracted but do your best to come back to observing until you can reach that point of detachment (between you and your mental activity and thoughts).
- Find that damaging or futile conversation, stop it, and switch it to something more useful and meaningful. Think of it like switching from one radio station to another. Replace the subject and the words with something more pleasant.

YOU AND I ARE CONNECTED; YOU ARE NOT ALONE

In spirituality, we understand that much of our suffering is enhanced by a sense of separation and being alone. So, one of the first steps to healing that self of loneliness is to reconnect oneself with life and others. Surprisingly, this can also alleviate the tension and nervousness we usually feel, especially if we are convinced that no one "gets us" or loves us. You need to realize that you are not alone. All of us have experienced that debilitating pain of living with anxiety, and though it manifests differently for each of us, we all share that pain. And those of us who have found a way to overcome and rebuild our lives are still connected to you and can be there for you if you will allow it. The same is true with your loved ones. If you can find a way to connect with those you care about deeply, whether they are alive or not, you can learn to tap into the same power taught by Buddha and all the other great spiritual teachers. How do you do this? You can sit in meditation regularly and connect yourself to the people you love and those across the world like me who support and cheer for your well-being. Focus on your breath and bring that mindfulness into the moment. Imagine yourself surrounded by people who love you. Feel yourself touching the shoulder of a loved one next to you and express your love, gratitude, and compassion. Breathe in the knowing that you are not alone, for we are all in this together. As you heal and bring your mind to a state of oneness, we all become better human beings, and the world becomes a healthier, brighter place.

WHY WOULD YOU WANT TO TAKE A MORE SPIRITUAL APPROACH?

Although you don't "have to" become spiritual or religious to heal from anxiety, many who have chosen to follow this path claim it was the best decision ever made (myself included). Why?

First and foremost, it moves one from a self-centeredness approach and that feeling of being alone into a state of connectedness. If you think about it, anxiety is rooted in fear and thoughts such as *"I'm not good enough. What will happen to me? What do people think of me? What's wrong with me?"* etc.

Notice that all these thoughts are very focused on ME. It's an ego-centered approach to living which hinges on external circumstances going right. When they don't, which is at least 50% of the time, anxiety kicks in. The problem with this way of being is that one can never get enough external validation. Also, life is full of both positive and adverse conditions. So, this approach can only keep recreating cause for hopelessness, fear, and anxiety.

When we turn our lives around and seek out spiritual solutions, we shift our focus to "something larger than ourselves." Some might call it God if they are religious. Others may settle for Higher Purpose, Higher Power, or Source. When the focus is taken away from the ego, the perspective changes. For example, we realize that death happens to all of us, and it happens every second of every minute. In fact, by the time I finish typing this sentence, at least two people have passed away somewhere in this world. We also shift from trying to protect and satiate the ego and start asking questions such as *"what is my purpose? Whom can I serve today? What can I do for another to make them feel that they are not alone? What is the right thing for me to think and do at this moment? What is this anxiety teaching me about myself?"*

By connecting to something larger than yourself, you are relieved from the bondage of the ego-self and all the self-obsessed fears and neuroses that typically accompany ego thoughts. Spiritual practices like meditation and prayer can help you recognize and detach from the emotional reactions that usually trigger panic. In essence, you learn how to connect to the part of yourself that is always calm, peaceful, and happy. You also learn to love yourself just as you are, including the dark aspects of your personality. And when it comes to your anxiety disorder, let's just say it's easier to change your viewpoint and emotions around having it in the first place. That health issue becomes an opportunity for growth and expansion instead of a hindrance. You begin to believe that nothing is going wrong, and you are moving through life precisely as your soul designed it to be so you can express and discover more of who you really are. Instead of succumbing to the torture of living with anxiety, you begin to rise stronger, better, wiser, and more compassionate than ever because you see your life through a different lens for the first time in your life. I am not advocating for any particular religion or spiritual approach. Whatever works for you is fine as long as you feel deep within that something larger than yourself is calling you into a new experience. And if spirituality is your path, follow it wholeheartedly and trust that your purpose will lead the way.

15

THE 1 LIFE-CHANGING PIECE OF ADVICE TO HELP MAKE YOUR NEW ANXIETY-FREE LIFESTYLE STICK, AND WHAT TO DO WHEN THE ANXIETY COMES BACK

The recovery path will come with challenges. Even after treatment is done and you find yourself experiencing fewer panic attacks and more joy-filled productive days, there's no guarantee you will never have another anxiety breakdown again. That might sound grim, but it is, in fact, good news for you because what that implies is that you don't need to concern yourself with never having anxiety again! Instead, you need to focus on taking each day at a time, doing the best you can to be present and in control of your emotions. Above all else, you need to set yourself up for success by developing the right habits and cultivating the right mindset.

If there's one bulletproof way to enjoy an anxiety-free lifestyle, it must be the cultivation of the right mindset. Your frame of mind will determine how healthy, happy, productive, and fulfilled you become. That includes training your mind to accept and embrace all emotions, including the negative ones without attachment. It's also about decluttering your inner and outer world. Notice your living space and working space. How serene and organized is it? Notice your internal dialogue and mental space. How chaotic and cluttered are things? Are you exposing yourself to negative news, gossip, and unhelpful conversations or feeding it rich, healthy, prosperous information? It's vital to keep analyzing your inner and outer environment so you can clean up and declutter whatever clogs that sense of serenity. In her book, The Life-Changing Magic of Tidying Up, by Marie Kondo tells us to "Focus on the things you want to keep, not on the things you want to get rid of." So, if you can identify what you want to keep doing and start getting rid of everything else that doesn't support or serve a purpose in your life, you'll feel a tremendous shift in your emotional, mental, and physical health.

THAT ONE LIFE-CHANGING ADVICE TO STICKING TO YOUR NEW LIFESTYLE

If there's one piece of advice I'd like you to carry for the rest of your life, it's this. It's okay to have a setback because setbacks don't make you a failure. There's nothing wrong with you if anxiety strikes a year or so after you've healed your mental disorder. The only time failure occurs is when you give up on taking care of your mental health. Most people assume they should only and always go forward in their healing process. But life is never that black and white. Sometimes you might take two steps forward and one step back. That "setback" is still progress in my eyes and should never be seen as a negative.

Recognize that leftover automatic negative thoughts (ANTs) may be playing a mind game with you, so you need to stop them as soon as you catch yourself and then calmly and gently redirect your focus. If you have therapy handouts of processes that have been helping you throughout this process, now would be the best time to implement some of those exercises to ground yourself in the present moment. You could even say something as simple as "Wait! I'm not going to give in to my negative thoughts and emotions. I've been so long without an incident, and I know my body is healing. These thoughts are just irrational lies that make things seem worse than they are. I know I will be okay no matter what, and it's okay if right now I don't feel so good. I will still be okay. I choose not to go down the pigpen. I'm tired of wallowing in the mud. Been there, done that. I don't need to torture myself like that. Instead, I will "make" myself sit here, embrace myself, and just breathe." Of course, this is easier said than done. Sometimes you might need a more impactful exercise to create that shift, so just be present and utilize one of the tools in your distress kit.

A SETBACK DOES NOT SET US BACK, BUT WHY DO WE HAVE IT?

As you go through your recovery, you will have a real glimpse of the fact that the old you is still there, especially when those leftover automatic negative thoughts kick in. And you'll also become reacquainted with the real you who got buried underneath all your symptoms. You will have days of total clarity, sharp thinking, and freedom, and that sense of joy and purpose that you've always wanted will fill you up. One day, you might wake up and feel like you're back to square one. On those days, everything will feel like a struggle, and you might feel like you're failing, and healing isn't really happening. When that happens, you need to remember that your mind and body go through cycles, and some seasons will be more challenging than others. When your mind starts to feel noisy, detached, and nervous, stay open to whatever is showing up. Don't make it wrong or try to manipulate the moment because setbacks happen even to the best of us. I am convinced that setbacks happen when real healing is taking place.

As your mind and body readjusts and frees up old energies, things will happen. You need to understand that there is no quick fix or shortcut for healing, and everyone takes however much time they need for a full recovery. The more you resist, fight, and interfere with the natural healing process, the harder it will be to transform your health and life.

Consider what happens when someone does a detox or goes into a physical fast. At first, everything feels okay, but you reach a point where it feels awful, and your body might even feel sick and worse than before. This seeming setback is actually the turning point. Usually, people will give up because it just gets too hard. But the few who stick with it and ride that discomfort always find themselves on the other side, ultimately victorious. Just as the body needs to get rid of the toxins before it can be cleansed and energized, so too will your mind. The best you can do is ride out these discomforts and seeming setbacks trusting that once that storm passes, you'll be stronger, better, and well on your way to that new lifestyle.

So, there's no need to worry about why setbacks happen or to feel bad when you're not mentally at your best. What matters is that you are accepting and understanding of your healing process. The ups and downs of recovery from anxiety are the natural processes of healing. It won't just be smooth sailing, and that is okay.

Ben, who I helped recover from panic attacks, shared this message based on his own experience with setbacks which might give you the comfort and perspective needed.

"Setbacks have always been an interesting experience for me. Hopefully, I'm not the only one who feels that way. My setbacks felt like they destroyed everything I had been fighting for. I'd be coming out of the pit, and then I'll wake up one morning only to be met with that profound sense of dread, despair, and loss. Good times can sometimes feel like a hoax, and that little evil voice often whispers that peace and happiness cannot be real. That the only reality was the nightmare of anxiety and panic attacks and all the symptoms that go along with it. When you have those episodes, it's easy to believe that nothing will ever get better. At a fundamental level, that was one of my biggest hurdles. Changing that belief that I am broken, and there's no hope for me has been a massive task. I think experts call it an automatic negative reaction. Willfully, I had very little power over just changing that belief. I would argue with it, try to read the same things that once gave me hope, only to fall flat on my face. At one point, my despair was so bad I literally felt like there was nothing more to do but die. But it was at that moment that I realized I had two choices. I could wallow in my despair and wait to die, or I could get up and take a step forward, fully accepting of the fact that I am having a rough patch, but my emotions are not the totality of my life. I believe that was my point of redemption. In recognizing the futility of fighting with my fears, symptoms, and thoughts, I started to live my life wholeheartedly regardless of my state. Then something crazy started happening. The dark clouds seemed to dissipate, and that awful feeling of failure lost its grip on me. How is this happening? I asked myself. Despite all those negative emotions, I started feeling that I wasn't broken. I felt that in time, this storm would pass. And indeed, it passed and has continued to do so ever since. It's almost like when I stopped fighting and resisting setbacks, that surrender allowed peace to enter my mind and body. And almost every time I had a setback, once I came out of it, it was like a little piece of me was restored back."

MOVING FORWARD WITH SETBACKS!

The length of your setback should never be an issue. What matters is that you have the right attitude and the willingness to accept, process, and keep moving forward, as Ben shared. Increase your awareness and understanding of what's happening when you have a setback so you can allow yourself to have a great life at last. If you would like some tips on how to handle those challenging moments in a healthy way, here are a few things to practice. Know that sometimes, none of these will work, and that's okay.

Find all your achievements no matter how small and celebrate:

Since most of us feel helpless and drained of the previously gained knowledge and progress, a good exercise is to remind yourself of how far you've come. There has been evidence of success (no matter how small), and it's important to recall or read from your journal all the days where things felt great. Did you manage to work out and hit all your weekly goals? Great. Celebrate that old win again. Show yourself all the times you've overcome a challenge.

Get back to basics:

Don't feel ashamed of going back to the basic techniques and principles that first got you moving if you have handouts from your therapy sessions or books that were helpful, re-read those.

Deep breathing techniques and mindfulness practices:

Go back to practicing breathing and relaxation techniques. Remember the deep breathing exercises, meditation, and grounding exercises that you learned earlier in the book? Implement those religiously.

Create your personalized flashcards:

It's hard to remember helpful affirmations, statements, or tips when in the midst of a setback. Consider creating some flashcards that you can pull out when you're about to fall into despair. You could write statements such as:

I have a setback which is why I feel like this, but it's okay. I am still OK.

I will feel better again. I've recovered before, and I will do it again.

Setbacks are a normal part of recovery.

CONCLUSION

Congratulations on making it to the end of this book. It's been a wild, emotionally challenging ride. Your commitment shall be greatly rewarded if you follow up and implement everything you've learned. Anxiety is like wearing dark-colored sunglasses. Everything seems gloomy no matter what you're looking at. I know going through this book has had its fair share of challenges, and so will completing your treatment. But once you find yourself on the other side of anxiety, those dark glasses will vanish, and you will finally enjoy the freedom and fulfillment you've been dreaming of.

Let's remind ourselves once more that negative thoughts and distorted thinking won't vanish forever. Along this journey, you will still find yourself thinking and feeling negatively toward yourself and others. When that happens, observe without judgment and allow them to drift on by. Negative thinking and beliefs are never easy to change and will require time. Positive affirmations are great, but they may not always work, so what you need is to develop the right awareness and practice mindfulness as a way of life. Be proactive and take steps on your own whether you work with a therapist or not. By the way, as we discussed earlier, getting professional help doesn't make you weak or crazy. If you need some support, consider hiring a therapist that feels like the right fit. Working with a therapist can provide you with the objectivity, accountability, and guidance most necessary in the healing process. It can be a way for you to create a "safe space" for you to explore, share, discuss, and examine the cause of your anxiety. It can also be the best solution to have a professional supporting you as you learn life skills for overcoming it.

In our volatile economy and social media-addicted society, mental health issues are a real challenge for many young adults, so don't feel there's something wrong with you. Treatment of emotional problems is critical for our generation if we wish to enjoy modern civilization and maintain a sense of peace and happiness.

The bottom line is, peace and happiness matter to us, and we should do everything we can to retrain our minds the same way we emphasize training our physical bodies. Some people can do it on their own at home with a YouTube video, while others require a gym membership with a personal trainer to make it work. There is no right or wrong. What matters is that it gets you the results you want. When it comes to mental health, you can choose to embark on this quest by yourself and follow the recommendations outlined in this book, or you can combine these ideas with the support of a community/ therapist, depending on what feels best. Here's what I know for sure. You cannot permanently heal and transform your life if all you're looking for are shortcuts or quick fixes. The mind cannot be cheated or short-changed into transformation. You will need to step up and take responsibility. Learn to face your fears, and accept your wild, unruly, and sometimes dark emotions. Invest in anything and everyone who helps you expand your self-awareness because everything begins and ends with you. The quality of life you will have as you take the next steps are not dependent on the economy, how bad your anxiety gets, or where you live. Your quality of life depends on you and the choices you make daily. So, my invitation is for you to start making life-giving choices. Decide that you will invest some time experimenting with new morning and nighttime rituals. Choose to adjust your current nutrition, workout habits, and sleep habits. Integrate mindfulness as a way of life. Invest in more books, teachers, events, or even group therapy sessions where you can have access to like-minded, inspiring people. Peace and happiness have never been missing in your life. You just need to learn ways of eliminating or avoiding the things that cause you to block out these beautiful states.

Most people will pick up this book with the perspective that anxiety is terrible, and they are flawed and broken. I hope that by now, you've started to see things differently. That you've realized anxiety, panic, or any other disorder cannot rule your life unless you hand over your mind and let it be on the driver's seat. I also hope that you realize that no matter how bad things have been, they can change for the better. Today can be the start of your new life. You can find peace and happiness now even as you recover and heal from anxiety. Make-believe that your new life is real and that it's time for you to have a better quality of life, and that is precisely what you will get.

Thank you for reading my story, the story of others just like us who have walked the same path and proven that freedom is possible. And last but not least, thank you for still believing in yourself. Go forth and heal.

RESOURCES PAGE

Oakley, A. (2016, August 24). Your Natural State Of Being. Retrieved February 27, 2021, from https://www.innerpeacenow.com/inner-peace-blog/natural-state-of-being

Three common misconceptions about anxiety. (n.d.). Retrieved February 27, 2021, from https://www.beyondblue.org.au/personal-best/pillar/in-focus/three-common-misconceptions-about-anxiety

Anxiety disorders - Symptoms and causes. (2018, May 4). Retrieved February 27, 2021, from https://www.mayoclinic.org/diseases-conditions/anxiety/symptoms-causes/syc-20350961

Three common myths about anxiety. (2018, August 10). Retrieved February 27, 2021, from https://www.trainingjournal.com/articles/features/three-common-myths-about-anxiety

Common Misconceptions About Anxiety Disorders. (2020, November 5). Retrieved February 27, 2021, from https://www. banyanmentalhealth.com/2018/08/02/common-misconceptions-about-anxiety-disorders/

Stöppler, M. C. (2007, January 1). Panic Attack Symptoms. Retrieved February 27, 2021, from https://www.webmd.com/anxiety-panic/ guide/panic-attack-symptoms

NIMH » Social Anxiety Disorder: More Than Just Shyness. (2021, March 3). Retrieved February 27, 2021, from https://www.nimh.nih. gov/health/publications/social-anxiety-disorder-more-than-just-shyness/index.shtml

Harvard Health Publishing. (2020b, October 13). Yoga for anxiety and depression. Retrieved February 27, 2021, from https://www.health. harvard.edu/mind-and-mood/yoga-for-anxiety-and-depression#:% 7E:text=By%20reducing%20perceived%20stress%20and,blood%20-pressure%2C%20and%20easing%20respiration.

High-Intensity Exercise Best Way To Reduce Anxiety, University Of Missouri Study Finds. (n.d.). Retrieved February 27, 2021, from https://www.sciencedaily.com/releases/2003/07/030715091511.htm

Bonfil, A. (2020, August 26). Mindfulness from a DBT Perspective. Retrieved February 27, 2021, from https://cogbtherapy.com/cbt-blog/mindfulness-in-dbt

Khoramnia, S. (n.d.). The effectiveness of acceptance and commit-ment therapy for social anxiety disorder: a randomized clinical trial.

Retrieved February 27, 2021, from http://www.scielo.br/scielo.php?script=sci_arttext&pid=S2237-60892020000100030

Gavlick, K. (2020, March 15). Breathe In, Breathe Out: Simple Breathwork Meditation For Beginners. Retrieved February 27, 2021, from https://www.organicauthority.com/energetic-health/breathe-in-breathe-out-simple-breathwork-meditation-for-beginners

nnection Between Mental and Physical Health. (n.d.). Retrieved ruary 27, 2021, from https://ontario.cmha.ca/documents/nnection-between-mental-and-physical-health/

ercise for Stress and Anxiety | Anxiety and Depression Association merica, ADAA. (n.d.). Retrieved February 27, 2021, from https://.org/living-with-anxiety/managing-anxiety/exercise-stress-and-ty

ow to Design the Ideal Bedroom for Sleep. (2020, October 23). Retrieved February 27, 2021, from https://www.sleepfoundation.org/bedroom-environment/how-to-design-the-ideal-bedroom-for-sleep

rockland-editor. (2016, July 26). How to Develop Coping Skills for Anger, Anxiety, and Depression. Retrieved February 27, 2021, from http://www.rocklandhelp.org/how-to-develop-coping-skills-for-anger-anxiety-and-depression/

Understanding Anxiety Disorders. (2017, September 8). Retrieved February 27, 2021, from https://newsinhealth.nih.gov/2016/03/understanding-anxiety-disorders

Rubinstein, B. L. N. (2007, May 14). How to Choose the Best Therapist or Counselor for You. Retrieved February 27, 2021, from https://www.goodtherapy.org/blog/how-to-find-a-therapist/

Signs You Are Healing From Anxiety and Depression. (2018, August 23). Retrieved February 27, 2021, from https://www.bayviewrecovery.com/rehab-blog/signs-you-are-healing-from-anxiety-and-depression/